Praise for

ORANGE IS THE NEW BLACK

BY PIPER KERMAN

One of Newsday's *ten best books of 2010*

"*Orange Is the New Black* reads like an estrogen-drenched version of Dostoevsky's *The House of the Dead,* as our gentlewoman protagonist becomes exalted by her exposure to the beautiful souls of trannie divas, Latina grandmothers, a West Indian roommate, even a few politicals— radical pacifists and nuns who managed against all odds to run afoul of the U.S. penal code (along with, of course, a good few of the truly damned). It's a fantastic tale from the Siberia of America's war on drugs and is a rippingly fun read right down to the unexpected moment of closure that arrives before Kerman goes home to Larry for good."

—*Elle*

"Fascinating."   —*O: The Oprah Magazine*

"Ten years after a fleeting post–Smith College flirtation with drug trafficking, Piper Kerman was arrested—a P.O.W. in the war on drugs. In *Orange Is the New Black,* Kerman presents—devoid of self-pity, and with novelistic flair—life in the clink as less *Caged Heat* and more *Steel Magnolias.*"   —*Vanity Fair*

"Kerman puts us inside, from the first strip search (yes, even women have to squat and cough). . . . This book is impossible to put down because she could be you. Or your best friend. Or your daughter."

—*Los Angeles Times*

"Beautifully written . . . destined to become a classic in the genre."

—*Columbia Journalism Review*

"Kerman neither sentimentalizes nor lectures. She keeps the details of her despair to a minimum along with her discussion of the outrages of the penal system, concentrating instead on descriptions of her direct experiences, both harrowing and hilarious, and the personalities of the women who shared them with her."   —*Boston Sunday Globe*

"An honest, insightful and often very funny book."   —Salon

"Don't let the irreverent title mislead: This is a serious and bighearted book that depicts life in a women's prison with great detail and—crucially—with empathy and respect for Piper Kerman's fellow prisoners, most of whom did not and do not have her advantages and options. With its expert reporting and humane, clear-eyed storytelling, *Orange Is the New Black* will join Ted Conover's *Newjack* among the necessary contemporary books about the American prison experience."
     —DAVE EGGERS, author of *Zeitoun* and co-author of
     Surviving Justice: America's Wrongfully Convicted and Exonerated

"In her memoir, *Orange Is the New Black,* Kerman recounts a year in which she learned to clean her cell with maxipads, to wire a light fixture, and to make prison cheesecake—all while finding camaraderie with women from all walks of life."   —NPR

"Vivid, revealing."   —*Entertainment Weekly* (Must List)

"An absorbing, meditative look at life behind bars."   —*Booklist*

"An original view into the prisoner's psyche."   —*The Onion* A.V. Club

"I can't stop thinking about this marvelous book, and about the generous and lovely women with whom Piper Kerman served her time. I never expected to pick up a memoir about prison and find myself immersed in a story of grace, of friendship, of loyalty and love. I have never read anything like this book, and I will read and reread it again and again."
     —AYELET WALDMAN, author of *Bad Mother* and *Daughter's Keeper*

ORANGE
Is the New
BLACK

ORANGE
Is the New
BLACK

| | | |

*My Year in a
Women's Prison*

PIPER KERMAN

Spiegel & Grau
New York
2011

Published in the United States by Spiegel & Grau,
an imprint of The Random House Publishing Group,
a division of Random House, Inc., New York.

SPIEGEL & GRAU and Design is a registered
trademark of Random House, Inc.

RANDOM HOUSE READER'S CIRCLE and colophon is a
trademark of Random House, Inc.

Originally published in hardcover and in slightly different
form in the United States by Spiegel & Grau, an imprint of
The Random House Publishing Group, a division of
Random House, Inc., in 2010.

Grateful acknowledgment is made to the following for permission to reprint
previously published material:

Sony/ATV Music Publishing LLC: Excerpt from "Anthem," written by
Leonard Cohen, © 1992 Stranger Music Inc. All rights administered by
Sony/ATV Music Publishing LLC, 8 Music Square West, Nashville,
TN 37203. All rights reserved. Used by permission.

SMITH Magazine: Interview with Piper Kerman by Whitney Joiner, which
was published on 4/6/2010 in the online storytelling magazine SMITH.
Reprinted by permission of SMITH Magazine, smithmag.net.

LIBRARY OF CONGRESS CATALOGING-IN-PUBLICATION DATA
Kerman, Piper.
Orange is the new black : my year in a women's prison /
Piper Kerman.
p.   cm.
ISBN 978-0-385-52339-4
eBook ISBN 978-0-385-53026-2
1. Federal Correctional Institution (Danbury, Conn.)
2. Kerman, Piper.   3. Women prisoners—Connecticut—
Danbury.   4. Reformatories for women—Connecticut—
Danbury.   I. Title.
HV9474.F66K47 2010
365'.43092—dc22   2009037936
[B]

Printed in the United States of America

www.randomhousereaderscircle.com

22 24 26 28 29 27 25 23 21

Book design by Donna Sinisgalli

To Larry
To my mother and father
And to Pop

Ring the bells that still can ring
Forget your perfect offering
There is a crack, a crack in everything
That's how the light gets in.

—from "Anthem" by Leonard Cohen

Author's Note

||||

This book is a memoir, and is drawn from my own experience. All of the names (and in some cases distinguishing characteristics) of the people who lived and worked inside of the prisons where I was held have been changed to afford them their privacy. The exceptions are Sister Ardeth Platte and Alice Gerard, who kindly granted me permission to use their real names.

ORANGE
Is the New
BLACK

CHAPTER 1

Are You Gonna Go My Way?

||||

International baggage claim in the Brussels airport was large and airy, with multiple carousels circling endlessly. I scurried from one to another, desperately trying to find my black suitcase. Because it was stuffed with drug money, I was more concerned than one might normally be about lost luggage.

I was twenty-four in 1993 and probably looked like just another anxious young professional woman. My Doc Martens had been jettisoned in favor of beautiful handmade black suede heels. I wore black silk pants and a beige jacket, a typical *jeune fille,* not a bit countercul-ture, unless you spotted the tattoo on my neck. I had done exactly as I had been instructed, checking my bag in Chicago through Paris, where I had to switch planes to take a short flight to Brussels.

When I arrived in Belgium, I looked for my black rollie at the baggage claim. It was nowhere to be seen. Fighting a rushing tide of panic, I asked in my mangled high school French what had become of my suitcase. "Bags don't make it onto the right flight sometimes," said the big lug working in baggage handling. "Wait for the next shuttle from Paris—it's probably on that plane."

Had my bag been detected? I knew that carrying more than $10,000 undeclared was illegal, let alone carrying it for a West African drug lord. Were the authorities closing in on me? Maybe I should try to get through customs and run? Or perhaps the bag really was just delayed, and I would be abandoning a large sum of money that belonged to someone who could probably have me killed with a simple phone call. I decided that the latter choice was slightly more terrifying. So I waited.

The next flight from Paris finally arrived. I sidled over to my new "friend" in baggage handling, who was sorting things out. It is hard to flirt when you're frightened. I spotted the suitcase. "Mon bag!" I exclaimed in ecstasy, seizing the Tumi. I thanked him effusively, waving with giddy affection as I sailed through one of the unmanned doors into the terminal, where I spotted my friend Billy waiting for me. I had inadvertently skipped customs.

"I was worried. What happened?" Billy asked.

"Get me into a cab!" I hissed.

I didn't breathe until we had pulled away from the airport and were halfway across Brussels.

My graduation processional at Smith College the year before was on a perfect New England spring day. In the sun-dappled quad, bagpipes whined and Texas governor Ann Richards exhorted my classmates and me to get out there and show the world what kind of women we were. My family was proud and beaming as I took my degree. My freshly separated parents were on their best behavior, my stately southern grandparents pleased to see their oldest grandchild wearing a mortarboard and surrounded by WASPs and ivy, my little brother bored out of his mind. My more organized and goal-oriented classmates set off for their graduate school programs or entry-level jobs at nonprofits, or they moved back home—not uncommon during the depths of the first Bush recession.

I, on the other hand, stayed on in Northampton, Massachusetts. I had majored in theater, much to the skepticism óf my father and grandfather. I came from a family that prized education. We were a clan of doctors and lawyers and teachers, with the odd nurse, poet, or judge thrown into the mix. After four years of study I still felt like a dilettante, underqualified and unmotivated for a life in the theater, but neither did I have an alternate plan, for academic studies, a meaningful career, or the great default—law school.

I wasn't lazy. I had always worked hard through my college jobs in restaurants, bars, and nightclubs, winning the affection of my bosses and coworkers via sweat, humor, and a willingness to work doubles. Those jobs and those people were more my speed than many of the people I had met at college. I was glad that I had chosen Smith, a college full of smart and dynamic women. But I was finished with what was required of me by birth and background. I had chafed within the safe confines of Smith, graduating by a narrow margin, and I longed to experience, experiment, investigate. It was time for me to live my own life.

I was a well-educated young lady from Boston with a thirst for bohemian counterculture and no clear plan. But I had no idea what to do with all my pent-up longing for adventure, or how to make my eagerness to take risks productive. No scientific or analytical bent was evident in my thinking—what I valued was artistry and effort and emotion. I got an apartment with a fellow theater grad and her nutty artist girlfriend, and a job waiting tables at a microbrewery. I bonded with fellow waitrons, bartenders, and musicians, all equally nubile and constantly clad in black. We worked, we threw parties, we went skinny-dipping or sledding, we fucked, sometimes we fell in love. We got tattoos.

I enjoyed everything Northampton and the surrounding Pioneer Valley had to offer. I ran for miles and miles on country lanes, learned how to carry a dozen pints of beer up steep stairs, indulged in numerous romantic peccadilloes with appetizing girls and boys, and journeyed to Provincetown for midweek beach excursions on my days off throughout the summer and fall.

When winter set in, I began to grow uneasy. My friends from school told me about their jobs and their lives in New York, Washington, and San Francisco, and I wondered what the hell I was doing. I knew I wasn't going back to Boston. I loved my family, but the fallout of my parents' divorce was something I wanted to avoid completely. In retrospect a EuroRail ticket or volunteering in Bangladesh would have been brilliant choices, but I stayed stuck in the Valley.

Among our loose social circle was a clique of impossibly stylish and cool lesbians in their mid-thirties. These worldly and sophisticated older women made me feel uncharacteristically shy, but when several of them moved in next door to my apartment, we became friends. Among them was a raspy-voiced midwesterner named Nora Jansen who had a mop of curly sandy-brown hair. Nora was short and looked a bit like a French bulldog, or maybe a white Eartha Kitt. Everything about her was droll—her drawling, wisecracking husky voice, the way she cocked her head to look at you with bright brown eyes from under her mop, even the way she held her ever-present cigarette, wrist flexed and ready for gesture. She had a playful, watchful way of drawing a person out, and when she paid you attention, it felt as if she were about to let you in on a private joke. Nora was the only one of that group of older women who paid any attention to me. It wasn't exactly love at first sight, but in Northampton, to a twenty-two-year-old looking for adventure, she was a figure of intrigue.

And then, in the fall of 1992, she was gone.

She reappeared after Christmas. Now she rented a big apartment of her own, furnished with brand-new Arts and Crafts–style furniture and a killer stereo. Everyone else I knew was sitting on thrift store couches with their roommates, while she was throwing money around in a way that got attention.

Nora asked me out for a drink, just the two of us, which was a first. Was it a date? Perhaps it was, because she took me to the bar of the Hotel Northampton, the closest local approximation to a swank hotel lounge, painted pale green with white trelliswork everywhere. I nervously ordered a margarita with salt, at which Nora arched a brow.

"Sort of chilly for a marg?" she commented, as she asked for a scotch.

It was true, the January winds were making western Massachusetts uninviting. I should have ordered something dark in a smaller glass—my frosty margarita now seemed ridiculously juvenile.

"What's that?" she asked, indicating the little metal box I had placed on the table.

The box was yellow and green and had originally held Sour Lemon pastilles. Napoleon gazed westward from its lid, identifiable by his cocked hat and gold epaulettes. The box had served as a wallet for a woman I'd known at Smith, an upperclasswoman who was the coolest person I had ever met. She had gone to art school, lived off campus, was wry and curious and kind and superhip, and one day when I had admired the box, she gave it to me. It was the perfect size for a pack of cigarettes, a license, and a twenty. When I tried to pull money out of my treasured tin wallet to pay for the round, Nora waved it away.

Where had she been for so many months? I asked, and Nora gave me an appraising once-over. She calmly explained to me that she had been brought into a drug-smuggling enterprise by a friend of her sister, who was "connected," and that she had gone to Europe and been formally trained in the ways of the underworld by an American art dealer who was also "connected." She had smuggled drugs into this country and been paid handsomely for her work.

I was completely floored. Why was Nora telling me this? What if I went to the police? I ordered another drink, half-certain that Nora was making the entire thing up and that this was the most hare-brained seduction attempt ever.

I had met Nora's younger sister once before, when she came to visit. She went by the name of Hester, was into the occult, and would leave a trail of charms and feathered trinkets made of chicken bones. I thought she was just a Wiccan heterosexual version of her sister, but apparently she was the lover of a West African drug kingpin. Nora described how she had traveled with Hester to Benin to meet the kingpin, who went by the name Alaji and bore a striking resemblance to MC Hammer. She had stayed as a guest at his compound, witnessed and been subject to "witch-doctor" ministrations, and was now considered his sister-in-law. It all sounded dark, awful, scary, wild—and exciting beyond belief. I couldn't believe that she, the keeper of so many terrifying and tantalizing secrets, was taking me into her confidence.

It was as if by revealing her secrets to me, Nora had bound me to her, and a secretive courtship began. No one would call Nora a classic beauty, but she had wit and charm in excess and was a master at the art of seeming effortlessness. And as has always been true, I respond to people who come after me with clear determination. In her seduction of me, she was both persistent and patient.

Over the months that followed, we grew much closer, and I learned that a number of local guys I knew were secretly working for her, which proved reassuring to me. I was entranced by the illicit adventure Nora represented. When she was in Europe or Southeast Asia for a long period of time, I all but moved into her house, caring for her beloved black cats, Edith and Dum-Dum. She would call at odd hours of the night from the other side of the globe to see how the kitties were, and the phone line would click and hiss with the distance. I kept all this quiet—even as I was dodging questions from my already-curious friends.

Since business was conducted out of town, the reality of the drugs felt like a complete abstraction to me. I didn't know anyone who used heroin; and the suffering of addiction was not something I thought about. One day in the spring Nora returned home with a brand-new white Miata convertible and a suitcase full of money. She dumped the cash on the bed and rolled around in it, naked and giggling. It was her biggest payout yet. Soon I was zipping around in that Miata, with Lenny Kravitz on the tape deck demanding to know, "Are You Gonna Go My Way?"

Despite (or perhaps because of) the bizarre romantic situation with Nora, I knew I needed to get out of Northampton and do something. My friend Lisa B. and I had been saving our tips and decided that we would quit our jobs at the brewery and take off for San Francisco at the end of the summer. (Lisa knew nothing about Nora's secret activities.) When I told Nora, she replied that she would love to have an apartment in San Francisco and suggested that we fly out there and house-hunt. I was shocked that she felt so strongly about me.

Just weeks before I was to leave Northampton, Nora learned that she had to return to Indonesia. "Why don't you come with me, keep me company?" she suggested. "You don't have to do anything, just hang out."

I had never been out of the United States. Although I was supposed to begin my new life in California, the prospect was irresistible. I wanted an adventure, and Nora had one on offer. Nothing bad had ever happened to the guys from Northampton who had gone with her to exotic places as errand boys—in fact, they returned with high-flying stories that only a select group could even hear. I rationalized that there was no harm in keeping Nora company. She gave me money to purchase a ticket from San Francisco to Paris and said there would be a ticket to Bali waiting for me at the Garuda Air counter at Charles de Gaulle. It was that simple.

Nora's cover for her illegal activities was that she and her partner in crime, a goateed guy named Jack, were starting an art and literary magazine—questionable, but it lent itself to vagueness. When I explained to my friends and family that I was moving to San Francisco and would be working and traveling for the magazine, they were uniformly surprised and suspicious of my new job, but I rebuffed their questions, adopting the air of a woman of mystery. As I drove out of Northampton headed west with my buddy Lisa, I felt as if I were finally embarking on my life. I felt ready for anything.

Lisa and I drove nonstop from Massachusetts to the Montana border, taking turns sleeping and driving. In the middle of the night we pulled into a rest stop to sleep, where we awoke to see the incredible golden eastern Montana dawn. I could not remember ever being so happy. After lingering in Big Sky country, we sped through Wyoming and Nevada until finally we sailed over the Bay Bridge into San Francisco. I had a plane to catch.

What would I need for my journey to Indonesia? I had no idea. I packed one small L.L. Bean duffel bag with a pair of black silk pants, a tank dress, blue-jean cutoffs, three T-shirts, a red silk shirt, a black miniskirt, my running gear, and a pair of black cowboy boots. I was so excited, I forgot to pack a bathing suit.

Upon arrival in Paris, I went straight to the Garuda counter to claim my ticket to Bali. They had never heard of me. Freaked out, I sat down at an airport restaurant, ordered a coffee, and tried to decide what to do. The days of cell phones and e-mail were still in the future, and I had no idea how to reach Nora; I assumed something must have gotten lost in translation. Finally I got up and went to the newsstand, bought a Paris guidebook, and picked out a cheap hotel that was centrally located in the sixth arrondissement. (My one credit card had a very low limit.) From my little room I could see the rooftops of Paris. I called Jack, Nora's old friend and now business partner in the States. Snide and superior and obsessed with prostitutes, Jack was not one of my favorite people.

"I'm stranded in Paris. Nothing Nora told me is right. What should I do?" I asked him.

Jack was annoyed but decided he could not leave me to my own devices. "Go find a Western Union. Tomorrow I'll wire you money for a ticket."

The wire didn't come for several days, but I didn't mind; I wandered Paris in a haze of excitement, taking everything in. Alongside most French women I looked like a teenager, so to counter this I bought a pair of spidery and beautiful black crochet stockings to go with my Doc Martens and miniskirt. I didn't care if I ever left Paris. I was in heaven, all alone.

WHEN I got off the smoky thirteen-hour flight from Paris to Bali, I was surprised to see my former brewery coworker Billy waiting for me, towering above the Indonesians with a big grin on his freckled face. Billy could have passed for my brother, strawberry blond with bright blue eyes. "Nora's waiting at the resort. You're going to love it here!" he said. Reunited with Nora in our luxurious room, I felt shy with her in this unfamiliar setting. But she acted as if this were all perfectly normal.

Bali was a bacchanalia: days and nights of sunbathing, drinking, and dancing until all hours with Nora's crew of gay boys, any pretty locals who wanted to help us spend money, and young Euros and Aussies we met in the clubs at Kuta beach. I went to the street market to buy a bikini and sarong, bartered for carved masks and silver jewelry, and walked the back roads of Nusa Dua talking to the friendly locals. Expeditions to temples, parasailing, and scuba diving offered other diversions—the Balinese scuba instructors loved the long-finned, jeweled, and elegant blue fish that had been tattooed on my neck back in New England and eagerly showed me their own tattoos. But the festivities were punctuated by tense phone calls between Nora and Alaji, or Nora and Jack.

The way their business worked was simple. From West Africa, Alaji would make it known to select people in the States that he had "contracts" for units of drugs (usually custom-built suitcases with heroin sewn into the linings) available—they could turn up at any number of places in the world. People like Nora and Jack (essentially subcontractors) would arrange to transport the suitcases into the States, where they were handed off to an anonymous pickup. It was up to them to figure out how to manage the transport—recruiting couriers, training them on how to get through customs undetected, paying for their "vacations" and their fees.

Nora and Jack were not the only people with whom Alaji worked; in fact, Nora was now competing with Jonathan Bibby, the "art dealer" who had originally trained her, for Alaji's business. The tension I observed in Nora derived from how many "contracts" were available, whether she and Jack could fulfill them, and whether the units of drugs would actually arrive as scheduled—all factors that seemed to change at a moment's notice. The job required lots of flexibility and lots of cash.

When cash ran low, I would be sent off to retrieve money wires from Alaji at various banks—a crime itself, although I did not realize it. Then I was sent on one such errand in Jakarta, one of the intended drug couriers asked to come along for the ride. He was a young gay guy from Chicago who was heavily into Goth but cleaned up well and looked the part of the perfect prepster; he was bored by the plush hotel. During the long, hot ride across the sprawling city, we were transfixed by the gridlock, the cages of barking puppies for sale at roadside, and the human strata that the Southeast Asian metropolis offers. At a traffic light a beggar lay in the street asking for alms. His skin was almost blackened by the sun, and he had no legs. I started to roll down my window to give him some of the hundreds of thousands of rupiah that I had with me.

My companion gasped and shrank back in his seat. "Don't!" he shouted.

I looked at him, disgusted and perplexed. Our taxi driver took the money from me and handed it out his window to the beggar. We rode on in silence.

WE HAD tons of time to kill. We blew off steam in Bali beach clubs, Jakarta military pool halls, and nightclubs like Tanamur that were borderline brothels. Nora and I shopped, got facials, or journeyed to other parts of Indonesia—just the two of us, girl time. We didn't always get along.

During a trip to Krakatoa we hired a guide to lead us on a hike in the mountains, which were covered by dense, humid jungle growth. It was hot, sweaty going. We stopped to eat lunch by a beautiful river pool at the top of a towering waterfall. After a skinny-dip, Nora dared me—double-dog-dared me, to be precise—to jump off the falls, which were at least thirty-five feet high.

"Have you seen people jump?" I asked our guide.

"Oh yes, miss," he said, smiling.

"Have you ever jumped?"

"Oh no, miss!" he said, still smiling.

Still, a dare was a dare. Naked, I began to crawl down the rock that seemed like the most logical jumping place. The falls roared. I saw the churning, opaque green water far below. I was terrified, and this suddenly seemed like a bad idea. But the rock was slippery, and as I tried in vain to edge back like a crab, I realized that I was going to have to jump; there was no other way. I gathered all of my physical strength and flung myself off the rock and into the air, shrieking as I plunged deep into the green gorge below. I burst the surface, laughing and exhilarated. Minutes later Nora came howling down the falls after me.

When she popped up, she gasped, "You are *crazy!*"

"You mean you wouldn't have gone if I had been too scared to jump?" I asked, surprised.

"No fucking way!" she replied. Right then and there I should have understood that Nora was not to be trusted.

Indonesia offered what seemed like a limitless range of experience, but there was a murky, threatening edge to it. I'd never seen such stark poverty as what was on display in Jakarta, or such naked capitalism at work in the enormous factories and the Texas drawls coming from across the hotel lobby where the oil company executives were drinking. You could spend a lovely hour chatting at the bar with a grandfatherly Brit about the charms of San Francisco and his prize greyhounds back in the U.K., and when you took his business card on the way out, he would explain casually that he was an arms dealer. When I rode the elevator to the top of the Jakarta Grand Hyatt at dusk, stepped into the lush garden there, and began to run laps on the track that circuited the roof, I could hear the Muslim call to prayer echoing from mosque to mosque throughout the entire city.

After many weeks I was both sad and relieved to say goodbye to Indonesia and head back to the West. I was homesick.

For four months of my life, I traveled constantly with Nora, occasionally touching down in the States for a few days. We lived a life of relentless tension, yet it was also often crushingly boring. I had little to do, other than keep Nora company while she dealt with her "mules." I would roam the streets of strange cities all alone. I felt disconnected from the world even as I was seeing it, a person without purpose or place. This was not the adventure I craved. I was lying to my family about every aspect of my life and growing sick and tired of my adopted drug "family."

During a brief stay in the States to visit with my real and very suspicious family, I received a call from Nora, who said that she needed me to meet her in Chicago. O'Hare Airport was known as a "safe" airport, whatever that meant, and it was where the drugs were flown. I met her at the Congress Hotel on Michigan Avenue. *What a dump,* I thought. I was used to the Mandarin Oriental. Nora explained tersely that she needed me to fly out the next day, carrying cash to be dropped off in Brussels. She had to do this for Alaji, and I had to do it for her. She never asked anything of me, but she was asking now. Deep down I felt that I had signed up for this situation and could not say no. I was scared. And I agreed to do it.

IN EUROPE things took a darker turn. Nora's business was getting harder for her to maintain, she was taking reckless chances with couriers, and that was a very scary thing. Her partner Jack joined us in Belgium, and things went downhill rapidly. I thought he was greedy, lecherous, and dangerous. And I could see that Nora trusted him far more than she cared for me.

I was scared and miserable, retreating into almost constant silence as we all moved from Belgium to Switzerland. I moped around Zurich alone, while Nora and Jack schemed. I saw *The Piano* three times in a row, gratefully transported to another place and time as I cried throughout the movie.

When Nora informed me in no uncertain terms that she wanted me to carry drugs, I knew that I was no longer valuable to her unless I could make her money. Obediently I "lost" my passport and was issued a new one. She costumed me in glasses, pearls, and a pair of ugly loafers. With makeup she tried in vain to cover up the fish tattooed on my neck. I was told to get a conservative haircut. Caught in a cold Saturday afternoon rainstorm trying to find a hairdresser who would transform my overgrown blond tresses into something presentable, I staggered dripping into a tiny salon, the fifth I had tried. I had been met with an arctic Swiss reception in the previous four, but now a soft familiar accent asked, "Y'all need some help?"

I almost cried when I saw the fellow who was asking—a sweet young southerner named Fenwick who looked like Terence Trent D'Arby. He took my wet coat, sat me down in his chair, and gave me hot tea and a haircut. He was curious but gentle when I balked at explaining myself or my presence in his salon. He talked about New Orleans, music, and Zurich. "It's a great city, but we have a terrible heroin problem here. You see people just lying in the streets, out of it." I felt ashamed. I wanted to go home. I thanked Fenwick profusely as I left his salon, the only friend I'd made in months.

At any time, with one phone call, my family would have helped rescue me from this mess of my own making, yet I never placed that call. I thought I had to tough it out on my own. I alone had signed up for this misadventure, and I alone would navigate it to some conclusion, although I was now petrified that it might be a very dismal end.

Nora and Alaji developed an elaborate and risky scheme to switch suitcases inside the Zurich airport, but mercifully the drugs she wanted me to carry never showed up, and I narrowly avoided becoming a drug courier. It seemed like it was only a matter of time before disaster would strike, and I was in way over my head. I knew I had to escape. When we got back to the States, I took the first flight to California I could get. From the safety of the West Coast I broke all ties with Nora and put my criminal life behind me.

CHAPTER 2

It All Changed in an Instant

||||

San Francisco was a welcome refuge—I might be a freak, but at least I was among many. I found a place on the Lower Haight with my old friend Alfie, a brewery coworker from back east who was now living in San Francisco. I was shell-shocked and felt like a smoking chunk of SkyLab that had crashed through the atmosphere back to Earth. When Alfie wasn't around, I would sit on the floor of our apartment and ponder what I had done, astonished by how far afield I had wandered and how willing I had been to abandon myself on the journey. I vowed that I would never relinquish my sense of self again, to anything or anyone.

After spending months in the underworld, it took a while to get used to a normal life. I had been living on room service, exoticism, and anxiety for a long time. But I had several great friends from college now in the Bay Area who took me under their wing, pulling me into a world of work, barbecues, softball games, and other wholesome rituals. I quit smoking.

I was terrified all the time about money and immediately got two jobs. I rose early in the morning to get to job one in the Castro, opening Josie's Juice Joint and Cabaret at seven A.M., and I got home late at night after hostessing at a swank Italian restaurant across town in Pacific Heights. Finally, I got a "real" job at a TV production company that specialized in infomercials. The job required coaxing passersby onto bizarre exercise equipment in public places, tending to the needs of C-list celebrities on set, and waxing facial hair off perfect strangers. I flew all over the country, filming people who wanted to be less fat, less poor, less wrinkled, less lonely, or less hairy. I found that I could talk to just about anyone, whether it was Bruce Jenner or a mom with a mustache, and find some common ground with them quickly—I wanted to be less poor, lonely, and hairy too. I worked my way up from Gal Friday to a real producer, working on preproduction, filming, and editing for broadcast. I loved my job, much to the amusement of my friends, who would tease me about the latest late-night life-changing widget, scheme, or cream.

I dated but still felt pretty crispy and gun-shy after the flame-out with Nora. I was fine being serially single, with the occasional crazy romance thrown in to distract me from work.

I never talked about my involvement with Nora to new friends, and the number of people who knew my secret remained very small. As time passed, I gradually relaxed inside my head. I started to feel as though there were no second shoe, and it had all been a crazy interlude. I thought I understood risk. I considered my time abroad with Nora as a crash course on the realities of the world, how ugly things can get, and how important it is to stay true to yourself even in the midst of an adventure or experiment. In my travels I had encountered all kinds of people whose dignity seemed to have a price—widely variable—and I thought that next time I had better set my price higher than anyone would pay.

With all that worldly wisdom secreted in my memory, I was feeling pretty damn lucky. Great job, great friends, great city, great social life. Through mutual friends I met Larry, the only pal I knew who worked as much as I did in leisure-loving San Francisco. He ran a wire service called AlterNet at a nonprofit media institute. When I would crawl, exhausted, out of the editing room after hours, I could always count on Larry for late dinner or later drinks.

In fact, Larry was always up for anything. Random tickets to a random music festival? Larry was in. Want to get up early on Sunday and go to church at Glide in the Tenderloin, and then go on a six-hour urban hike with pit stops for bloody Marys? He was Jewish, but sure, he'd come to church and lip-sync the hymns. He wasn't my only straight male friend, but we shared a particularly simpatico sense of humor, and he quickly became the most reliable source of fun that I knew.

As Larry's new best lesbian buddy, I got to hear about his every romantic conquest and reversal in gory detail, which was both appalling and entertaining. I spared him nothing in my evaluations of his progress. He returned the favor by treating me like a queen. One evening a bike messenger arrived at my office with a parcel that yielded a real Philadelphia soft pretzel, complete with spicy mustard, which Larry had personally imported just for me from a trip back east. How sweet, I thought, chewing.

But then a disturbing thing happened. Larry got hung up on one of his attempted conquests, and a rather drippy one at that. He became distinctly less fun. I was not the only one who noticed this. "She's leading him around by his nose!" other friends smirked. We mocked him mercilessly, but that didn't seem to have much effect. So I had to take matters into my own hands, and in a dark corner of a dirty nightclub, I sacrificed myself for Larry's dignity, kissing him squarely on his surprised, wisecracking mouth.

That got his attention. And mine. What the hell was I thinking? I proceeded to pretend for several months that nothing had happened, while I tried to sort out my feelings. Larry was nothing like any guy I'd been involved with in the past. For one thing, I liked him. For another, he was a short, scrappy, eager-to-please guy with big blue eyes, a big grin, and exceedingly big hair. I had deigned to sleep only with tall, exotically handsome narcissists in the past. I didn't particularly want to date a man, and this man wasn't even my type!

Except that he was. Larry was completely my type. Even after the weirdness of our barroom kiss, we were still inseparable, although he was understandably confused. But he didn't push, he didn't demand answers or clarity, he just waited. When I remembered that pretzel, I realized that Larry had been in love with me back then, and I was in love with him. Within months we were a real, official couple, much to the shock of our skeptical friends.

In fact, it was the easiest relationship I had ever been in, by far. Being with him made me undeniably happy, so when Larry came to me, conflicted and confused, to tell me that he had been offered a great magazine job back east, it didn't really disturb my equilibrium. My next step seemed·so obvious, so natural, that the decision practically made itself. I quit my beloved job to move back east with him— by far the best risk I have ever taken.

LARRY AND I landed in New York in 1998—he was an editor at a men's magazine, I worked as a freelance producer—and settled in a West Village walk-up. One warm May afternoon the doorbell rang. I was working at home, still in my pajamas.

"Who is it?" I asked over the intercom.

"Miss Kerman? It's Officers Maloney and Wong."

"Yes?" I wondered what the local cops wanted in the building.

"Can we speak with you a moment?"

"What is this about?" I was suddenly suspicious.

"Miss Kerman, I think it would be better if we spoke face-to-face."

Maloney and Wong, large men dressed in street clothes, walked up five flights of stairs and sat themselves down in the living room. Maloney did all the talking while Wong looked at me impassively. "Miss Kerman, we are U.S. Customs officers. We are here to notify you that you've been indicted in federal court in Chicago, on charges of drug smuggling and money laundering." He handed me a sheet of paper. "You need to appear in court on that date, at that place. If you do not appear, you will be taken into custody."

I blinked at him silently, and the veins in my temples suddenly pounded as if I had run miles at top speed. The noise in my head scared me. I had put my past behind me, had kept it secret from just about everyone, even Larry. But that was over. I was shocked at how physical my fear was.

Maloney took out a pad and paper and conversationally asked, "Would you like to make a statement, Miss Kerman?"

"I think I'd better speak with a lawyer, don't you, Officer Maloney?"

I staggered uptown to Larry's office, barely remembering to change out of my pajamas. Babbling, I pulled him out onto West Twenty-second Street.

"What's wrong? Are you mad at me?" he asked.

I drew a deep breath, because I couldn't talk otherwise. "I've been indicted in federal court for money laundering and drug trafficking."

"What?" He was amused. He looked around, as if perhaps we were participating in some secret street theater.

"It's true. I'm not making it up. I just came from the house. The feds were there. I need to use a phone. I need a lawyer. Can I use a phone?"

Wait, maybe I couldn't use the phone. Maybe all the phones remotely associated with me, including all of Larry's office phones, were tapped. Every crazy, paranoid thing that Nora had ever told me was screaming for attention inside my head. Larry was looking at me as if I had lost my mind.

"I need to use someone else's cell phone! Whose phone can I use??"

Minutes later I was on the fire escape outside Larry's office, using Larry's coworker's phone to call a friend in San Francisco who was the biggest big-shot lawyer I knew. He got on the line.

"Wallace, it's Piper. Two federal agents just came to my door and told me that I've been indicted for money laundering and drug trafficking."

Wallace laughed. This was a reaction I would eventually get used to when friends first learned of my predicament.

"Wallace, I'm totally fucking serious. I have no idea what to do. I'm freaking out!! You have to help me."

"Where are you calling me from?"

"The fire escape."

"Go find a pay phone."

I walked back into Larry's office. "I need to find a pay phone."

"Honey, what the hell is going on?" he said. He looked exasperated, worried, and a little annoyed.

"I really don't know. I gotta go make this call. I'll come back and find you."

Later, when he heard a condensed (and probably less than coherent) explanation of the situation, Larry was uncharacteristically quiet. He didn't yell at me for not telling him I was a former criminal before we combined our lives. He didn't chastise me for being a reckless, thoughtless, selfish idiot. As I emptied my savings account for lawyer's fees and bond money, he didn't suggest that perhaps I had ruined my life and his too. He said, "We'll figure it out." He said, "It will all work out. Because I love you."

THAT DAY was the beginning of a long, torturous expedition through the labyrinth of the U.S. criminal justice system. Wallace helped me find a lawyer. Confronted with the end of my life as I knew it, I adopted my standard pose when in over my head and scared: I closed myself off, telling myself that I had gotten into this mess and it was no one's fault but my own. I would have to figure out a solution on my own.

But I wasn't in this alone—my family and my unsuspecting boyfriend came along for the miserable ride. Larry, my parents, my brother, my grandparents—they all stood by me the entire way, though they were appalled and ashamed by my heretofore hidden criminal past. My father came to New York, and we spent an excruciating four hours driving up to New England, where my grandparents were spending the summer. I wasn't feeling hip, cool, adventurous, counterculture, or rebellious. All I felt was that I had willfully hurt and disappointed everyone I loved most and carelessly thrown my life away. What I had done was beyond their comprehension, and I sat in my grandparents' living room rigid with shame at the emergency family meeting, while they questioned me for hours, trying to make some sort of sense of what was happening. "What on earth did you do with the money?" my grandmother asked me finally, mystified.

"Well, Grandmother, I wasn't really in it for money," I answered lamely.

"Oh, Piper, for heaven's sake!" she snapped. Not only was I a shame and a disappointment, I was an idiot too.

She didn't say I was an idiot. No one actually said I was a shame or a disappointment either. They didn't have to. I knew it. Incredibly, my mother, my father, and my grandparents—all my family—said they loved me. They were worried for me. They would help me. When I left, my grandmother hugged me hard, her tiny arms circling my rib cage.

Although my family and the few friends I told took my situation seriously, they doubted that a "nice blond lady" like me could ever end up in prison, but my lawyer quickly impressed upon me the severity of my situation. My indictment in federal court for criminal conspiracy had been triggered by the collapse of my ex-lover's drug-smuggling operation. Nora, Jack, and thirteen others (some of whom I knew and some I did not), including African drug lord Alaji, shared my indictment. Nora and Jack were both in custody, and someone was pointing fingers and naming names.

No matter how badly things had ended between us, I never dreamed that Nora would turn me in to try to save her own skin. But when my lawyer sent me the prosecutor's discovery materials—the evidence the government had gathered against me—it included a detailed statement from her that described me carrying cash to Europe. I was in a whole new world, one where "conspiracy charges" and "mandatory minimum sentencing" would determine my fate.

I learned that a conspiracy charge, rather than identifying individual lawless acts, accuses a group of people of plotting to commit a crime. Conspiracy charges are often brought against a person just on the strength of testimony from a "coconspirator" or, even worse, a "confidential informant," someone who has agreed to rat out others in exchange for immunity. Conspiracy charges are beloved by prosecutors, because they make it much easier to obtain indictments from grand juries and are a great lever for getting people to plead guilty: once one person on a conspiracy indictment rolls over, it's pretty easy to convince their codefendants that they won't stand a chance in open trial. Under a conspiracy charge, I would be sentenced based on the total amount of drugs involved in the operation, not on my small role in it.

In the United States mandatory minimum sentencing was a critical part of the late-twentieth-century "War on Drugs." Guidelines established by Congress in the 1980s required federal judges to impose set sentences for drug crimes, regardless of the specific circumstances of a case, and without discretion to evaluate the person being sentenced. The federal laws have been widely duplicated by state legislatures. The length of the sentences completely freaked me out: ten, twelve, twenty years. Mandatory minimum sentences for drug offenses are the primary reason that the U.S. prison population has ballooned since the 1980s to over 2.5 million people, a nearly 300 percent increase. We now lock up one out of every hundred adults, far more than any other country in the world.

Gently but firmly, my lawyer explained to me that if I wished to go to trial and fight the conspiracy charge, I would be one of the best defendants he had ever worked with, sympathetic and with a story to tell; but if I lost, I risked the maximum sentence, probably over a decade in prison. If I pleaded guilty, make no mistake, I was going to prison, but for a much shorter time.

I chose the latter. There were some agonizing conversations with Larry and with my still-reeling family. But it was my decision to make. My lawyer negotiated hard and smartly on my behalf, and ultimately the U.S. Attorney's Office allowed me to plead guilty to money laundering rather than conspiracy, for which they would require a minimum sentence of thirty months in federal prison.

On Halloween Day 1998, Larry and I traveled to Chicago in costume as "teenagers"; maybe my misery was masked by the disguise. That night we hit the town with our friends Gab and Ed, who had no clue about my predicament and thought I was in Chicago for work. The next morning I was standing tall, if pale, in my best suit as we went to the federal building where the court was located. With Larry looking on, I choked out three words that sealed my fate: "Guilty, Your Honor."

. . .

SHORTLY AFTER I pleaded guilty, something surprising happened. Alaji, the West African drug kingpin, was arrested in London on a U.S. warrant. Suddenly my date with prison was postponed— indefinitely—while the United States tried to extradite him to stand trial. They wanted me in street clothes, not an orange jumpsuit, to testify against him.

There was no end in sight. I spent almost six years under supervision by the feds, reporting monthly to my pretrial supervisor, an earnest young woman with an exuberantly curly mullet and an office in the federal court building down on Pearl Street in Manhattan. Once a month I would go through building security, ride the elevator up to Pretrial Services, and sign in, waiting in a dingy room decorated with inspirational and cautionary posters that reminded me about Perseverance and to Use Condoms. I was often alone in the waiting room. Sometimes I was joined by young black or Latino men, who either sized me up silently or stared straight ahead. The occasional thick-necked older white guy with lots of gold jewelry would appear—and he would look at me with frank surprise. Once in a while there would be another female, never white, sometimes accompanied by children. They always ignored me. When my Miss Finnegan would finally appear and beckon, I would trail her to her office, where we would sit awkwardly for a few minutes.

"So . . . any news on your case?"

"Nope."

"Well . . . this sure is a long one."

Every now and then she would apologetically drug-test me. I always tested clean. Eventually Miss Finnegan left the department to go to law school, and I was transferred to the equally mild-mannered Miss Sanchez. She had long Frito-chip fingernails painted Barbie pink. "You're my easiest one!" she would say every month, cheerfully.

Over more than five years of waiting, I thought about prison in every imaginable way. My predicament remained a secret from almost everyone I knew. Initially it was too terrible, too overwhelming, and too uncertain to tell anyone what was happening. When the extradition delay struck, the situation grew too weird to broach with friends who didn't know: "I'm going to prison . . . someday?" I felt that I just had to gut it out in silence. My friends who did know were mercifully quiet on the subject as the years dragged on, as if God had put me on hold.

I worked hard at forgetting what loomed ahead, pouring my energies into working as a creative director for Web companies and exploring downtown New York with Larry and our friends. I needed money to pay my huge ongoing legal fees, so I worked with the clients my hipster colleagues found unsexy and unpalatable—big telecom, big petrochemicals, and big shadowy holding companies.

With everyone but Larry, in my interactions I was partially absent. Only to him could I reveal my fear and shame. With folks who knew nothing of my criminal secret and looming imprisonment, I was simply not quite myself—pleasant, sometimes charming, but aloof, distant, perhaps even indifferent. Even with close friends who knew what was happening, I wasn't fully engaged—I was always observing myself with an unstated foresight, a sense that whatever was happening now didn't matter much given what was to come. Somewhere on the horizon was coming devastation, the arrival of Cossacks and hostile Indians.

As the years passed, my family almost began to believe that I would be miraculously spared. My mother was certainly logging a lot of hours in church. But never for a minute did I allow myself to indulge in that fantasy—I knew that I would go to prison. There were times when I was pretty damn depressed. But the revelation was that my family and Larry still loved me despite my massive fuckup; that my friends who knew my situation never turned away from me; and that I could still function in the world professionally and socially, despite having ostensibly ruined my life. I began to grow less fearful about my future, my prospects for happiness, and even about prison, as more and more time passed.

The main reason was Larry. When I was indicted, we were definitely in love, but just twenty-eight and freshly arrived in New York, we were not thinking about the future beyond where we would move when the guy we were subletting from reappeared from London. When my criminal past reappeared, who could have blamed him if he had sat me down and said, "I did not sign up for this crazy shit. I thought you were good crazy, not scary-crazy"? Who could predict how a nice Jewish boy from New Jersey would process the information that his ex-lesbian, boho-WASP girlfriend was also a soon-to-be-convicted felon?

Who knew that my extroverted, mercurial, overcaffeinated boyfriend would be so patient, so capable, and so resourceful? That when I cried myself into hyperventilation, he would hold my head and comfort me? That he would guard my secret and make it his own? That when I moped for too long, letting the poor-me blues clamp around my ankles and drag me down to very bad places, he would fight to get me back, even if it meant terrible battles and tough days and nights at home?

In July 2003 we were in Massachusetts at my family's beach shack. On a beautifully sunny day Larry and I kayaked out to Pea Island, a speck of rock and sand set in a small cove off Buzzard's Bay. The island was placid and deserted. We swam and then sat on a rock looking back at the cove. Larry was fumbling with his swimming trunks, and I eyed him sideways, wondering why he was being so weird. He withdrew a plastic Baggie from his swim trunks and from it a metal box. "P, I got you these rings, because I love you, and I want you to have them because you mean so much to me. There's seven of them, for every year we've been together. We don't have to get married if you don't want to. But I want you to have them . . ."

Of course I can't remember another word he said, because I was so surprised and astonished and touched and thrilled that I couldn't hear anything anymore. I just shouted, "Yes!" The box held seven hammered-gold rings, each as thin as manila paper, to be worn stacked. And he had gotten himself a ring too, a thin silver band that he worried nervously on his finger.

My family was ecstatic. Larry's parents were too, but despite the length of my relationship with their son, there was a lot they didn't know about their future daughter-in-law. They had always been kind and welcoming to me, but I was terrified of what their reaction would be to my nasty secret. Carol and Lou were different from my former-hippie parents: they were 1950s high school sweethearts who predated the counterculture. They still lived in the bucolic county where they grew up, and they went to football games and bar association dinners. I didn't think they were going to understand my adolescent fascination with the underbelly of society, my involvement in international drug trafficking, or my impending incarceration.

By now more than five years had passed since I had been indicted. Larry thought it was important to tell his parents what was happening. We decided to practice on some other people, a tactic Larry described as "tell the truth and run." Reactions were pretty consistent—our friends would laugh uproariously, then have to be persuaded of the truth, then be horrified and worried for me. Despite our friends' responses, I was deeply frightened that my luck would run out with my future in-laws.

Larry called his parents and told them there was something important we needed to discuss with them in person. We drove down on an August evening, arrived late, and ate a classic summer dinner—steak, corn on the cob, big juicy Jersey tomatoes, delicious peach cobbler. Larry and I sat opposite each other at their kitchen table. Carol and Lou looked far more than nervous but not quite terrified. I think they assumed it was about me and not about Larry. Finally Larry said, "Bad news, but it's not cancer."

The story spilled out of me, with interruptions from Larry, not entirely coherent, but at least it was out, like a splinter.

Carol was sitting next to me and she took my hand, squeezed it hard, and said, "You were young!"

Lou tried to organize this radical new information in his head by switching into lawyer mode, asking about my indictment, my lawyer, the court in question, and what he could do to help. And was I a heroin addict?

The beautiful irony of Larry's family was that when something minor was amiss, it was as if the *Titanic* were going down, but when a real disaster struck, they were the people you wanted in your life raft. I had expected an explosion of recrimination and rejection and instead got a big hug.

ULTIMATELY BRITAIN declined to extradite the kingpin Alaji to America and instead set him free. My lawyer explained that as a Nigerian, he was a citizen of the British Commonwealth and enjoyed certain protections under British law. A little bit of Web research revealed that he was a wealthy and powerful businessman-gangster in Africa, and I could certainly imagine that he might have connections that could make pesky things like extradition treaties go away.

Finally, the U.S. Attorney in Chicago was willing to move forward with my case. To prepare for my sentencing, I wrote a personal statement to the court and broke my silence with more friends and coworkers, asking them to write letters vouching for my character and asking the judge for leniency. It was an incredibly humbling and difficult experience to approach people I had known for years, confess my situation, and ask for their help. Their collective response was devastating; I had steeled myself for rejection, knowing that it would be perfectly reasonable for someone to decline on any number of grounds. Instead, I was overwhelmed by kindness and concern and cried over every letter, whether it described my childhood, my friendships, or my work ethic. Each person strived to convey what they thought was important and great about me, which flew in the face of how I felt: profoundly unworthy.

One of my dearest friends from college, Kate, wrote this to the judge:

> I believe that her decision to enter into criminal activity was partially motivated by a sense that she was alone in the world and had to look out for herself. Since the time that she made those decisions, her relationships with others have changed

and deepened. I believe that she now knows that her life is entwined with those of people who love her . . .

Finally my sentencing date drew near. While the cliché "what doesn't kill you makes you stronger" had been echoing in my brain over the almost six years of waiting, I had to consider the truth it offers, like most hoary, oft-repeated ideas. I had dealt myself the cards of deceit, exposure, shame, near-bankruptcy, and self-imposed isolation. It was a pretty crappy hand to try to play. And yet somehow I was not alone at this stage of the game. My family, my friends, my coworkers—these good people had all refused to abandon me despite my rotten, wild, reckless behavior all those years ago and my I-am-an-island-fortress method of dealing with my problems. Maybe, because all these good people loved me enough to help me, maybe I wasn't quite as bad as I felt. Maybe there was a part of me that was worthy of their love.

Larry and I again flew to Chicago, and I met with my lawyer, Pat Cotter, the day before my sentencing. We hoped for a shorter sentence than thirty months, and with Pat's careful, painstaking, and persuasive legal work the U.S. Attorney had agreed not to oppose our motion in light of the lengthy delay. I showed Pat my options for courtroom wardrobe: one of my sleek "creative director" pantsuits; a militaristic navy coatdress that had to be the most conservative piece of clothing I owned; and a bonus choice, a skirt suit from the 1950s that I had won on eBay, soft cream with a delicate blue windowpane check, very country club. "That's the one," said Pat, pointing at the skirt suit. "We want him to be reminded of his own daughter or niece or neighbor when he looks at you." I couldn't sleep that night, and Larry flicked on the hotel television to a yoga channel, where a smooth, handsome yogi struck pretzel poses on a hypnotic Hawaiian beach. I wished fervently that I were there instead.

On December 8, 2003, I stood in front of Judge Charles Norgle with a small group of my family and friends sitting behind me in the courtroom. Before he handed down my sentence, I made a statement to the court.

"Your Honor, more than a decade ago I made bad decisions, on both a practical and a moral level. I acted selfishly, without regard for others, I knowingly broke the law, I lied to my loving family, and I distanced myself from my true friends.

"I am prepared to face the consequences of my actions, and accept whatever punishment the court decides upon. I am truly sorry for all the harm I have caused to others and I know the court will deal fairly with me.

"I would like to take this opportunity to thank my parents, my fiancé, and my friends and colleagues who are here today and who have loved and supported me, and to apologize to them for all the pain, worry, and embarrassment I have caused them.

"Your Honor, thank you for hearing my statement and considering my case."

I was sentenced to fifteen months in federal prison, and I could hear Larry, my parents, and my friend Kristen crying behind me. I thought it was a miracle it wasn't a longer sentence, and I was so exhausted by waiting that I was eager to get it over with as quickly as possible. Still, my parents' suffering was worse than any strain, fatigue, or depression that the long legal delay caused me.

But the wait continued, this time for my prison assignment. It felt a lot like waiting for my college acceptance letter—I hope I get into Danbury in Connecticut! Anywhere else would have proved disastrous in respect to seeing Larry or my family with any frequency. West Virginia, five hundred miles away, had the next closest federal women's prison. When the thin envelope arrived from the federal marshals telling me to report to the Federal Correctional Institution (FCI) in Danbury on February 4, 2004, my relief was overwhelming.

I tried to get my affairs in order, preparing to vanish for over a year. I had already read the books on Amazon about surviving prison, but they were written for men. I paid a visit to my grandparents, nervously fighting off the fear that I might not see them again. About a week before I was to report, Larry and I met a small group of friends at Joe's Bar on Sixth Street in the East Village, for an impromptu going-away. These were our good friends from the city, who had known my secret and done whatever they could to help. We had a good time—shot pool, told stories, drank tequila. The night went on—I wasn't slowing down, I wasn't going to exercise any tequila restraint, I wasn't going to be a bummer. Night turned into morning, and finally someone had to go home. And as I hugged them as hard and relentlessly as only a girl drunk on tequila can, it sank in on me that this was really goodbye. I didn't know when I would see any of my friends again or what I would be like when I did. And I started to cry.

I never wept in front of anyone but Larry. But now I cried, and then my friends started to cry. We must have looked like lunatics, a dozen people sitting in an East Village bar at three in the morning, sobbing. I couldn't stop. I cried and cried, as I said goodbye to every one of them. It took forever. I would calm down for a minute and then turn to another friend and start to sob again. Completely beyond embarrassment, I was so sad.

The next afternoon I could barely see myself between the puffy slits that were my eyes. I had never looked worse. But I felt a little better.

My lawyer, Pat Cotter, had sent his share of white-collar clients off to prison. He advised me, "Piper, I think for you the hardest thing about prison will be chickenshit rules enforced by chickenshit people. Call me if you run into trouble. And don't make any friends."

CHAPTER 3

#11187–424

IIII

On February 4, 2004, more than a decade after I had committed my crime, Larry drove me to the women's prison in Danbury, Connecticut. We had spent the previous night at home; Larry had cooked me an elaborate dinner, and then we curled up in a ball on our bed, crying. Now we were heading much too quickly through a drab February morning toward the unknown. As we made a right onto the federal reservation and up a hill to the parking lot, a hulking building with a vicious-looking triple-layer razor-wire fence loomed up. If that was minimum security, I was fucked.

Larry pulled into one of the parking areas. We looked at each other, saucer-eyed. Almost immediately a white pickup with police lights on its roof pulled in after us. I rolled down my window.

"There's no visiting today," the officer told me.

I stuck my chin out, defiance covering my fear. "I'm here to surrender."

"Oh. All right then." He pulled out and drove away. *Had he looked surprised?* I wasn't sure.

In the car I stripped off all my jewelry—the seven gold rings; the diamond earrings Larry had given me for Christmas; the sapphire ring from my grandmother; the 1950s man's watch that was always around my wrist; all the earrings from all the extra holes that had so vexed my grandfather. I had on jeans, sneakers, and a long-sleeved T-shirt. With false bravado I said, "Let's do this."

We walked into the lobby. A placid woman in uniform was sitting behind the raised desk. There were chairs, some lockers, a pay phone, and a soda machine. It was spotless. "I'm here to surrender," I announced.

"Hold on." She picked up a phone and spoke to someone briefly. "Have a seat." We sat. For several hours. It got to be lunchtime. Larry handed me a foie gras sandwich that he had made from last night's leftovers. I wasn't hungry at all but unwrapped it from the tinfoil and munched every gourmet bite miserably. I am fairly certain that I was the first Seven Sisters grad to eat duck liver chased with a Diet Coke in the lobby of a federal penitentiary. Then again, you never know.

Finally, a considerably less pleasant-looking woman entered the lobby. She had a dreadful scar down the side of her face and neck. "Kerman?" she barked.

We sprang to our feet. "Yes, that's me."

"Who's this?" she said.

"This is my fiancé."

"Well, he's gotta leave before I take you in." Larry looked outraged. "That's the rule, it prevents problems. You have any personal items?"

I had a manila envelope in my hands, which I handed to her. It contained my self-surrender instructions from the U.S. Marshals, some of my legal paperwork, twenty-five photographs (an embarrassing number of my cats), lists of my friends' and family's addresses, and a cashier's check for $290 that I had been instructed to bring. I knew that I would need money in my prison account to make phone calls and buy . . . something? I couldn't imagine what.

"Can't take that," she said, handing the check to Larry.

"But I called last week, and they told me to bring it!"

"He has to send it to Georgia, then they'll process it," she said with absolute finality.

"*Where* do we send it?" I asked. I was suddenly furious.

"Hey, do you have that Georgia address?" the prison guard asked over her shoulder to the woman at the desk while poking through my envelope. "What are these, pictures? You got any nudie Judies in here?" She raised an eyebrow in her already-crooked face. Nudie Judies? Was she for real? She looked at me as if to ask, *Do I need to go through all these photos to see if you're a dirty girl?*

"No. No nudie Judies," I said. Three minutes into my self-surrender, and I already felt humiliated and beaten.

"Okay, are you ready?" I nodded. "Well, say goodbye. Since you're not married, it could be a while until he can visit." She took a symbolic step away from us, I guess to give us privacy.

I looked at Larry and hurled myself into his arms, holding on as tight as I could. I had no idea when I would see him again, or what would happen to me in the next fifteen months.

He looked as if he was going to cry; yet at the same time he was also furious. "I love you! I love you!" I said into his neck and his nice oatmeal sweater that I had picked for him. He squeezed me and told me he loved me too.

"I'll call you as soon as I can," I croaked.

"Okay."

"Please call my parents."

"Okay."

"Send that check immediately!"

"I know."

"I love you!"

And then he left the lobby, rubbing his eyes with the heel of his hand. He banged the doors hard and walked quickly to the parking lot.

The prison guard and I watched him get into the car. As soon as he was out of sight, I felt a surge of fear.

She turned to me. "You ready?" I was alone with her and whatever else was waiting for me.

"Yeah."

"Well, come on."

She led me out the door Larry had just exited from, turning right and walking along that vicious, towering fence. The fence had multiple layers; between each layer was a gate through which we had to be buzzed. She opened the gate, and I stepped in. I looked back over my shoulder at the free world. The next gate buzzed. I stepped through again, wire mesh and barbed metal soaring all around me. I felt fresh, rising panic. This was not what I had expected. This was not how minimum-security camps had been described; this didn't look at all like "Club Fed." This was scaring the crap out of me.

We reached the door of the building and again were buzzed in. We walked through a small hallway into an institutional tiled room with harsh fluorescent light. It felt old, dingy, clinical, and completely empty. She pointed into a holding cell with benches bolted to the walls and metal screens over all visible sharp edges. "Wait in there." Then she walked through a door into another room.

I sat on a bench facing away from the door. I stared at the small high window through which I could see nothing but clouds. I wondered when I would see anything beautiful again. I meditated on the consequences of my long-ago actions and seriously questioned why I was not on the lam in Mexico. I kicked my feet. I thought about my fifteen-month sentence, which did nothing to quell my panic. I tried not to think about Larry. Then I gave up and tried to imagine what he was doing, with no success.

I had only the most tenuous idea of what might happen next, but I knew that I would have to be brave. Not foolhardy, not in love with risk and danger, not making ridiculous exhibitions of myself to prove that I wasn't terrified—really, genuinely brave. Brave enough to be quiet when quiet was called for, brave enough to observe before flinging myself into something, brave enough to not abandon my true self when someone else wanted to seduce or force me in a direction I didn't want to go, brave enough to stand my ground quietly. I waited an unquantifiable amount of time while trying to be brave.

"Kerman!" As I was unaccustomed to being called like a dog, it took her a number of shouts before I realized that meant "Move." I jumped up and peered cautiously out of the holding cell. "Come on." The prison guard's rasp made it hard for me to understand what she was saying.

She led me into the next room, where her coworkers were lounging. Both were bald, male, and white. One of them was startlingly big, approaching seven feet tall; the other was very short. They both stared at me as if I had three heads. "Self-surrender," my female escort said to them by way of explanation as she started my paperwork. She spoke to me like I was an idiot yet explained nothing during the process. Every time I was slow to answer or asked her to repeat a question, Shorty would snort derisively, or worse, mimic my responses. I looked at him in disbelief. It was unnerving, as it was clearly intended to be, and it pissed me off, which was a welcome switch from the fear I was battling.

The female guard continued to bark questions and fill out forms. As I stood at attention and answered, I could not stop my eyes from turning toward the window, to the natural light outdoors.

"Come on."

I followed the guard toward the hallway outside the holding cell. She pawed through a shelf filled with clothing, then handed me a pair of granny panties; a cheap nylon bullet bra; a pair of elastic-waist khaki pants; a khaki top, like hospital scrubs; and tube socks. "What size shoe are you?" "Nine and a half." She handed me a little pair of blue canvas slippers like you would buy on the street in any Chinatown.

She indicated a toilet and sink area behind a plastic shower curtain. "Strip." I kicked off my sneakers, took off my socks, my jeans, my T-shirt, my bra, and my underpants, all of which she took from me. It was cold. "Hold your arms up." I did, displaying my armpits. "Open your mouth and stick out your tongue. Turn around, squat, spread your cheeks and cough." I would never get used to the cough part of this drill, which was supposed to reveal contraband hidden in one's privates—it was just so unnatural. I turned back around, naked. "Get dressed."

She put my own clothes in a box—they would be mailed back to Larry, like the personal effects of a dead soldier. The bullet bra, though hideous and scratchy, did fit. So in fact did all the khaki prison clothes, much to my amazement. She really had the eye. In minutes I was transformed into an inmate.

Now she seemed to soften toward me a bit. As she was fingerprinting me (a messy and oddly intimate process), she asked, "How long you been with that guy?"

"Seven years," I replied sullenly.

"He know what you were up to?"

Up to? What did she know! My temper flared again as I said defiantly, "It's a ten-year-old offense. He had nothing to do with it." She seemed surprised by this, which I took as a moral victory.

"Well, you're not married, so you probably won't be seeing him for quite a while, not until he gets on your visitor list."

The horrifying reality that I had no idea when I would see Larry again shut me right down. The prison guard was indifferent to the devastating blow she had just dealt me.

She had been distracted by the fact that no one seemed to know how to use the ID machine camera. Everyone took a turn poking at it, until finally they produced a photo that made me look remarkably like serial killer Aileen Wuornos. My chin was raised defiantly, and I looked like hell. I later figured out that everyone looks either thuggish and murderous or terrified and miserable in their prison ID photo. I'm proud to say that, against all odds, I fell into the former category, though I felt like the latter.

The ID card was red, with a bar code and the legend "U.S. Department of Justice Federal Bureau of Prisons—INMATE." In addition to the unflattering photo, it also bore my new registration number in large numerals: 11187–424. The last three numbers indicated my sentencing district—Northern Illinois. The first five numbers were unique to me, my new identity. Just as I had been taught to memorize my aunt and uncle's phone number when I was six years old, I now silently tried to commit my reg number to memory. 11187–424, 11187–424, 11187–424, 11187–424, 11187–424, 11187–424, 11187–424, 11187–424, 11187–424, 11187–424.

After the ID debacle, Ms. Personality said, "Mr. Butorsky's gonna talk to you, but first go into medical." She pointed into another small room.

Mr. Who? I went and stared out the window, obsessing about the razor wire and the world beyond it from which I had been taken, until a medic—a round Filipino man—came to see me. He performed the most basic of medical interviews, which went quickly, as I have been blessed with more or less perfect health. He told me he needed to perform a TB test, for which I extended my arm. "Nice veins!" he said with very genuine admiration. "No track marks!" Given his total lack of irony, I thanked him.

Mr. Butorsky was a compact, mustachioed fiftyish man, with watery, blinky blue eyes and, unlike the prison staff I had met so far, of discernible intelligence. He was leaning back in a chair, with paperwork spread out in front of him. It was my PSI—the presentencing investigation that the Feds do on people like me. It is supposed to document the basic facts of one's crime, one's prior offenses, one's family situation and children, one's history of substance abuse, work history, everything important.

"Kerman? Sit down," he gestured, looking at me in a way that I suspect was much practiced to be calculating, penetrating, and measuring. I sat. He regarded me for several seconds in silence. I kept my chin firm and didn't look at him. "How are you doing?" he asked.

It was startling to have anyone show the slightest interest in how, exactly, I was doing. I felt a flood of gratitude in spite of myself. "I'm okay."

"You are?"

I nodded, deciding this was a good situation for my tough act.

He looked out the window. "In a little bit I'm going to have them take you up to the Camp," he began.

My brain relaxed a bit and my stomach unclenched. I followed his gaze out the window, feeling profound relief that I wouldn't have to stay down here with evil Shorty.

"I'll be your counselor at the Camp. You know I've been reading your file." He gestured at my PSI on the desk. "Sort of unusual. Pretty big case."

Was it? I realized I had absolutely no idea if it was a big case or not. If I was a big-time criminal, who exactly would my cellmates be?

"And it's been a long time since you were involved in all that," he continued. "That's pretty unusual. I can tell you've matured since then." He looked at me.

"Yeah, I guess so," I muttered.

"Well, look, I've been working up at that Camp for ten years. I run that Camp. It's my Camp, and there's nothing that goes on up there that I don't know about."

I was embarrassed by how relieved I felt: I didn't want to see this man, or any prison staffer, as my protector, but at the moment he was the closest thing to human I had encountered.

"We've got all types up there. What you really have to watch is the other inmates. Some of them are all right. No one's going to mess with you unless you let them. Now, women, they don't fight much. They talk, they gossip, they spread rumors. So they may talk about you. Some of these girls are going to think you think you're better than them. They're going to say, 'Oh, she's got money.' "

I felt uncomfortable. Was that how I came across? Was I going to be pegged as a snotty rich bitch?

"And there's lesbians up there. They're there, but they're not gonna bother you. Some are gonna try and be your friend, whatever—just stay away from them! I want you to understand, you do not have to have lesbian sex. I'm old-fashioned. I don't approve of any of that mess."

I tried very hard not to smirk. Guess he didn't read my file that closely. "Mr. Butorsky?"

"Yes?"

"I'm wondering when my fiancé and my mother can come to visit me?" I could not control the querulous tone in my voice.

"They're both in your PSI, right?" My PSI detailed all the members of my immediate family, including Larry, who had been interviewed by the probation department.

"Yes, they're all in there, and my father too."

"Anyone who's in your PSI is cleared to visit. They can come this weekend. I'll make sure the list is in the visiting room." He stood up. "You just keep to yourself, you're gonna be fine." He gathered up my paperwork and left.

I went out to retrieve my new creature comforts from the prison guard: two sheets, a pillowcase, two cotton blankets, a couple of cheap white towels, and a face cloth. These items were crammed into a mesh laundry bag. Add to that an ugly brown stadium coat with a broken zipper and a sandwich bag that contained a stubby mini-toothbrush, tiny packets of toothpaste and shampoo, and a rectangle of motel soap.

Heading out through the multiple gates of the monster fence, I felt elated that I would not be behind it, but now the mystery of the Camp was rushing toward me, unstoppable. A white minivan waited. Its driver, a middle-aged woman in army-issue-looking street clothes and sunglasses, greeted me warmly. She wore makeup and little gold hoops in her ears, and she looked like she could be a nice Italian-American lady called Ro from New Jersey. *The prison guards are getting friendlier,* I thought as I climbed into the passenger seat. She closed the door, and smiled encouragingly at me. She was chipper. I stared back at her.

She flipped up the sunglasses. "I'm Minetta. I'm an inmate too."

"Oh!" I was flabbergasted that she was a prisoner, and she was driving—and wearing makeup!

"What's your name—your last name? People go by their last names here."

"Kerman," I replied.

"Is this your first time down?"

"My first time here?" I was confused.

"Your first time in prison."

I nodded.

"You doin' okay, Kerman?" she asked as she guided the minivan up a small hill. "It's not so bad, you're going to be all right. We'll take care of you. Everyone's okay here, though you've gotta watch out for the stealing. How much time do you have?"

"How much time?" I bleated.

"How long is your sentence?"

"Oh! Fifteen months."

"That's not bad. That'll be over in no time."

We circled to the back entrance of a long, low building that re-sembled a 1970s elementary school. She pulled up next to a handi-capped ramp and stopped the car. Clutching my laundry bag, I followed her toward the building, picking through patches of ice while the cold penetrated my thin rubber soles. Small knots of women wearing identical ugly brown coats were smoking in the February chill. They looked tough, and depressed, and they all had on big, heavy black shoes. I noticed that one of them was hugely preg-nant. *What was a woman that pregnant doing in prison?*

"Do you smoke?" Minetta asked.

"No."

"Good for you! We'll just get you your bed assignment and get you settled. There's the dining hall." She gestured to her left down several stairs. She was talking the entire time, explaining everything about Danbury Federal Prison Camp, none of which I was catching. I followed her up a couple of stairs and into the building.

" . . . . TV room. There's the education office, that's the CO's of-fice. Hi, Mr. Scott! CO, that's the correctional officer. He's all right. Hey, Sally!" She greeted a tall white woman. "This is Kerman, she's new, self-surrender." Sally greeted me sympathetically with another "Are you okay?" I nodded, mute. Minetta pressed on. "Here's more offices, those are the Rooms up there, the Dorms down there." She turned to me, serious. "You're not allowed down there, it's out of bounds for you. You understand?"

I nodded, not understanding a thing. Women were surging all around me, black, white, Latino, every age, here in my new home, and they made a tremendous collective din in the linoleum and cinder-block interior. They were all dressed in khaki uniforms different from the one I was wearing, and they all wore huge, heavy-looking black work shoes. I realized that my attire made it glaringly obvious that I was new. I looked down at my little canvas slippers and shivered in my brown coat.

As we proceeded up the long main hall, several more women

came up and greeted me with the standard "You're new . . . are you all right?" They seemed genuinely concerned. I hardly knew how to respond but smiled weakly and said hello back.

"Okay, here's the counselor's office. Who's your counselor?"

"Mr. Butorsky."

"Oh. Well, at least he does his paperwork. Hold on, let me see where they put you." She knocked on the door with some authority. Opening it, she stuck her head in, all business. "Where did you put Kerman?" Butorsky gave her a response that she understood, and she led me up to Room 6.

We entered a room that held three sets of bunk beds and six waist-high metal lockers. Two older women were lying on the lower bunks. "Hey, Annette, this is Kerman. She's new, a self-surrender. Annette will take care of you," she told me. "Here's your bed." She indicated the one empty top bunk with a naked mattress.

Annette sat up. She was a small, dark fiftyish woman with short, spiky black hair. She looked tired. "Hi," she rasped in a Jersey accent. "How are you? What's your name again?"

"It's Piper. Piper Kerman."

Minetta's work was apparently done. I thanked her profusely, making no effort to hide my gratitude, and she exited. I was left with Annette and the other, silent woman, who was tiny, bald, and seemed much older, maybe seventy. I cautiously placed my laundry bag on my bunk and looked around the room. In addition to the steel bunk beds and lockers, everywhere I looked there were hangers with clothes, towels, and string bags dangling from them. It looked like a barracks.

Annette got out of bed and revealed herself to be about five feet tall. "That's Miss Luz. I've been keeping stuff in your locker. I gotta get it out. Here's some toilet paper—you gotta take it with you."

"Thank you." I was still clutching my envelope with my paperwork and photos in it, and now a roll of toilet paper.

"Did they explain to you about the count?" she asked.

"The count?" I was getting used to feeling completely idiotic. It was as if I'd been home-schooled my whole life and then dropped into a large, crowded high school. *Lunch money? What's that?*

"The count. They count us five times a day, and you have to be here, or wherever you're supposed to be, and the four o'clock count is a standing count, the other ones are at midnight, two A.M., five A.M., and nine P.M. Did they give you your PAC number?"

"PAC number?"

"Yeah, you'll need it to make phone calls. Did they give you a phone sheet? NO? You need to fill it out so you can make phone calls. But maybe Toricella will let you make a call if you ask him. It's his late night. It helps if you cry. Ask him after dinner. Dinner's after the four o'clock count, which is pretty soon, and lunch is at eleven. Breakfast is from six-fifteen to seven-fifteen. How much time do you have?"

"Fifteen months . . . how much time do you have?"

"Fifty-seven months."

If there was an appropriate response to this information, I didn't know what it was. What could this middle-class, middle-aged Italian-American lady from Jersey possibly have done to get fifty-seven months in federal prison? Was she Carmela Soprano? Fifty-seven months! From my presurrender due diligence, I knew it was *verboten* to ask anyone about their crime.

She saw that I was unsure what to say and helped me out. "Yeah, it's a lot of time," she said sort of drily.

"Yeah." I agreed. I turned to start pulling items out of my laundry bag.

That's when she shrieked, "Don't make your bed!!!"

"What?" I spun around, alarmed.

"We'll make it for you," she said.

"Oh . . . no, that's not necessary, I'll make it." I turned back to the thin cotton-poly sheets I'd been issued.

She came over to my bunk. "Honey. We'll. Make. The. Bed." She was very firm. "We know how."

I was completely mystified. I looked around the room. All five beds were very tidily made, and both Annette and Miss Luz had been lying on top of their covers.

"I know how to make a bed," I protested tentatively.

"Listen, let us make the bed. We know how to do it so we'll pass inspection."

Inspection? No one told me anything about inspections.

"Inspection happens whenever Butorsky wants to do them—and he is insane," Annette said. "He will stand on the lockers to try to see dust on the light fixtures. He will walk on your bed. He's a nut. And that one"—she pointed to the bunk below mine—"doesn't want to help clean!"

Uh-oh. I hated cleaning too but was certainly not about to risk the ire of my new roommates.

"So we have to make the beds every morning?" I asked, another penetrating question.

Annette looked at me. "No, we sleep on top of the beds."

"You don't sleep in the bed?"

"No, you sleep on top with a blanket over you." Pause.

"But what if I want to sleep in the bed?"

Annette looked at me with the complete exasperation a mom shows a recalcitrant six-year-old. "Look, if you wanna do that, go ahead—you'll be the only one in the whole prison!"

This sort of social pressure was irresistible; getting between the sheets wasn't going to happen for the next fifteen months. I let go of the bed issue—the thought of hundreds of women sleeping on top of perfectly made military-style beds was too strange for me to deal with at that moment. Plus, somewhere nearby a man was bellowing. "Count time, count time, count time! Count time, ladies!" I looked at Annette, who looked nervous.

"See that red light?" Out in the hallway, over the officers' station, was a giant red bulb that was now illuminated. "That light comes on during count. When that red light is on, you better be where you're supposed to be, and don't move until it goes off."

Women were streaming back and forth in the hallway, and two young Latinas came hurrying into the room.

Annette did a brief round of introductions. "This is Piper." They barely glanced at me.

"Where's the woman who sleeps here?" I asked about my missing bunkmate.

"That one! She works in the kitchen, so they count her down there. You'll meet her." She grimaced. "Okay, shhhhh! It's a stand-up count, no talking!"

The five of us stood silent by our bunks, waiting. The entire building was suddenly quiet; all I could hear was the jangling of keys and the thud of heavy boots. Eventually a man stuck his head into the room and . . . counted us. Then, several seconds later, another man came in and counted us. When he left, everyone sat down on beds and a couple of footstools, but I figured it wouldn't be cool to sit on my absent bunkmate's bed, so I leaned on my empty locker. Minutes passed. The two Latina women began to whisper to Miss Luz in Spanish.

Suddenly we heard, "Recount, ladies!" Everyone leaped back on their feet, and I stood at attention.

"They always screw it up," muttered Annette under her breath. "How hard is it to count?"

We were counted again, this time with seeming success, and the payoff of inspections became apparent to me. "It's suppertime," said Annette. It was 4:30 in the afternoon, by New York City standards an unimaginably uncivilized time to eat dinner. "We're last."

"What do you mean, last?"

Over the PA system the CO was calling out numbers: "A12, A10, A23, go eat! B8, B18, B22, go eat! C2, C15, C23, go eat!"

Annette explained, "He's calling honor cubes—they eat first. Then he calls the Dorms in order of how well they did in inspection. Rooms are always last. We always do the worst in inspection."

I peered out the door at the women heading to the chow hall and wondered what an honor cube was but asked, "What's for dinner anyway?"

"Liver."

After the liver-and-lima-beans dinner, served in a mess hall that brought back every dreadful school-age cafeteria memory, women of every shape, size, and complexion flooded back into the main hall of the building, shouting in English and Spanish. Everyone seemed to be lingering expectantly in the hall, sitting in groups on the stairs or lining the landing. Figuring that I was supposed to be there too, I tried to make myself invisible and listen to the words swirling around me, but I couldn't figure out what the hell was going on. Finally, I timidly asked the woman next to me.

"It's mail call, honey!" she answered.

A very tall black woman up on the landing seemed to be handing out toiletries. Someone on my right gestured toward her. "Gloria's going home, she's down to a wake-up!" I stared at Gloria with renewed interest, as she tried to find someone to take a small purple comb off her hands. *Going home!* The idea of leaving was riveting to me. She looked so nice, and so happy, as she gave away all her things. I felt a tiny bit better, knowing that it was possible someday to go home from this awful place.

I wanted her purple comb very badly. It looked like the combs we used to carry in the back pockets of our jeans in junior high, that we'd whip out and use to fix our winged bangs. I stared at the comb, too shy to reach up and ask, and then it was gone, claimed by another woman.

A guard, different from the one Minetta had pointed out earlier, emerged from the CO's office. He looked like a gay pornstar, with a bristling black crew cut and a scrub-brush mustache. He started bellowing "Mail call! Mail call!" Then he started giving out the mail. "Ortiz! Williams! Kennedy! Lombardi! Ruiz! Skelton! Platte! Platte! Platte! Wait a minute, Platte, there's more. Mendoza! Rojas!" Each woman would step up to claim her mail, with a smile on her face, and then skitter away somewhere to read it—perhaps someplace with more privacy than I had yet observed? The hall's population thinned as he worked through the bin of mail, until there were only hopefuls left. "Maybe tomorrow, ladies!" he shouted, turning the empty bin upside down.

After mail call I crept around the building, feeling vulnerable in my stupid little canvas slippers that so obviously marked me as new. My head was spinning with new information, and for the first moment in hours I was sort of alone with my own thoughts, which turned immediately to Larry and my parents. They must be freaking. I had to figure out how to let them know that I was okay.

Very timidly, I approached the closed door to the counselors' office, clutching a blue phone sheet that Annette had shown me how to fill out, bubbling in the numbers of people I wanted permission to call on the pay phones at some future date. Larry's cell phone, my family, my best friend Kristen, my lawyer. The lights in the office were on. I rapped softly, and there was a muffled snort from within. Gingerly I turned the handle.

The counselor named Toricella, who always wore a look of mild surprise, was blinking his little eyes at me, annoyed at my interruption.

"Mr. Toricella? I'm Kerman, I'm new. They said I should come talk to you . . ." I trailed off, swallowing.

"Is something wrong?"

"They said I should turn in my phone list . . . and I don't have a PAC number . . ."

"I'm not your counselor."

My throat was getting very tight, and there was no need to fake tears—my eyes were threatening to spill. "Mr. Toricella, they said maybe you might let me call my fiancé and let him know that I'm okay?" I was begging.

He looked at me, silent. Finally he grunted. "Come in and close the door." My heart started pounding twice as hard. He picked up the phone and handed the receiver to me. "Tell me the number and I'll dial it. Just two minutes!"

Larry's cell phone rang, and I closed my eyes and willed him to answer it. If I lost this opportunity to hear his voice, I might die right on the spot.

"Hello?"

"Larry! Larry, it's me!!"

"Baby, are you okay?" I could hear how relieved he was.

Now the tears were falling, and I was trying not to screw up my two minutes or scare Larry by totally losing it. I snuffled. "Yes, I'm okay. I'm really okay. I'm fine. I love you. Thank you for taking me today."

"Honey, don't be crazy. Are you sure you're okay, you're not just saying that?"

"No, I'm all right. Mr. Toricella let me call you, but I won't be able to call you again for a while. But listen, you can come visit me this weekend! You should be on a list."

"Baby! I'll come on Friday."

"So can Mom, please call her, and call Dad, call them as soon as we get off the phone and tell them you talked to me and tell them I'm okay. I won't be able to call them for a while. I can't make phone calls yet. And send in that money order right away."

"I mailed it already. Baby, are you sure you're okay? Is it all right? You would tell me if it wasn't?"

"I'm okay. There's a lady from South Jersey in my room, she's nice. She's Italian."

Mr. Toricella cleared his throat.

"Darling, I have to go. I only have two minutes. I love you so much, I miss you so much!"

"Baby! I love you. I'm worried about you."

"Don't worry. I'm okay, I swear. I love you, darling. Please come see me. And call Mom and Dad!"

"I'll call them as soon as we get off the phone. Can I do anything else, baby?"

"I love you! I have to go, honey!"

"I love you too!"

"Come see me on Friday, and thank you for calling my folks . . . I love you!"

I hung up the phone. Mr. Toricella watched me with something that looked like sympathy in his beady little eyes. "It's your first time down?" he said.

After thanking him, I headed out into the hall wiping my nose on my arm, depleted but exponentially happier. I looked down at the doors of the forbidden Dorms and studiously examined the bulletin boards covered with incomprehensible information about events and rules I didn't understand—laundry schedules, inmate appointments with various staffers, crochet permits, and the weekend movie schedule. This weekend's film was *Bad Boys II*.

I avoided eye contact. Nonetheless women periodically accosted me: "You're new? How are you doing, honey? Are you okay?" Most of them were white. This was a tribal ritual that I would see play out hundreds of times in the future. When a new person arrived, their tribe—white, black, Latino, or the few and far between "others"—would immediately make note of their situation, get them settled, and steer them through their arrival. If you fell into that "other" category—Native American, Asian, Middle Eastern—then you got a patchwork welcome committee of the kindest and most compassionate women from the dominant tribes.

The other white women brought me a bar of soap, a real toothbrush and toothpaste, shampoo, some stamps and writing materials, some instant coffee, Cremora, a plastic mug, and perhaps most important, shower shoes to avoid terrible foot fungi. It turned out that these were all items that one had to purchase at the prison commissary. You didn't have the money to buy toothpaste or soap? Tough. Better hope that another prisoner would give it to you. I wanted to bawl every time another lady brought me a personal care item and reassured me, "It'll be okay, Kerman."

By now conflicting things were churning around in my brain and my guts. Had I ever been so completely out of my element as I was here in Danbury? In a situation where I simply didn't know what to say or what the real consequences of a wrong move might be? The next year was looming ahead of me like Mount Doom, even as I was quickly learning that compared with most of these women's sentences, fifteen months were a blip and I had nothing to complain about.

So though I knew I shouldn't complain, I was bereft. No Larry, no friends, no family to talk to, to keep me company, to make me laugh, to lean on. Every time a random woman with a few missing teeth gave me a bar of deodorant soap I swung wildly from elation to despair at the loss of my life as I knew it. Had I ever been so completely at the mercy of the kindness of strangers? And yet they were kind.

The young woman who furnished my new shower shoes had introduced herself as Rosemarie. She was milky pale, with short curly brown hair and thick glasses over mischievous brown eyes. Her accent was instantly familiar to me—educated, but with a strong whiff of working-class Massachusetts. She knew Annette, who said she was Italian, and had made a point of greeting me several times already, and now she came by Room 6 to bring me reading material. "I was a self-surrender and I was terrified. You're going to be okay," she assured me.

"Are you from Massachusetts?" I asked shyly.

"My Bahston accent must be wicked bad. I'm from Nawhwood." She laughed.

That accent made me feel a lot better. We started talking about the Red Sox and her stint as a volunteer on Kerry's last senatorial campaign.

"How long are you here for?" I asked innocently.

Rosemarie got a funny look on her face. "Fifty-four months. For Internet auction fraud. But I'm going to Boot Camp, so when you take that into account . . ." and she launched into a calculation of good time and reduction of sentence and halfway house time. I was shocked again, both by her casual revelation of her crime and by her sentence. Fifty-four months in federal prison for eBay fraud?

Rosemarie's presence was comfortingly familiar—that accent, the love for Manny Ramirez, her *Wall Street Journal* subscription, all reminded me of places other than here.

"Let me know if you need anything," she said. "And don't feel bad if you need a shoulder to cry on. I cried nonstop for the first week I was here."

I made it through the first night in my prison bed without crying. Truth was, I didn't really feel like it anymore, I was too shocked and tired. Earlier I had sidled my way into one of the TV rooms with my back to the wall, but news of the Martha Stewart trial was on, and no one was paying any attention to me. Eyeing the bookshelf crammed with James Patterson, V. C. Andrews, and romance novels, I finally found an old paperback copy of *Pride and Prejudice* and retired to my bunk—on top of the covers, of course. I fell gratefully into the much more familiar world of Hanoverian England.

My new roommates left me alone. At ten P.M. the lights were turned off abruptly, and I slipped Jane Austen onto my locker and stared at the ceiling, listening to Annette's respirator machine—she had suffered a massive heart attack shortly after arriving in Danbury and had to use it at night to breathe. Miss Luz, almost imperceptible in the other bottom bunk, was recovering from breast cancer treatment and had no hair on her tiny head. I was beginning to suspect that the most dangerous thing you could do in prison was get sick.

CHAPTER 4

Orange Is the New Black

||||

The next morning I and eight other new arrivals reported for a day-long orientation session, held in the smallest of the TV rooms. Among the group was one of my roommates, a zaftig Dominican girl who was an odd combination of sulky and helpful. She had a little tattoo of a dancing Mephistopheles figure on her arm, with the letters *JC*. I tentatively asked her if they stood for Jesus Christ—maybe protecting her from the festive devil?

She looked at me as if I were completely insane, then rolled her eyes. "That's my boyfriend's initials."

Sitting on my left against the wall was a young black woman to whom I took an instant liking, for no reason. Her rough cornrows and aggressively set jaw couldn't disguise the fact that she was very young and pretty. I made small talk, asking her name, where she was from, how much time she had to do, the tiny set of questions that I thought were acceptable to ask. Her name was Janet, she was from Brooklyn, and she had sixty months. She seemed to think I was weird for talking to her.

A small white woman on the other side of the room, on the other hand, was chatty. About ten years my senior, with a friendly-witch aspect, straggly red hair, aquiline nose, and weathered creases in her skin, she looked as if she lived in the mountains, or by the sea. She was back in prison on a probation violation. "I did two years in West Virginia. It's like a big campus, decent food. This place is a dump." She said this all pretty cheerfully, and I was stunned that anyone returning to prison could be so matter-of-fact and upbeat. Another white woman in the group was also back in for a violation, and she was bitter, which made more sense to me. The rest of the group was a mixed bag of black and Latino women who leaned against the walls, staring at the ceiling or floor. We were all dressed alike, with those stupid canvas slippers.

We were subjected to an excruciating five-hour presentation from all of Danbury FCI's major departments—finance, phones, recreation, commissary, safety, education, psychiatry—an array of professional attention that somehow added up to an astonishingly low standard of living for prisoners. The speakers fell into two categories: apologetic or condescending. The apologetic variety included the prison psychiatrist, Dr. Kirk, who was about my age and handsome. He could have been one of my friends' husbands. Dr. Kirk sheepishly informed us that he was in the Camp for a few hours each Thursday and "couldn't really supply" any mental health services unless it was "an emergency." He was the only provider of psychiatric care for the fourteen hundred women in the Danbury complex, and his primary function was to dole out psych meds. If you wanted to be sedated, Dr. Kirk was your guy.

In the condescending category was Mr. Scott, a cocky young corrections officer who insisted on playing a question-and-answer game with us about the most basic rules of interpersonal behavior and admonished us repeatedly not to be "gay for the stay." But worst of all was the woman from health services, who was so unpleasant that I was taken aback. She firmly informed us that we had better not dare to waste their time, that they would determine whether we were sick or not and what was medically necessary, and that we should not expect any existing condition to be addressed unless it was life-threatening. I silently gave thanks that I was blessed with good health. We were fucked if we got sick.

After the health services rep was out of the room, the red-headed violator piped up. "Jesus F. Christ, who peed in her Cheerios?"

Next a big bluff man from facilities with enormously bushy eyebrows entered the room. "Hello, ladies!" he boomed. "My name is Mr. Richards. I just wanted to tell you all that I'm sorry you're here. I don't know what landed you here, but whatever happened, I wish things were different. I know that may not be much comfort to you right now, but I mean it. I know you've got families and kids and that you belong home with them. I hope your time here is short." After hours of being treated as ungrateful and deceitful children, this stranger showed us remarkable sensitivity. We all perked up a bit.

"Kerman!" Another prisoner with a clipboard stuck her head into the room. "Uniforms!"

I was lucky to arrive at prison on a Wednesday. Uniform issue was done on Thursdays, so if you self-surrendered on a Monday, you might be pretty smelly after a few days, depending on whether you sweat when you are nervous. I followed the clipboard down the hall to a small room where uniforms were distributed, leftovers from when the place had been a men's facility. I was given four pairs of elastic-waist khaki pants and five khaki poly-blend button-down shirts, which bore the names of their former wearers on the front pockets; Marialinda Maldonado, Vicki Frazer, Marie Saunders, Karol Ryan, and Angel Chevasco. Also: one set of white thermal underwear; an itchy boiled-wool hat, scarf, and mittens; five white T-shirts; four pairs of tube socks; three white sports bras; ten pairs of granny panties (which I soon discovered would lose their elastic after a couple washings); and a nightgown so enormous it made me giggle—everyone referred to it as a muu-muu.

Finally, the guard who was silently handing me the clothing asked, "What size shoe?"

"Nine and a half."

He pushed a red and black shoebox toward me, containing my very own pair of heavy black steel-toed shoes. I hadn't been so happy to put on a pair of shoes since I found a pair of peep-toed Manolo Blahniks at a sample sale for fifty dollars. These beauties were solid and held the promise of strength. I loved them instantly. I handed back those canvas slippers with a huge smile on my face. Now I was a for-real, hardened con. I felt infinitely better.

I strutted back into orientation in my steel-toes. My fellows were still there, their eyes rolling back into their heads from the endless droning. The nice man from facilities had been replaced by Toricella, the counselor who partnered with Butorsky and had allowed me to call Larry the night before. I came to think of him as "Mumbles." His walruslike visage rarely changed; I never heard him raise his voice, but it was difficult to read his mood, beyond mild aggravation. He informed us that Warden Kuma Deboo would be gracing us with her presence momentarily.

Suddenly I was interested: I knew nothing of the warden, the big boss, who was a woman, and one with an unusual name to boot. I had not heard a word about her in the twenty-four hours I had been in prison. Would she resemble Wendy O. Williams or Nurse Ratched?

Neither. Warden Deboo sailed into the room and took a seat facing us. She was only ten years older than me, tops, and she was fit, olive-skinned, and good-looking, probably of Middle Eastern extraction. She was wearing a dowdy pantsuit and hideous costume jewelry. She spoke to us in an informal, faux-warm fashion that instantly reminded me of someone running for office.

"Ladies, I am Warden Kuma Deboo, and I am here to welcome you to Danbury, which I know is not an ideal scenario for any of you. While you are here, I am responsible for your well-being. I am responsible for your safety. I am responsible for you successfully completing your sentences. So, ladies, the buck stops here."

She went on for a while in this vein, with some mention of personal responsibility (ours) thrown in, and then she got down to the sex part.

"If anyone at this institution is pressuring you sexually, if anyone is threatening you or hurting you, I want you to come directly to me. I come to the Camp every Thursday at lunch, so you can come up and talk to me about anything that is happening to you. We have a zero-tolerance policy for sexual misconduct here at Danbury."

She was talking about prison guards, not marauding lesbians. Clearly sex and power were inseparable behind prison walls. More than a few of my friends had voiced their fears that in prison I would be in more danger from the guards than the inmates. I looked around the room at my fellow prisoners. Some looked scared; most looked indifferent.

Warden Deboo finished her spiel and left us. One of the other prisoners tentatively volunteered, "She seems nice."

The bitter violator who had previously been locked up at Danbury snorted, "Miss Slick. Don't expect to see her again, except for fifteen minutes every other Thursday on the line. She talks a good game, but she might as well not be here. She don't run this place. That zero-tolerance shit? Just remember this, *ladies* . . . it's gonna be your word against theirs."

NEW ARRIVALS in Federal prison are stuck in a sort of purgatory for the first month or so, when they are "A&Os"—admissions and orientation status. When you are an A&O, you can't do anything—can't have a job, can't go to GED classes, can't go to chow until everyone else goes, can't say a word when ordered to shovel snow at odd hours of the night. The official line is that your medical tests and clearances must come back from whatever mysterious place they go before your prison life can really start. Nothing involving paperwork happens quickly in prison (except for lockups in solitary), and a prisoner has no way to get speedy resolution with a prison staffer. Of anything.

There are a dizzying number of official and unofficial rules, schedules, and rituals. Learn them quickly, or suffer the consequences, such as: being thought an idiot, being called an idiot, getting on another prisoner's bad side, getting on a guard's bad side, getting on your counselor's bad side, being forced to clean the bathrooms, eating last in line when everything edible is gone, getting a "shot" (or incident report) put in your record, and getting sent to the Special Housing Unit or SHU (aka Solitary, the Hole, or Seg). Yet the most common response to a query about anything other than an official rule is "Honey, don't you know you don't ask questions in prison?" Everything else— the unofficial rules—you learn by observation, inference, or very cautious questioning of people you hope you can trust.

Being an A&O that February—a leap year, no less—was a strange combination of confusion and monotony. I prowled around the Camp building, trapped not only by the feds but also by the weather. With no job, no money, no possessions, no phone privileges, I was verging on a nonperson. Thank God for books and the gifts of paper and stamps from other prisoners. I couldn't wait for the weekend, and the prospect of seeing Larry and my mother.

Friday, there was snow. A worried-looking Annette woke me by wiggling my foot.

"Piper, they've been calling the A&Os for snow duty! Get up!"

I sat up, confused. It was still dark. Where was I?

"KERMAN! KERMAN! REPORT TO THE CO'S OFFICE, KERMAN!" The PA boomed.

Annette was bug-eyed. "You have to go now! Get dressed!"

I tumbled into my new steel-toed shoes and presented myself at the correctional officers' office, totally disheveled and with un-brushed teeth. The CO on duty was a dykey blond woman. She looked as if she ate new fish like me for breakfast after her triathlon workouts.

"KERMAN?"

I nodded.

"I called the A&Os a half-hour ago. There's snow duty. Where were you?"

"I was asleep."

She looked at me like I was a worm squirming on the sidewalk after spring rain. "Oh yeah? Get your coat on and shovel."

What about breakfast? I put on my thermal underwear and the ugly stadium coat with the broken zipper and headed out to meet my compadres in the whipping, icy wind, clearing the walks. By now the sun had risen, and there was a gloomy half-light. There were not enough shovels for everyone to use, and the one I used was broken, but no one could go back inside until the work was done. We had more salt-scatterers than shovelers.

One of the A&Os was a little Dominican lady in her seventies, who barely spoke a word of English. We gave her our scarves, wrapped her up, and put her out of the wind in a doorway—she was too scared to go inside, although it was insane for her to be out there in the cold with us. One of the other women told me over the wind that the old lady had a four-year sentence for a "wire charge," taking phone messages for her drug-dealing male relative. I wondered what U.S. Attorney was enjoying that particular notch in his or her belt.

I worried that the weather would prevent Larry from driving up from New York, but I had no way of knowing, so before visiting hours began at three P.M., I tried to pull myself together. Freshly showered and wearing the uniform that I thought was the least un-flattering, I stood in the fluorescent light of the decrepit bathroom and looked at the unfamiliar woman in the mirror. I looked undeco-rated and to my eye unfeminine—no jewelry, no makeup, no embell-ishments at all. Someone else's name was on the breast pocket of my khaki shirt. What would Larry think when he saw me now?

I went to wait outside the big recreation room where visits were held. A red light was mounted on the wall of the visiting room. After a prisoner saw her people walk up the hill and into the Camp build-ing, or if she heard her name called over the PA system, she would flip a light switch by the side of the room's double doors, and a red light on the other side of the doors would go on too, alerting the vis-iting room CO that the prisoner was in place, waiting to see their vis-itor. When the CO felt like it, they would get up, go to the doors, pat down the inmate, and allow her into the visiting room.

After an hour or so on the landing next to the visiting room, I began to wander the main hall, bored and nervous. When I heard my name called over the PA system—"Kerman, report to visitation!"—I racewalked up to the landing. A female guard with curly hair and bright blue eye shadow was waiting for me on the landing. I spread my arms and legs, and she skimmed her fingertips along my extrem-ities, under my collar, below my sports bra, and around my waistband.

"Kerman? First time, right? Okay, he's in there waiting for you. Watch the contact!" She pulled open the visiting room door.

For visits the large room was set up with card tables and folding chairs. When I arrived, they were about half filled, and Larry was sitting at one of them, looking anxious and expectant. When he saw me, he jumped to his feet. I walked as quickly as I could to him and threw my arms around him. I was so grateful that he looked happy. I felt like myself again.

Hugging and kissing your visitors (no tongue!) was permitted at the beginning and end of the visit. Some guards would allow hand-holding; some would not. If a guard was having a bad day, week, or life, we would all feel it in that bleak, linoleum-floored visiting room. There were always two prisoners working in the visiting room too, assisting the CO, and they were stuck making small talk with the guard for hours.

Larry and I took our seats at the card table, and he just stared at me, smiling. I felt suddenly shy, and wondered if he saw a difference in me. Then we started to talk, trying to cover an impossible amount of ground all at once. I told him what had happened after he left the prison lobby, and he told me what it had been like for him to have to leave. He said that he had talked to my parents, that they were holding up, and that my mother was coming to visit tomorrow. He listed all the people who had called to try to find out how I was and who had sent in requests to be approved as visitors. I explained to him that there was a twenty-five-person limit on my visitor list. Our friend Tim had set up a website, www.thepipebomb.com, and Larry was posting all the relevant information (including an FAQ) there.

We talked for hours (visiting hours were three to eight P.M. on Fridays), and Larry was curious about every detail of prison so far. Together at the card table, I could relax the taut watchfulness and caution that had governed my every move for the last three days and almost forget where I was, even as I shared every discovery that my new life offered. I felt so loved sitting there with him, and more confident that someday I would be able to leave this horrible place behind. I reassured Larry countless times that I was okay. I told him to look around—did the other prisoners look so bad? He thought they did not.

At seven forty-five it was time for Larry and the other visitors to leave. My whole heart clutched up. I had to leave the bubble of love around our card table. I wouldn't see him for another week.

"Did you get my letters?" he asked.

"No, not yet, no mail. Everything here is on prison time . . . slow motion."

Departures were tough, and not just for us. A toddler didn't want to leave her mother and wailed as her father struggled to get her into her snowsuit. Visitors and prisoners shifted from one foot to another as they tried to say' goodbye. We were all permitted a final hug, and then watched as our loved one's backs disappeared into the night. The more experienced prisoners were already unlacing their shoes, getting ready for the strip search.

This ritual, which I'd repeat hundreds of times in the next year, never varied. Remove shoes and socks, shirt, pants, T-shirt. Pull up your sports bra and display your breasts. Show the soles of your feet. Then turn your back to the female prison guard, pull down your underpants and squat, exposing yourself. Finally, force a cough, which would theoretically cause any hidden contraband to clatter to the floor. I always found the interchange between the person who has no choice but to strip naked and the guard who gives the order to be brisk and businesslike, but some women found strip searches so humiliating that they would forgo visits in order to avoid it. I would never have survived without my visits and so would grit my teeth and rush through the motions. It was the prison system's quid pro quo: You want contact with the outside world? Be prepared to show your ass, every time.

With my clothes back on, I walked back out into the main hall, floating on air and memories of everything Larry had said. Someone said, "Hey Kerman, they called your name at mail call!" I headed straight to the CO's station, and he handed me sixteen wonderful letters (including Larry's!) and a half-dozen books. Somebody out there loved me.

The next day my mother was due to arrive. I could only guess at how awful the last seventy-two hours had been for her, and I worried what she would think when she saw that razor-wire fence—it evoked a primal fear. When they called my name on the PA, I could barely stand still for the pat-down. I flew through the doors of the visiting room, scanning for my mother's face. When I saw her, it was as if all our surroundings faded into a distant background. She burst into tears when she saw me. In thirty-four years I couldn't remember her ever looking more relieved.

I spent most of the next two hours trying to reassure Mom that I was okay; that no one was bothering me, or hurting me; that my room-mates were helping me; and that the guards were leaving me alone. The presence of other families in the visiting room, many with little kids, was a reminder to me that we were not the only ones. In fact, we were just one of millions of American families trying to cope with the prison system. My mother fell silent as she watched a little girl playing with her parents at another card table. The strain on her face wiped away any complaint or self-pity I might have had. She was putting on a brave front, but I knew she would cry all the way to the car.

The hours I would spend in the prison visiting room were among the most comforting of my life. They sped by, the only occasion at the Camp in which time seemed to move quickly. I could completely forget about the human stew that lay on the other side of the visiting room doors, and I carried that feeling with me for many hours after each visit was over.

But I could see how awful and scary it was for my family to see me in my khaki uniform and get a tiny taste of what I was experiencing, surrounded by guards, strangers, and powerful systems of control. I felt terrible for exposing them to this world. Every week I needed to renew my promises to my mother and Larry that I was going to make it, that I was okay. I felt more guilt and shame witnessing their worry than when I stood in front of the judge—and it had been terrible standing in that courtroom.

THE CAMP had distinct rhythms of frenzied action and lulls of calm, like a high school or an ER ward. In bursts of activity the polyglot of women came and went, clustered in groups, hurried, loitered, very often waited, and almost always chattered in an overwhelming rush of noise, accents, and emotions mixing into swirling eddies of language.

Other times the place was still and silent . . . sleepy during some hours of the day, when most of the campers were off at their job assignments and the orderlies had already hustled through their cleaning assignments and gone off to nap, crochet, or play cards. At night, after ten P.M. lights out, the halls were quiet, haunted by the occasional woman in her muu-muu heading to the bathroom or the mail drop box, navigating by the distant light from a common room where someone was sitting, perhaps illicitly watching after-hours TV.

My understanding of the causes of these patterns of movement—meals, mail call, work call, pill line, commissary days, phone time—was still tenuous. But I learned more every day, filing away the information and trying to figure out where I fit in.

Letters and good books—an overwhelming number of good books—started to pour in from the outside world. At mail call almost every day the Gay Pornstar would bellow "Kerman!" and shove a plastic bin overflowing with a dozen books toward me with his boot, half disgusted and half perplexed. The entire population of the Camp would watch me claim my mail, with the occasional wisecrack—"You keeping up?"

On the one hand, folks were impressed at this evidence that people on the outside cared about me. On the other hand, the literary avalanche was proof that I was different, a freak: "She's the one with the books." Annette and a few other women were delighted by the influx of new reading material and borrowed from my library with abandon (and permission). Jane Austen, Virginia Woolf, and *Alice in Wonderland* definitely served to fill the time and keep me company inside my head, but I was really lonely in my actual physical life. I was cautiously trying to make friends, but like everything else in prison it was tricky; there were too many places where a newbie like me could easily misstep. Like the chow hall.

The chow hall was like a high school cafeteria, and who has fond memories of that? A vast linoleum room filled with tables with four attached swivel chairs, it was lined on two sides by windows that looked out toward the main back entrance to the Camp, where there were parking spaces, a handicapped ramp, and a forlorn and unused basketball hoop. Breakfast was a quiet affair, attended by only a fraction of the prisoners, mostly the older ones who appreciated the almost meditative peace of the morning ritual at six-thirty A.M. There was never a wait at breakfast—you grabbed a tray and plastic cutlery and approached the kitchen line from which food was dished out by other prisoners, some blank-faced, some chatty. It could be cold cereal or oatmeal or, on a really good day, boiled eggs. Usually there was a piece of fruit for every person, an apple or banana, or sometimes a rock-hard peach. Big vats of watery coffee sat next to cold drink dispensers filled with water and something like weak Kool-Aid.

I got in the habit of going to breakfast, where I would sit alone peacefully, not drinking the terrible coffee, observing the other prisoners come and go and watching the sun rise through the east-facing windows.

Lunch and dinner were altogether different: the line of women waiting for their food stretched the length of the wall below the windows and sometimes out the door, and the noise was tremendous. I found these meals nerve-racking and would cautiously advance with my tray, darting my eyes around for someone I knew near an empty chair, or even better, an empty table that I could grab. Sitting with someone you didn't know was a dicey proposition. You could be met with the hairy eyeball and a resounding silence, or a pointed, "This seat is saved." But you could also be met with a chatterer or a questioner, and when I ventured afield, I was often nabbed after the meal by Annette: "You wanna stay away from that one, Piper. She'll be after you to buy her commissary in no time."

Annette had a maternal instinct that was a force of nature and helped me navigate the official rules, like remembering the counts, and the PAC numbers, and what day I was allowed to bring my clothes to the laundry to be washed. But she was leery of most other prisoners who were not middle class and white. It turned out that early on Annette had been gamed by a young girl who had gotten the older woman to buy her lots of commissary items, playing on her pity. The girl was in fact notorious for her hustles of new prisoners, so Annette felt burned, and her caution was outsize. Annette included me in endless Rummy 500 games with her set of Italians, who grudgingly tolerated my poor play. The black women played far more boisterous games of Spades a few tables over; the Italians sniffed that they all cheated.

Annette introduced me to Nina, a fellow Italian, who was my age and lived a few rooms down, and she also took me under her wing. Nina had just returned from a month in the SHU (she had refused to shovel snow) and was waiting to get put back in the Dorms. Annette seemed scared of most other prisoners, but not Nina, who was Brooklyn street-smart, and just as wary of others as Annette: "They're all wackos—they make me sick." She had lived a tough life and was prison-savvy, funny as hell, and surprisingly tolerant of my naïveté, and I followed her around like a puppy. I paid close attention to her advice about how not to get rooked by another prisoner. I was definitely interested in figuring out who the nonwackos were.

I got along well with some of the women in my A&O group (plus I could remember their names): the tattooed Latina from my room, who was doing just six months for getting caught with six keys of coke in her car (made no sense to me); the salty redhead, who was still going on about how much better the prison in West Virginia was than Danbury, "although there's more of us northerners here, if you know what I mean . . ."

Then there was little Janet from Brooklyn, who was slowly warming up to me, although she still seemed to think I was strange for being friendly. She was just twenty years old, a college girl who had been arrested on vacation as a drug mule. She had been locked in a Caribbean jail for an entire harrowing year before the feds came to get her. Now she was doing sixty months—more than half of her twenties would be spent behind bars.

One day I was joined at lunch by a different Janet, who was fifty-ish, tall, fair, and striking. I had been watching her and wondering what her story was—she reminded me of my aunt. Janet was like me—a middle-class drug criminal. She was doing a two-year sentence on a marijuana charge. As we made conversation, she was friendly but never pushy, explicitly respectful of other people's space. I learned that she was a world traveler, a classic eco-peacenik intellectual, a fitness fanatic and yoga expert, and a devout Buddhist possessed of a wry sense of humor, all incredibly welcome attributes to encounter in a fellow prisoner.

Institutional food required a Zen outlook. The mess hall lunch was sometimes hot, sometimes not, the most popular meals being McDonald's-style hamburger patties or the ultimate, and rare, deep-fried chicken sandwich. People went crazy for chicken in any form. Far more often lunch was bologna and rubbery orange cheese on white bread and endless amounts of cheap and greasy starch in the form of rice, potatoes, and horrible frozen pizzas. Dessert was wildly variable, sometimes really good home-baked cookies or cake, sometimes Jell-O, and sometimes bowls of pudding, which I was warned off of: "It comes out of cans marked DESERT STORM, and if there's mold on the top, they just scrape it off and serve the rest." For the few vegetarians, there was texturized vegetable protein. TVP was a repulsive reconstituted soy powder that someone back in the kitchen would fruitlessly try to make edible. It usually looked like worms. Sometimes if they had added a list of onions, you could choke it down. Poor Yoga Janet was a vegetarian and resigned herself to a subsistence diet most of the time.

Both lunch and dinner featured a salad bar that offered iceberg lettuce, sliced cucumbers, and raw cauliflower. Only certain women, like Yoga Janet, were regulars at the salad bar. I said hello to them shyly, my sisters in roughage. Occasionally other vegetables would appear on the bar—broccoli florets, canned bean sprouts, celery, carrots, and very rarely, raw spinach. These would quickly be raided and spirited out of the dining hall for prisoners' cooking projects, which went on in force in the two microwaves near the Dorms. The only food available was what we got in the dining hall and what prisoners were able to buy from the commissary.

A constant presence in the dining hall was Italian Nina's former bunkie Pop, the imposing fiftyish wife of a Russian gangster who ruled the kitchen with an iron fist. One evening I was sitting with Nina as the dinner hour was drawing to a close, when Pop sat down with us, clad in her customized burgundy kitchen smock adorned with POP over the heart in white yarn, *à la* Laverne and Shirley. I, knowing less than nothing, began maligning the food. It didn't occur to me at that point that anyone would put any pride into their prison job, but Pop did. When I made a joke about a hunger strike, that was it.

Pop fixed me with a ferocious glare and a pointed finger. "Listen, honey, I know you just got here, so I know that you don't understand what's what. I'm gonna tell you this once. There's something here called 'inciting a riot,' and that kind of shit you're talking about, hunger strikes, that kind of shit, that's inciting a riot. You can get in big trouble for that, they will lock your ass up in the SHU in a heartbeat. Now, me, I don't care, but you don't know these people, honey. The wrong one hears you saying that shit, she goes and tells the CO, you're going to be shocked how quickly the lieutenant is coming to lock your ass up. So take a tip from me, and watch what you say." And with that, she left. Nina looked at me, silently telegraphing, *You asshole.* From then on I stayed out of Pop's path, ducking my head to avoid her eyes on the chow line.

February is Black History Month, and someone had festooned the dining hall with posters of Martin Luther King, Jr., George Washington Carver, and Rosa Parks. "They didn't put shit up for Columbus Day," groused a woman named Lombardi behind me in line one day. Was she really objecting to Dr. King? I kept my mouth shut. The minimum-security camp at Danbury housed approximately 200 women at any given time, though sometimes it climbed to a nightmarishly cramped 250. About half were Latino (Puerto Rican, Dominican, Colombian), about 24 percent white, 24 percent African-American and Jamaican, and then a very random smattering: one Indian, a couple of Middle Eastern women, a couple of Native Americans, one tiny Chinese woman in her sixties. I always wondered how it felt to be there if you lacked a tribe. It was all so very *West Side Story*—stick to your own kind, Maria!

The racialism was unabashed; the three main Dorms had organizing principles allegedly instituted by the counselors, who assigned housing. A Dorm was known as "the Suburbs," B Dorm was dubbed "the Ghetto," and C Dorm was "Spanish Harlem." The Rooms, where all new people went first, were a strange mix. Butorsky wielded housing assignments as a weapon, so if you got on his bad side, you would be stuck into rooms. The most physically ill women in the Camp, or pregnant women like the one I had seen when I first arrived, occupied the bottom bunks; the top bunks were full of newbies, or behavior problems, of which there was never a shortage. Room 6, where I lived, was serving as a sick ward rather than a punishment room—I was lucky. At night I would lie in the dark in my bunk over the snoring Polish woman, listening to the thrum of Annette's breathing apparatus and gazing past the sleeping top-bunk shapes out the windows, which were level with my bunk. When there was a moon, I could see the tops of fir trees and the white hills of the far valley.

I spent as many hours as I could standing out in the cold, staring to the east over an enormous Connecticut valley. The Camp sat perched atop one of the highest hills in the area, and you could see rolling hills and farms and clusters of towns for miles over the giant basin of the valley below. I saw the sunrise every day in February. I braved the rickety icy stairs that led down to a field house gym and the Camp's frozen track, where I'd crunch around bundled in my ugly brown coat and itchy army-green hat, muffler, and mittens before heading into the cold gym to lift weights, almost always mercifully alone. I wrote letters and read books. But time was a beast, a big, indolent immovable beast that wasn't interested in my efforts at hastening it in any direction.

Some days I barely spoke, keeping eyes open and mouth shut. I was afraid, less of physical violence (I hadn't seen any evidence of it) than of getting cursed out publicly for fucking up, either breaking a prison rule or a prisoner's rule. Be in the wrong place at the wrong time, sit in "someone's" seat, intrude where you were not wanted, ask the wrong question, and you'd get called out and bawled out in a hurry, either by a terrifying prison guard or by a terrifying convict (sometimes in Spanish). Except to pester Nina with questions, and to theorize and trade notes with my fellow A&O newbies about what was what, I kept to myself.

But my fellow prisoners were in fact looking out for me. Wormtown Rosemarie brought me her *Wall Street Journal* every day and checked on how I was. Yoga Janet would make a point of sitting with me at meals, and we would chat about the Himalayas and New York and politics. She was appalled when a subscription to *The New Republic* showed up for me at mail call. "You might as well read the *Weekly Standard*!" she said with disgust.

ONE COMMISSARY day—shopping was twice a week in the evening, half the Camp on Monday, the other half on Tuesday—Nina appeared in the door of Room 6. Still without money in my prison account, I was washing with loaned soap and was deeply envious of the other prisoners' weekly shopping excursions.

"Hey Piper, how about a root beer float?" said Nina.

"What?" I was dumbfounded, and hungry. Dinner had been roast beef with an eerie metallic-green cast. I had eaten rice and cucumbers.

"I'm gonna get ice cream at commissary, we can make root beer floats." My heart soared, then crashed.

"I can't shop, Nina. My account didn't clear yet."

"Would you shut up? Come on."

You could get a pint of cheap ice cream at the commissary— vanilla, chocolate, or strawberry. You had to eat it right away, because of course there was no freezer, just a big ice dispenser for prisoners. Woe to the inmate who stuck a pint into the ice machine and got caught by another inmate! You would get yelled at for being disgustingly unsanitary. Like many things, it just wasn't done.

Nina bought vanilla ice cream and two cans of root beer. My

mouth was watering as she prepared our floats in plastic coffee mugs, the foam a luscious rich brown. She handed me one, and I sipped, wearing a foam mustache. It was the best thing I had tasted since I got to prison. I felt tears pricking behind my eyes. I was so happy.

"Thank you, Nina. Thank you so much."

AT MAIL call I continued to be blessed with an avalanche of letters, every one of which I savored. Some were from my closest friends, some were from family, and some were from people I had never met, friends of friends who had heard about me and taken the time to offer some solace with pen and paper to a total stranger. Larry told me that one of our friends had told her folks about me, and her father had decided to read every one of the books on my Amazon wish list. In short order I had accumulated, via the mail: beautiful postcards from my old coworker Kelly and letters written on my friend Arin's exquisitely decorated writing paper, which were a treasure in the drab ugliness of the facility; seven printout pages of Steven Wright jokes from Bill Graham; a little book about coffee, hand-illustrated by my friend Peter; and a lot of photographs of other people's cats. These were all of my riches and in fact my only valuable possessions.

My uncle Winthrop Allen III wrote to me:

Pipes,

Your Web page was well received. I forwarded it to a few of my friends and acquaintances, so don't be surprised to get bundles of old books from unknown sources.

Enclosed is *Japanese Street Slang.* You never know when you're going to need just the right insult. *Joe Orton,* he needs no introduction, but there is one in the front of the book, anyhow. *Parkinson* was an amusing old duffer, inventor of Parkinson's Law, which I kinda forget. No, I remember now, it's about tasks expanding to fill the available time. When you are finished getting your group therapy sessions, safe-sex lectures, and 12-step sermons, you may be able to test the hypothesis.

The Prince, Mach's my all-time fave. Like you and me, he's forever maligned.

Gravity's Rainbow, all my literary friends consider this the greatest since *Under the Volcano.* I couldn't finish either of 'em.

I enclose a couple of posters so that you could get a start on decorating the digs before Martha shows up with all her bundles of frou-frou.

Regards, Winthrop, the Worst Uncle

I began to receive letters from a man named Joe Loya, a writer and a friend of a friend back in San Francisco. Joe explained that he had served over seven years in federal prison for bank robbery, that he knew what I was going through, and that he hoped I would write him back. He told me that the act of writing literally saved his life when he spent two years in solitary confinement. I was startled by the intimacy of his letters, but also touched, and it was reassuring to know that there was someone on the outside who understood something about the surreal world I now inhabited.

Only the nun got more mail than me. On my first day in the Camp someone had helpfully informed me that there was a nun there—in my side-smacked daze, I vaguely assumed they meant a nun who had chosen to live among prisoners. I was correct, sort of. Sister Ardeth Platte was a political prisoner, one of several nuns who are peace activists and served long federal sentences for trespassing in a nonviolent protest at a Minuteman II missile silo in Colorado. Everyone respected Sister (as she was known to all), who was sixty-nine years old and one tough nun, an adorable, elfin, twinkling, and loving presence. Appropriately enough, Sister was Yoga Janet's bunkie— she liked to be tucked into bed by Janet every night, with a hug and kiss on her soft, wrinkled forehead. The Italian-American prisoners were the most outraged by her predicament. "The fucking feds have nothing better to do than to lock up *nuns?*" they would spit, disgusted.

Sister received copious amounts of mail from pacifists around the world.

One day I got a new letter from my best friend, Kristen, whom I had met in our first week at Smith. In the envelope was a short note, penned on an airplane, and a newspaper clipping. I unfolded it to reveal Bill Cunningham's "On the Street" fashion column from the Sunday *New York Times,* February 8. Covering the half-page were over a dozen photographs of women of every age, race, size, and shape, all clad in brilliant orange. "Oranginas Uncorked" was the headline, and Kristen had noted on a blue stickie, "NYers wear orange in solidarity w/ Piper's plight! xo K." I carefully stuck the clipping inside my locker door, where every time I opened it I was greeted by my dear friend's handwriting, and the smiling faces of women with orange coats, hats, scarves, even baby carriages. Apparently, orange was the new black.

CHAPTER 5

Down the Rabbit Hole

| | | |

After two weeks I was getting much better at cleaning, as inspections took place twice a week and there was considerable social pressure not to fuck up—the winners of inspection got to eat first, and certain extra-tidy "honor cubes" were first among the first. It was amazing how many uses sanitary napkins had—they were our primary cleaning tools.

There was tension in Room 6 over who cleaned and who did not. Miss Luz, who was in her seventies and sick with cancer, was not expected to clean. The Puerto Rican woman in one of the top bunks spoke no English, but she would silently help me and Annette dust and scrub. The bigoted Polish woman who occupied the bunk below me refused to clean, much to Annette's fury. My tattooed A&O pal pitched in halfheartedly—until she discovered she was pregnant and was quickly moved to a bottom bunk in another room. The BOP doesn't like lawsuits.

The new girl who took her place in Room 6 was a big Spanish girl. At first I used the politically correct term "Latina," as I had learned to do at Smith, but everyone, regardless of color, looked at me as if I were insane. Finally I was firmly corrected by a Dominican woman: "We call ourselves Spanish around here, honey, Spanish mamis."

This new young Spanish mami sat on the naked mattress of the top bunk, looking dazed. It was my turn to show someone else the ropes.

"What's your name?"

"Maria Carbon."

"Where are you from?"

"Lowell."

"In Massachusetts? I'm from there, I grew up in Boston. How much time do you have?" She looked at me blankly. "That means, how long is your sentence?"

"I don't know."

That stopped me cold. How could you not know your own sentence? I didn't think this was a language problem—her English was unaccented. I got worried. She looked like she was in shock. "Listen, Maria, it's going to be okay. We'll help you. You need to fill out your paperwork, and people will give you the stuff you need right away. Who's your counselor?"

Maria just looked at me helplessly, and finally I retreated to enlist one of the other Spanish mamis to assist with the new arrival.

ONE EVENING the PA system boomed "Kerman!" and I scurried to Mr. Butorsky's office. "You're moving down into B Dorm!" he barked, "Cube Eighteen! Miss Malcolm will be your bunkie!"

I hadn't been down into the Dorms (which were "out of bounds" for A&Os). In my imagination they were murky caves populated with seasoned convicts. "He likes you," said Nina, my expert on all things prison, who was still waiting to get back into her A Dorm cube with Pop. "That's why he put you with Miss Malcolm. She's been down a long time. Plus you'll always be honor cube." I had no idea who Miss Malcolm was, but I had learned that in prison "Miss" was an honorific conferred only on the elderly or on those who were highly respected.

I gathered my few belongings and nervously advanced down the stairs to B Dorm, aka "The Ghetto," clutching my pillow and laundry bag stuffed with uniforms. I would have to retrieve my pile of books on a second trip. The Dorms turned out to be large, semisubterranean basement rooms that were a maze of beige cubicles, each housing two prisoners, a bunk bed, two metal lockers, and a stepladder. Cube 18 turned out to be next to the bathroom, on the sole wall with narrow windows. Miss Malcolm was waiting for me in her cube, a petite dark-skinned middle-aged woman with a heavy Caribbean accent. She was all business.

"That's your locker." She indicated the empty one, "and these are your hooks. Those hooks are mine, and that's just the way it's gonna be." Her clothes were neatly hung, with her checkered cook's pants and burgundy smock. She worked in the kitchen. "I don't care if you're gay or what, but I don't want no foolishness in the bunk. I clean on Sunday nights. You have to help clean."

"Of course, Miss Malcolm," I agreed.

"Call me Natalie. I'll make your bed."

Suddenly a blond head popped up over the cubicle wall. "Hi, new neighbor!" It was the tall, baby-faced white girl who washed dishes in the dining hall. "I'm Colleen!" Colleen looked at my new bunkie cautiously. "How are you, Miss Natalie?"

"Hello, Colleen." Natalie's tone expressed tolerance for silly girls, but tolerance with limits. It wasn't unfriendly or mean, just a bit stern.

"What's your name, neighbor?"

I introduced myself, and she bounced out of the top bunk and around to the opening of the cube I now shared with Miss Malcolm. I was pelted with questions about my cool weird name, how much time I had, and where I was from, and I tried to answer them one at a time. Colleen was the resident Camp artist, specializing in flowers, fairy princesses, and fancy lettering, and she said, "Oh shit, neighbor, I gotta make your name tag! Write down the spelling for me." Colleen illustrated cubicle name tags for all new B Dorm arrivals in feminine script with sparkle details on each one—except for the people who had spent time down the hill in the FCI, and thus already had official-looking black plastic ones with white lettering, like Natalie's.

I had won the bunkie lottery. Natalie, a woman near the end of an eight-year sentence, was a reserve of quiet dignity and good counsel. Because of her heavy accent, it took careful listening on my part to understand everything she said, but she never said anything unnecessary. She was the head baker in the kitchen. She rose at four A.M. to begin her shift and kept largely to herself with a few select friends among the West Indian women and her kitchen coworkers. She spent quiet time reading, walking the track, and writing letters, and went to bed early, at eight P.M. We spoke very little about our lives outside of prison, but she could answer just about any question I had about life at Danbury. She never said what had landed her there, and I never asked.

How Natalie got to sleep at eight P.M. was a complete mystery to me, because it was LOUD down in B Dorm. My first evening there I was quiet as a mouse in my top bunk, trying to follow the hooting and hollering that took place across the big room filled with women. I was worried that I would never get any sleep, and that I would lose my marbles in the cacophony. When the main lights were shut off, though, it quieted down pretty quickly, and I could fall asleep, lulled by the breathing of forty-seven other people.

The next morning something woke me before dawn. Groggy and confused, I sat up in my bed, the room still dark, the collective slumber of its residents blanketing everything. Something was going on. I could hear someone, not shouting exactly, but angry. I looked below me—Natalie was already gone, at work. I leaned forward very slowly, very cautiously, and peeped out of my cubicle.

Two cubes away I could see a Spanish woman who'd been particularly loud the night before. She was not happy. What was pissing her off, I could not figure out. Suddenly she squatted for a few moments, then stood up and stalked off, leaving behind a puddle in front of my neighbor's cubicle.

I rubbed my eyes. Did I just see what I thought I saw? About a minute later a black woman emerged from the cubicle.

"Lili! Cabrales! *Lili Cabrales!* Get back here this minute and clean this up! LILIIIIIIIIIIII!!!" People were not happy to be awakened this way, and a smattering of "SHUT THE FUCK UP!" broke out across the big room. I ducked my head back out of sight—I didn't want either woman to know that I had seen the whole thing. I could hear someone cursing quietly. I cautiously stole a glance: the black woman quickly cleaned up the puddle with an enormous wad of toilet paper. She caught me peeking and seemed sheepish. I flopped back down on my bunk and stared at the ceiling. I had fallen down the rabbit hole.

The next day was Valentine's Day, my first holiday in prison. Upon arrival in Danbury, I was struck by the fact that there did not seem to be any lesbian activity. The Rooms, so close by the guard's station, were bastions of propriety. There was no cuddling or kissing or any obvious sexual activity on display in any of the common rooms, and while someone had told me a story about a former inmate who had made the gym her own personal love shack, it was always empty when I went there.

Given that, I was taken aback by the explosion of sentiment around me on Valentine's Day morning in B Dorm. Handmade cards and candy were exchanged, and I was reminded of the giddy intrigue of a fifth-grade classroom. Some of the "Be Mines" that were stuck on the outside of cubicles were clearly platonic. But the amount of effort that had gone into some of the Valentines, carefully constructed from magazine clippings and scavenged materials, suggested real ardor to me.

I had decided from the beginning to reveal nothing about my sapphic past to any other inmate. If I had told even one person, eventually the whole Camp would know, and no good could come of it. So I talked a lot about my darling fiancé, Larry, and it was known in the Camp that I was not "that way," but I was not at all freaked out by women who were "that way." Frankly, most of these women were not even close to being "real lesbians" in my mind. They were, as Officer Scott put it, "gay for the stay," the prison version of "lesbian until graduation."

It was hard to see how a person could conduct an intimate relationship in such an intensely overcrowded environment, let alone an illicit relationship. On a practical level, where on earth could you be alone in the Camp without getting caught? A lot of the romantic relationships I observed were more like schoolgirl crushes, and it was rare for a couple to last more than a month or two. It was easy to tell the difference between women who were lonely and wanted comfort, attention, and romance and a real, live lesbian: there were a few of them. There were other big barriers for long-term lovers, like having sentences of dramatically different lengths, living in different Dorms, or becoming infatuated with someone who wasn't actually a lesbian.

Colleen and her bunkie next door got lots of Valentines from other prisoners. I got none, but that evening's mail call yielded plenty of evidence that I was loved. Best of all was a little book of Neruda poems from Larry, *Twenty Love Poems and a Song of Despair*. I resolved to read a poem every day.

> *We have lost even this twilight.*
> *No one saw us this evening hand in hand*
> *While the blue night dropped on the world.*
>
> *I have seen from my window*
> *the fiesta of sunset in the distant mountain tops.*
>
> *Sometimes a piece of sun*
> *burned like a coin between my hands.*
>
> *I remembered you with my soul clenched*
> *in that sadness of mine that you know.*
>
> *Where were you then?*
> *Who else was there?*
> *Saying what?*
> *Why will the whole of love come on me suddenly*
> *when I am sad and feel you are far away?*
>
> *The book fell that is always turned to at twilight*
> *and my cape rolled like a hurt dog at my feet.*

*Always, always you recede through the evenings
towards where the twilight goes erasing statues.*

I WAS finally able to shop commissary on February 17, when I bought:

XL sweatpants, $24.70, given to me in error and which they
    would not let me return
A stick of cocoa butter, $4.30
Packets of tuna, sardines, and mackerel, each about $1
Ramen noodles, $0.25
Squeeze cheese, $2.80
Pickled jalapeños, $1.90
Hot sauce, $1.40
Legal pads, pens, envelopes, and stamps, priceless.

I desperately wanted to buy a cheap little portable headset radio for $42.90. The radio would have cost about $7 on the street. At the base pay for federal prisoners, which is $0.14 an hour, that radio could represent more than three hundred hours of labor. I needed the radio to hear the weekend movie or anything on television, and to use down in the gym, but the officer who ran the commissary brusquely told me they were out of radios. *No mas,* Kerman.

Because I could count on money from the outside world, I could buy items to return to each person who had helped me upon my arrival—soap, toothpaste, shampoo, shower shoes, packets of instant coffee. Some women tried to wave them away, "Don't worry about it, Kerman," but I insisted. "Please, forget it!" said Annette, who had loaned me so many things in my first several weeks. "You're like my daughter! Hey, did you get any new books today?"

The books continued to pour in at mail call. It had gotten to the point where I was embarrassed, and also it made me nervous; it was a clear demonstration that I "had it like that" on the outside, a network of people who had both a concern for me and the time and money to buy me books. So far no one had threatened me with anything more intimidating than a scowl or a harsh word, and no other prisoner had asked anything of me. Still, I was guarded against getting played, used, or targeted. I saw that some of the women had little or no resources from the outside to help make their prison life livable, and many of my fellow prisoners were seasoned hustlers.

One day right after I moved into B Dorm, a woman I didn't know popped her head into my cube. Miss Natalie was absent, and I was putting still more books away in my small footlocker, which was threatening to overflow. I looked at this woman—black, middle-aged, ordinary, yet unfamiliar. My guard went up.

"Hey there, new bunkie. Where's Miss Natalie?"

"Um, she's in the kitchen, I think."

"What's your name? I'm Rochelle."

"Piper. Kerman."

"What's your name?"

"You can call me Piper." What did she want from me? I felt trapped in my cube. I was sure she was sniffing around.

"Oh, you're the one with the books . . . you got all them books!" In fact, I had a book in my hand and a pile of them on top of the locker. By now I was scared as to what this woman wanted from me and what she was going to do to me.

"D-do you want a book?" I was always happy to lend a book, but only a few people took me up on it, checking my haul at every mail call.

"Okay—whatcha got?" I scanned the selection. The collected works of Jane Austen. A biography of John Adams. *Middlesex*. *Gravity's Rainbow*. I didn't want to assume that she wouldn't want any of these books, but how could I know what she liked?

"What kind of stuff do you like? You can borrow any of them, take your pick." She looked through the titles uncertainly. It was a long, slow, squirmy moment for both of us.

"How about this one? It's really, really fantastic." I seized up a copy of *Their Eyes Were Watching God* by Zora Neale Hurston. I felt racist on every level of my being by picking "the black book" from the stack for Rochelle, but there was a good shot that she might like it, might take it, and might leave me alone, at least for the moment.

"Looks good, looks good. Thanks, Pipe!" And she disappeared from my cube.

About a week later Rochelle came back around. She was returning the book.

"It seems good, but I couldn't really get into it," she said. "You got *The Coldest Winter Ever*? Sister Souljah?" I did not, and she wandered away. When I thought about how terrified I had been of Rochelle, and why, I felt like a complete jackass. I had gone to school with, lived with, dated, and worked with middle-class black people my whole life, but when faced by a black woman who hadn't "been where I've been," I felt threatened, absolutely certain she was going to take something from me. In truth, Rochelle was one of the most mild-mannered and pleasant people around, with a deep love for church and trashy novels. Ashamed, I resolved not to be a jackass again.

While I was meeting all these new players in my life, I made an extra effort to hang out with Annette. When I was moved down to B Dorm, she had sighed, resigned. "Now I'm never going to see you anymore."

"Annette, that's ridiculous. I'm literally yards away from you."

"I've seen it before . . . once girls get moved down to Dorms, they don't have time for me anymore." Annette was trapped in the Rooms because of her medical problems, so I made a point of going around to Room 6 to say hi and play cards in the recreation room. But I was officially bored with Rummy 500 and less inclined to spend time with a small handful of often-cranky middle-aged white women than I once had been. Perhaps I would learn Spades. Those players looked like they were having more fun.

NATALIE HAD the respect of everyone in B Dorm, and as I was clearly not going to give her any trouble, she seemed to take to me too. Despite her reserve and discretion, she had a dry but lively sense of humor and treated me to her sharp, sidelong observations on our daily life in B Dorm: "You in the Ghetto now, bunkie!" Ginger Solomon, her best friend who was also Jamaican, was like the yang to Natalie's yin: antic, combustible, and loud. Miss Solomon was also a fantastic cook, and once she and Natalie had decided that I was all right, she would make me a plate of her special Saturday night dinner, usually a knockout curry prepared with kitchen contraband. On special occasions, Natalie would magically make roti appear.

Extracurricular prison cooking happened primarily in two communal microwaves that were placed in kitchenette areas between the Dorms; their use was a privilege the staff constantly (and with great enjoyment) threatened to revoke. Remarkable concoctions came out of those microwaves, especially from homesick Spanish and West Indian women. This impressed me deeply, given the limited resources these cooks were working with—junk food and poly-bagged chicken, packets of mackerel and tuna, and whatever fresh vegetable one could steal from the kitchen. Corn chips could be reconstituted into mash with water and transformed into delectable "chilaquiles," my new prison favorite. Contraband onions were at a particular premium, and the chefs had to keep an eye peeled for guards with quivering nostrils. No matter what they were cooking, it smelled like food prepared with love and care.

Unfortunately Miss Solomon only cooked on Saturdays. I had lost ten pounds in a month, thanks to the prison diet—all the liver, lima beans, and iceberg lettuce you want! The day I walked into prison I looked all of my thirty-four years, if not worse. In the months before my surrender I'd drowned my sorrows in wine and New York comfort food; now my greatest comforts were time alone on the icy track and lifting weights in the gym. It was the only place in the Camp where freedom and control seemed in my grasp.

ONE OF the good things about living in B Dorm was that you had your choice of two bathrooms. Both were equipped with six showers, five sinks, and six toilet stalls. That's where their similarities ended. Natalie and I lived next to the bathroom that I liked to call the

Hell-mouth. The tiles and Formica were various shades of gray, the shower curtain rods were rusted, the plastic shower curtains were practically in ribbons, and not all of the stall door locks worked. None of this was what made the C Dorm bathroom a Hell-mouth, though. It was the infestations that made the place unacceptable for anything but a quick pee or toothbrushing. During the warmer months when the ground was not frozen, little black maggots would periodically appear in the shower area, squirming on the tiles. Nothing could make them disappear, although the bathroom orderlies did not have much of an arsenal—the cleaning supplies were stingily doled out. Eventually the maggots would hatch into evil little flies. They were the sign that the bathroom had been built over a direct route to Hell.

I showered instead in the bathroom on the other side of B Dorm, which connected to A Dorm. It was spalike by comparison and had been recently refurbished in shades of beige. The fixtures were new. The light was better. The mood was brighter, even if the shower curtains were just as ratty.

Showers were a complex ritual. It was necessary to schlep all your hygiene products to the bathroom—shampoo, soap, razor, washcloth, and whatever else you might need. This required either great minimalism or some sort of shower caddy. Some women had illegal crocheted bags to carry their stuff; some had mesh nylon bags from commissary; and one woman had a large pink plastic shower caddy, an actual shower caddy. I wasn't about to ask, knowing that it had either come from some long-ago and distant commissary or was contraband. Morning and evening were peak shower hours, with gradually diminishing stores of hot water. If you showered in the afternoon or early evening, you would have less competition. We were not supposed to be in the showers after lights out at ten P.M., to discourage people from having sex in them.

Many women would wait in line three deep for "their" shower to be free. In the good bathroom there was one shower stall that indisputably had the best water pressure. Some big shots, like Pop, would send an emissary to see if that stall was free or else dibs them a place in the waiting line. If you interfered with one of the early-morning risers' shower ritual by getting into "their" shower, you would be met with an icy stare when you emerged.

Once you had secured your shower stall, you faced a moment of truth. Some women would disappear behind the stall's plastic curtain still fully clad in their muu-muus, out of modesty; others would whip off their clothes in front of everyone and climb in and out unabashed. A handful would shower with the curtain open, giving everyone a show.

At first I was among the former, but the water was always freezing initially, and I would yelp as it rained down on my naked skin. "What's going on in there, Kerman?" someone would inevitably joke. "Piper's getting busy!" After a while I became convinced that the Linda Blair rape scene in *Born Innocent* was never going to be re-created in the Camp, so I took to starting my shower before I got in, checking to see that it was at least lukewarm before I whipped off my muu-muu and jumped in. This won me a couple of fans, notably my new neighbor Delicious, who shouted with surprise, "P-I Piper! You got some nice titties! You got those TV titties!! They stand up on they own all perky and everything! Damn!"

"Um, thanks, Delicious."

There was absolutely nothing threatening about Delicious's attention. In fact, it was mildly flattering that she noticed me at all.

All cleaning in the Camp was highly ritualized, including the all-hands-on-deck Sunday-night scrubdown of our cubicles. One day a week B Dorm's laundry was done for us (laundress was a prison job, captained by an elderly woman everyone called Grandma), and so the night before, I'd stuff my bag with sweat socks and a packet of laundry soap. Natalie would wake me at five-fifteen before the laundry opened so that I could get mine in before everyone else. Otherwise I'd have been part of the usual stampede of half-asleep women in the still-dark hallway getting in line to drop off their laundry bags. Why the urgency? Unclear. Did I need my laundry back in the early afternoon, as opposed to the evening? No. I found myself participating in the meaningless rituals of avoiding the laundry rush because prison is all about waiting in line. For many women, I realized, this was nothing new. If you had the misfortune of having the government intimately involved with your life, whether via public housing or Medicaid or food stamps, then you'd probably already spent an insane amount of your life in line.

I had twice made the monthly pilgrimage out to the warehouse to collect my eight packets of laundry soap powder from the unsmiling inmate in charge of issuing them. Laundry soap days happened once a month—on one appointed weekday all the "evens" would troop out to the warehouse during the lunch hour to claim their eight packets; the next day the "odds" would go. The prisoners who worked in the warehouse, a secretive bunch, took this enterprise very seriously. They treated soap days as an invasion of their turf and would all sit or stand silently while other prisoners lined up to collect the one handout that the prison gave to prisoners.

I never understood why laundry soap was the one free thing provided to us (other than our toilet paper rations, which were passed out once a week, and the sanitary napkins and tampons stocked in the bathroom). Laundry soap was sold on commissary; some women would buy Tide and give away their eight free soap packets to others who had nothing. Why not soap to clean your body? Why not toothpaste? Somewhere within the monstrous bureaucracy of the Bureau of Prisons, this all made sense to someone.

I CAREFULLY studied long-timers like Natalie. How had she done it? How had she served eight years in this rotten place with her grace, her dignity, her sanity intact? What had she drawn on to make it through, with only nine months until her release to the outside world? The advice I got from many quarters was "do your time, don't let the time do you." Like everyone in prison, I was going to have to learn from the masters.

I settled into rituals, which improved the quality of my existence immeasurably. The ritual of coffee-making and drinking was one of the first. The day I arrived a brassy former stockbroker had given me instant coffee in a foil bag and a can of Cremora. Larry, an insufferable coffee snob, was insanely particular about brewing methods, preferring a French press. I wondered what he would do if he was locked up—would he give up coffee entirely, or adapt to Nescafé? I would make my cup in the morning at the temperamental hot water dispenser and carry it down to the chow hall for breakfast.

After our late-afternoon dinner, Nina would often appear, inquiring whether I wanted to "get coffee." I always did. We would mix up our cups and find seats where the weather allowed, sometimes sitting out behind A Dorm looking south toward New York. We would talk about Brooklyn, her kids, Larry, and books; we'd gossip about other prisoners; I would ask her my endless questions about how to do time. Sometimes Nina wasn't in the mood to get coffee. I'm sure that my tagalong tendencies got old for her, but when I needed her wisdom, she was always there.

I TORE through every book I received, stayed out of the TV rooms, and watched with envy as people went off to their prison jobs. One could rearrange a footlocker only so many ways. I suspected work would help slaughter time. I tried to figure out who did what, and why some of them got to wear nifty army-green jumpsuits. Some prisoners worked in the Camp's kitchen; others, working as orderlies, washed floors and cleaned the bathroom and common areas. The benefit of the orderly jobs was that you worked only a few hours a day, usually alone. A handful of prisoners worked as trainers for seeing-eye dogs with whom they lived 24–7, a program tragically known as Puppies Behind Bars. Some women worked in CMS (Construction and Maintenance Services), getting on a bus every morning to do jobs like plumbing and grounds maintenance. An elite crew trooped off to the warehouse, the stopping point for everything that either entered or left the prison, and where the contraband opportunities were rich.

Certain prisoners worked in Unicor, the prison industries company that operates within the federal prison system. Unicor manufactures a wide range of products that are then sold within the government for many millions of dollars. In Danbury the FCI made radio components for the army. Unicor paid significantly more than other prison jobs, over one dollar an hour as opposed to the regular base pay rate of fourteen cents an hour, and the Unicor workers were always dressed in pressed, tidy uniforms. Unicor people would disappear into a large warehouse building that always had semis parked outside. Some girls enjoyed silent flirtation with the truckers, who looked nervous but intrigued.

Rosemarie had secured herself a job in the Puppy Program, which was housed in A Dorm. That meant she lived with a Labrador retriever that was being trained to be a seeing-eye dog or a bomb-sniffer. The dogs were beautiful, the little puppies adorable. A warm, squirming lapful of golden puppy, licking and biting and unabashedly happy, made despair dissolve no matter how hard you were hanging on to it.

I wasn't eligible for Puppies Behind Bars—my fifteen-month sentence was too short. Initially disappointed, on reflection I decided it wasn't necessarily a bad thing. The program attracted some of the most obsessive-compulsive women in the Camp, and their OCD could really come into full flower as they trained the dogs, forming intense bonds with their canine companions and feuding with their human neighbors. Rosemarie quickly became consumed with the training of her dog, Amber. I didn't mind because she would usually let me play with the puppy, which some of her fellow dog trainers frowned upon.

The doyenne of the Puppy Program was Mrs. Jones, the only person in Camp that anyone called "Mrs." Mrs. Jones had been in prison for a long time, and it was obvious. A grizzled, steel-haired Irish woman with enormous breasts, she had been down for almost fifteen years on a drug sentence. Her husband was said to have beaten her viciously on the outside and to have died in prison. Good riddance to bad rubbish. Mrs. Jones was a little crazy, but most prisoners and guards gave her more leeway than they might extend to others—after fifteen years, anyone would have gone a little crazy. People liked to sing a few bars of "Me and Mrs. Jones" from time to time. Some of the younger women from the street called her the OG, Original Gangster, and she loved that. "That's me . . . the OG! I'm crazy . . . like a fox!" she would cackle, tapping her temple. She seemed to lack any filter and would say exactly what she thought at any time. Although interacting with Mrs. Jones required patience, I liked her, and her candor too.

I wasn't allowed to be a dog trainer, but surely the right job for me was here somewhere? Danbury had a distinct labor hierarchy, and I was at the bottom of it. I wanted to teach in the GED program, which was overseen by a staff teacher and augmented by prisoners who were "tutors."

The handful of middle-class, educated prisoners with whom I often ate meals warned me against it. Although the program's female staffer was well liked, they said the combination of a bad program with captive and often surly students made for a crappy work environment. "Not a pleasant experience!" "Cluster fuck." "I copped out after a month." It sounded like my friend Ed's job teaching public high school in New York City. Nevertheless I requested the job, and Mr. Butorsky, who controlled assignments, said that should work out just fine. As it turned out, he was not as good as his word.

CHAPTER 6

High Voltage

||||

One morning my A&O pal Little Janet found me and said, "We have jobs!" We were assigned to the electric shop, in Construction and Maintenance Services. I was disappointed. What about teaching—feeding the hungry minds of the downtrodden, who were waiting to break free?

The mandatory GED program had been temporarily shut down. The two classrooms had been overrun with a virulent toxic killer mold that crawled over textbooks, walls, and furniture and made many people sick. The inmate teachers had reportedly sneaked samples of the mold to a sympathetic outsider for analysis and filed a grievance. The staff teacher had sided with the prisoners, to the fury of prison management. The students were gleeful about the shutdown, most of them not wanting to be there in the first place. So it was voltage for me instead.

The next day Little Janet and I followed the other CMS workers out into the March chill to a big white school bus parked behind the chow hall. After more than a month of being trapped in the confines of the Camp, the bus ride was exhilarating. We rode around to the back of the FCI and were deposited amid an assembly of low buildings. These were the CMS shops—garage, plumbing, safety, construction, carpentry, grounds, and electric, each housed in its own building.

Janet and I entered the electric shop, blinking in the sudden dim-ness we found there. The room had a cement floor half-filled with chairs, many broken; a desk with a television sitting on it; and blackboards where someone was keeping a large hand-drawn monthly calendar, crossing off the days. There was a refrigerator and a microwave and a feeble-looking potted plant. One alcove was caged off and brightly lit, filled with enough tools to stock a small hardware store. An enclosed office had a door plastered with union stickers. My fellow prisoners grabbed all the functional seats. I sat on the desk next to the TV.

The door banged open. "Good morning." A tall, bearded man with buggy eyes and a trucker hat strode through to the office. Joyce, who was friendly with Janet, said, "That's Mr. DeSimon."

About ten minutes later DeSimon emerged from the office and took roll call. He sized up each of us as he read out our names. "The clerk will explain the tool room rules," he said. "Break the rules, you're going to the SHU." He went back into the office.

We looked at Joyce. "Are we going to do any work?"

She shrugged. "Sometimes we do, sometimes we don't. It just depends on his mood."

"Kerman!" I jumped. I looked at Joyce.

She widened her eyes at me. "Go in there!" she hissed.

I cautiously approached the office door.

"Can you read, Kerman?"

"Yes, Mr. DeSimon, I can read."

"Good for you. Read this." He dropped a primer on his desk. "And get your convict buddies who are new to read it too. You'll be tested on it."

I backed out of the office. The packet was a basic course in electrics: power generation, electrical current, and basic circuitry. I thought for a moment about the safety requirements of the job and looked around at my coworkers with some concern. There were a couple of old hands like Joyce, who was Filipina and sarcastic as hell. Everyone else was new like me: in addition to Little Janet, there was Shirley, an extremely nervous Italian who seemed to think she was going to be shanked at any moment; Yvette, a sweet Puerto Rican

who was halfway through a fourteen-year sentence and yet still had
(at most) seventeen words of English at her command; and Levy, a
tiny French-Moroccan Jew who claimed to have been educated at
the Sorbonne.

For all her preening about her Sorbonne education, Levy was totally useless at our electrical studies. We spent a couple of weeks
studying those primers (well, some of us did), at which point we were
given a test. Everyone cheated, sharing the answers. I was pretty sure
there would be no repercussions to either flunking the test or being
caught cheating. It all seemed absurd to me—no one was going to get
fired for incompetence. However, simple self-preservation demanded
that I read and remember the explanations of how to control electric
current without frying myself. This was not how it was all going to
end for me, sprawled in polyester khaki on linoleum, with a tool belt
strapped to my waist.

ONE SNOWY day just a week later we reported to the electric shop
after lunch to find DeSimon jingling the keys to the big white electric shop van. "Kerman . . . Riales . . . Levy. Get in the van."

We trundled out and climbed in after him. The van sped down a
hill, past a building that housed a day care for the children of COs,
and through a cluster of about a dozen little white government
houses where some COs lived. We often spent our workdays changing exterior light bulbs or checking the electric panels in these buildings, but today DeSimon didn't stop. Instead he pulled off of prison
property and onto the main thoroughfare that skirted the institution.
Little Janet and Levy and I looked at each other in astonishment.
Where on earth was he taking us?

About a quarter mile from the prison grounds, the van pulled up
next to a small concrete building in a residential neighborhood. We
followed DeSimon up to the building, which he unlocked. A mechanical din came from inside.

"What ees this place, Mr. DeSimon?" asked Levy.

"Pump house. Controls water to the facility," he replied. He looked around the interior, and then locked the door again. "Stay here." And with that he climbed into the van and drove away.

Little Janet, Levy, and I stood there outside the building with our mouths open. Was I hallucinating? Had he really just left us here in the outside world? Three uniformed prisoners, out and about—was this some sort of sick test? Little Janet, who before Danbury had been locked up for over two years in extremely poor conditions, looked like she was in shock.

Levy was agitated. "What ees he sinking? What eef people see us? Zey will know we are prisoners!"

"There is *no way* that this is not against the rules," I said.

"We're gonna get in trouble!" Little Janet wailed.

I wondered what would happen if we left. Obviously we would be in massive trouble and be sent to the SHU and probably catch a new charge for "escape," but how long would it take them to nab us?

"Look at zeez houses! Oh my god . . . a school bus! Aieee! I mees my children!" Levy started to cry.

I felt terrible for anyone who was separated from her children by prison, but I also knew that Levy's kids lived nearby and that she would not allow them to come visit her because she didn't want them to see her in prison. I thought this was horrible and that for a kid the unpleasantness of the prison setting would be more than off-set by the eyewitness reassurance that their mother was okay. Anyway, I wanted Levy to stop crying.

"Let's look around." I said.

"No!!" Little Janet practically shouted. "Piper, we are gonna get in so much trouble! Don't even move your feet!" She looked so stressed that I acquiesced.

We stood there like idiots. Nothing was happening. The suburban neighborhood was quiet. Every couple of minutes a car would drive by. No one pointed or screeched to a halt at the sight of three convicts off the plantation. Eventually a man walked by with an enormous shaggy dog.

I perked up. "I can't tell if that's a Newfoundland or a Great Pyrenees . . . good-looking dog, huh?"

"I can't believe you—you're looking at the dog!?" said Little Janet.

The man was looking at us.

"He sees us!"

"Of course he sees us, Levy. We're three female inmates standing on a street corner. How's he going to miss. us?"

The man raised his hand and waved cheerfully as he passed.

After about forty-five minutes DeSimon returned with brooms and set us to work cleaning the pump house. The next week we were made to clean out the root cellar, a long low barn on the prison grounds. The root cellar contained a hodgepodge of equipment from all the shops. In the dark shadows we discovered enormous snake-skins that had been shed, which freaked us out and made DeSimon cackle with glee. An outside inspection was coming soon, and the prison staff wanted to be ready.

There was actual trash to be removed from the root cellar, a dirty and often heavy job, and we spent days hauling huge metal pipes, stockpiles of hardware, fixtures, and components out to the giant Dumpsters. Into the Dumpster went ceramic bathtubs and sinks still in their boxes, new baseboard heating components, and unopened fifty-pound boxes of nails.

"Your family's tax dollars at work," we muttered under our breath. I had never worked so physically hard in my life. By the time we were finished, the root cellar was empty, spotless, and tidy for in-spection.

While I was quickly learning that even in prison rules were made to be broken by staff and prisoners alike, there was one aspect of work in the electric shop that was meticulously observed and enforced. A large "cage" of tools, where the shop clerk sat, contained everything from band saws to Hilti drills and myriad types of special screw-drivers, pliers, wire cutters, and individual tool belts loaded with complete sets of the basics—a whole room filled with potentially murderous objects. There was a system for checking out those tools: each prisoner had an assigned number and a bunch of corresponding metal chits that looked like dog tags. When we went out to do a job, each prisoner signed out a tool with a chit, and was responsible for returning it. At the end of each shift DeSimon would inspect the tool cage. He made it clear that if a tool went missing the prisoner whose chit occupied the empty space and the shop clerk were both going to the SHU. It was the only rule that appeared to matter to him. One day a drill bit went missing and we tore the shop and the truck apart looking for it while he watched, the clerk on the edge of tears, until finally we found the twisted piece of metal rolling around in the lid of one of the toolboxes.

DeSimon was relentlessly unpleasant to many of the prison staff as well, who called him "Swamp Yankee" (and worse). He may have been widely disliked, but he was also the head of the institution's union chapter, which meant that management let him do as he pleased. "DeSimon's a prick," one of the other shop heads told me candidly. "That's why we elected him." Under the Prick's indifferent tutelage, I learned the rudimentary basics of electric work.

A group of totally inexperienced women working with high voltage and nearly no supervision did yield moments of broad comedy and only occasional bodily injury. In addition to a butch tool belt, prison work gave me a greater sense of normalcy, another way of marking time, and people with whom I had something in common. Best of all, I was sent over to the garage to obtain my prison driving license, which allowed me to drive the CMS vehicles. Although I loathed DeSimon, I was glad to be kept semibusy five days a week, and ecstatic at the freedom of movement I had driving the electric shop van around the prison grounds.

On a Friday when we returned from work to the Camp, Big Boo Clemmons from B Dorm came out to meet the CMS bus. "Guilty on all four counts!" she reported with great excitement. Inside we found the TV rooms packed, because a jury had found Martha Stewart guilty on four counts of obstructing justice and lying to investigators about a well-timed stock sale. The style diva was going to have to do fed time. Her case had been followed with keen interest at Danbury—most prisoners thought she was being targeted because she was a famous female: "Guys get away with that shit all the time."

. . .

ONE AFTERNOON Levy, our nervous coworker Shirley, and I, geared up in our tool belts, were shuttling around the staff housing on the grounds, checking the circuit panels in every house. DeSimon escorted us from house to house, where he would make small talk with the occupants while we did our thing. It was bizarre to go into the homes of our jailers and see their angel collections and family photos and pets and laundry and messy basements.

"Zey have no class," sneered Levy. I didn't like prison guards, but she was insufferable.

When we got back to the shop, DeSimon left, and it was up to us to clean out the truck and return the tools to the cage. That's when I discovered the extra screwdriver in my belt.

"Levy, Shirley, I've got one of your screwdrivers." They both checked their belts—no, they had theirs. I held two screwdrivers in my hands, confused. "But if you've got yours, then where . . ." I was mystified. "I must have . . . picked this one up in one of the houses?"

My eyes met Levy and Nervous Shirley's, which were huge.

"What are you going to do?" Shirley hissed.

My stomach dropped. I started to sweat. I saw myself in the SHU, with no visits from Larry, with another criminal charge for stealing a CO's potentially deadly screwdriver. And I had these two fools in on the game, no one's choice for accomplices.

"I don't know what I'm going to do, but you don't know a thing about this, understand?" I hissed back.

They hurried into the shop, and I stood outside, looking around wildly. What the fuck was I going to do with this screwdriver? I was terrified, because I knew it could be construed as a weapon. How could I get rid of it? If I found a hiding place, what if someone found it? How did you destroy a screwdriver?

My eyes fixed on the CMS dumpster. It was big, and all the shops threw their garbage, all kinds of garbage, in there. It got emptied often, and the garbage was taken away, to Mars as far as I was concerned. I grabbed the shop garbage and strode toward the

Dumpster. I fiddled with the garbage bag while I surreptitiously wiped the screwdriver like a maniac, trying to get rid of fingerprints. Then I flung both into the Dumpster, which unfortunately didn't sound very full. It was done. Heart pounding, I returned to the shop and put away my tool belt. I didn't even look at Nervous Shirley or Levy.

That night I went over the screwdriver problem again and again in my mind. What if the CO noticed it was missing and remembered that inmates had been in his house? He would raise the alarm, and then what? An investigation, interrogations, and then Levy and Nervous Shirley would give me up in a hot second. I closed my eyes. I was dead.

The next morning at the shop, an eerie air-raid siren went off. I almost vomited. Shirley looked faint. Levy appeared completely unconcerned. Usually the siren was used for "recalls"—sending us back to our housing units for either emergency or special practice counts. But this time nothing happened; the alarm went off for many excruciating minutes until it just stopped. Shirley went outside to smoke a cigarette with trembling hands.

At lunch I found Nina and told her what had happened, deeply rattled.

She rolled her eyes. "Jesus Christ, Piper. Let's go look for it after lunch. You'll just give it to DeSimon and explain. They ain't gonna lock you up."

But the Dumpster was empty. Nina frowned, and looked at me.

I wanted to cry. "Nina, you don't think the siren this morning . . . ?"

Although she was concerned, this struck her as hilarious. "No, Piper, I don't think the siren this morning was for you. I think the garbage is gone, and the screwdriver's gone, and if the evidence is gone, then they can't prove shit. Most likely nothing at all's gonna happen, and if it does, it's your word against Levy or Shirley, and let's face it, they're wackos, who's gonna believe them?"

. . .

ONE AFTERNOON I returned to B Dorm to find my neighbor Colleen in a state of great excitement.

"My girls Jae and Bobbie just got here from Brooklyn! Pipestar, you got any extra toothpaste I can give them, or any other stuff?" Colleen explained that before she'd been designated to Danbury, she had spent time with her two friends in the Brooklyn Metropolitan Correctional Center, aka a federal jail. Now her pals had just arrived off the transport bus. "They're both real cool, Piper, you'll like them."

On my way to the gym, I saw a black woman and a white woman standing out behind the Camp building in the early spring drizzle, staring up at the clouds. I didn't recognize them; I decided they must be Colleen's friends.

"Hey, I'm Piper. Are you guys Colleen's friends? I live next to her. Let me know if you need anything."

They lowered their faces from the sky and looked at me. The black woman was about thirty, pretty, and solidly built with high cheekbones. She looked like she had been carved out of supersmooth wood. The white woman was smaller and older, maybe forty-five, and had coarse skin like a coral reef and eyes with as many shades of blue as the ocean. Right now they looked aquamarine.

"Thanks," she said. "I'm Bobbie. This is Jae. You got any ciga-rettes?" Her heavy New York accent suggested many late nights and many cigarettes.

"Hi, Jae. No, sorry, I don't smoke. I've got toiletries, though, if you need." I was getting wet, and it was cold. Still, I was curious about these two. "Kinda crap weather out here."

At this they looked at each other. "We ain't felt the rain for two years," said Jae, the black woman.

"What?"

"In Brooklyn there's a little rec deck they take us up on, but it's covered over, barbed wire and shit, and you don't really see the sky," she explained. "So we don't mind the rain. We love it." And she put her head back again, face up, as close to the sky as it could get.

. . .

IN THE electric shop things were changing. Vera, the woman with the most experience, left to go to the only women's Boot Camp program, in Texas. Boot Camp (an early-release program that has since been eliminated) was six hard months in the Texas heat, where rumor had it that you were housed in a giant tent and required to shave your pubic hair to make insect detection easier.

Vera's departure to Texas meant that the leadership in the electric shop shifted to Joyce. Joyce was a reasonably confident replacement, having learned from Vera how to do the electric work that was required on a frequent or daily basis—changing eight-foot-long fluorescents, replacing the ballasts of light fixtures, installing new exit signs and fixtures, and checking circuit boards.

Levy soon became the unifying factor in the shop: the rest of us united against her. She was insufferable, crying daily and complaining loudly and constantly about her measly six-month sentence, asking inappropriate personal questions, trying to boss people around, and making appalling and loud statements about other prisoners' appearance and lack of education, sophistication, or "class," as she put it. More than once Campers had to be talked out of kicking her ass, which was done by reminding them that she was not worth the trip to the SHU. Most of the time she was nervous-verging-on-hysterical, which manifested in dramatic physical symptoms; an astonishing hive-like swelling made her look like the Elephant Man, and her always-sweating hands made her particularly useless for working with electricity.

DeSimon kept a television in the shop. He would periodically emerge from his office, toss a VHS tape at us, and grunt, "Watch this," then leave us for hours. These instructional videos explained the rudiments of electrical current and also very basic wiring procedures. While uninterested in the content of the videos, my coworkers quickly figured out how to rig up the TV with an illegal makeshift antenna. That way we could watch Jerry Springer; one con would man the lookout post by the window to spot any approaching COs.

I was trying to learn some Spanish, and my coworker Yvette was very patiently trying to teach me, but what I managed to pick up was almost exclusively about food, sex, or curses. Yvette was by far the most competent of my coworkers, and she and I would often work together on any electrical job requiring proficiency with tools. This occasioned conversations where every sentence suffered from multiple fractures, coupled with a lot of cautious mime—neither of us wanted to get shocked. I had already learned the hard way what that was like—your head snaps back as if you've been kicked under the chin.

Jae, my neighbor Colleen's pal, was assigned to the electric shop—she had been cleared to work back in the Brooklyn MCC, so her paperwork didn't take long. She got the clerk job. "As long as I don't have to touch wires and shit, I'm cool," she said.

By default, she hung out with me at work—I was best buddies with Little Janet, and Little Janet was the only other black person in electric. As the New England spring took its sweet time arriving, the three of us occupied the bench in front of the shop, smoking and watching the comings and goings of other prisoners. The guards went in and out of their deluxe gym, which was located directly across from the electric building. There were long stretches of inactivity during which we shot the shit . . . about the drug game (distant memories for me), about New York City (where we all were from), about men, about life.

Little Janet could hold her own with us, despite being fifteen years younger, and I could hold my own with them, despite being white. Little Janet was excitable, eager to argue a point or show off a dance move or just act silly, while Jae was funny and mellow, with an easy laugh. She had served just two years of a ten-year sentence, but she never seemed bitter, just measured and mindful. But she had a quiet sadness about her, and a deep, still quality that seemed to be the part of her that she would not allow her surroundings and circumstances to destroy. When she talked about her sons, a teenager and an eight-year-old, her face shone.

I admired the humor and calm with which she handled her losses and our prison world—her dignity was not as quiet as Natalie's but was just as lovely.

. . .

JOYCE, FROM the electric shop, was going home soon. She had drawn the calendar on the blackboard in the shop and would cross off every day that passed with chalk. About a week before she was due for release she asked if I would color her hair. I must have shown my surprise at the intimate request. "You're the only one I know who seems like they won't fuck it up," she explained in her sharp, matter-of-fact way.

We went into the salon room off the camp's main hallway, a space that occupied as much room as the law library—about the size of a large closet. There were two old pink hair sinks with nozzles for rinsing, a couple of salon chairs in almost total disrepair, and some standing driers that looked like they were from the early 1960s. Shears and other cutting instruments were kept in a locked cage mounted on the wall—only the CO could unlock it. One of the chairs was occupied by a woman having her hair set by a friend. As I worked on the sections of Joyce's straight shiny hair, carefully following the directions on the box, I felt proud that she had asked me, and I also felt a bit more like a normal girl, performing beauty chores with girlfriends. When I accidentally sent the sink nozzle shooting out of control, spraying water everywhere, to my surprise everyone laughed instead of cursing me out. Maybe, just a little, I was starting to fit in.

IN THE free world your residence can be a peaceful retreat from a long day at work; in prison, not so much. A loud discussion of farting was happening in B Dorm. It had been initiated by Asia, who didn't actually live in B and was chased out. "Asia, you're out of bounds! Get your grimy ass outta here, ya project ho!" someone bawled after her.

I was surviving just fine in "the Ghetto" of B Dorm, due to my luck in having been paired with Natalie, and maybe to my stubborn conviction that I would be acting like a racist baby if I tried to get moved, and perhaps also to the fact that I had gone to an elite women's college. Single-sex living has certain constants, whether it's upscale or down and dirty. At Smith College the pervasive obsession with food was expressed at candlelight dinners and at Friday-afternoon faculty teas; in Danbury it was via microwave cooking and stolen food. In many ways I was more prepared to live in close quarters with a bunch of women than some of my fellow prisoners, who were driven crazy by communal female living. There was less bulimia and more fights than I had known as an undergrad, but the same feminine ethos was present—empathetic camaraderie and bawdy humor on good days, and histrionic dramas coupled with meddling, malicious gossip on bad days.

It was a weird place, the all-female society with a handful of strange men, the military-style living, the predominant "ghetto" vibe (both urban and rural) through a female lens, the mix of every age, from silly young girls to old grandmas, all thrown together with varying levels of tolerance. Crazy concentrations of people inspire crazy behavior. I can just now step back far enough to appreciate its surreal singularity, but to be back with Larry in New York, I would have walked across broken glass barefoot in a snowstorm, all the way home.

MR. BUTORSKY, my counselor, had a policy he had come up with all by himself. Once a week he would put every prisoner he supervised— half the Camp—on the callout for a one-minute appointment with him. You had to report to the office he shared with Toricella and sign a big log book to acknowledge you had been there.

"Anything going on?" he would ask. That was your chance to ask questions, spill your guts, or complain. I only asked questions, usually to have a visitor approved.

Sometimes he was feeling curious. "How are you doing, Kerman?" I was fine. "Everything going all right with Miss Malcolm?" Yes, she was great. "She's a nice lady. Never gives me any problems. Not like some of her kind." Er, Mr. Butorsky—? "It's a big adjustment for someone like you, Kerman. But you seem to be handling it." Is there anything else, Mr. Butorsky? 'Cause if not I'm going to go. . . .

Or chatty.

"I'm almost done here, Kerman. Almost twenty years I've been at this. Things have changed. People at the top have different ideas about how to do things. 'Course they have no idea what really goes on here with these people." Well, Mr. Butorsky, I'm sure you'll enjoy retirement. "Yeah, I'm thinking of someplace like Wisconsin . . . where there's more of us northerners, if you know what I mean."

Minetta, the town driver who had brought me up to Camp on my first day, was due to be released in April. As her date was nearing, the line of succession was the hot topic around Camp, as the town driver was the one prisoner who was allowed off the plantation on a daily basis. She was responsible for doing errands for the prison staff in town, ferrying inmates and their CO escorts to hospital appointments, and driving prisoners to the bus station after they had been released—plus any other mission that was handed to her. Never, ever had a town driver been chosen who was not a "northerner."

One day I went into the counselors' office for my callout minute. As I was signing the book, Mr. Butorsky stared at me. "Kerman, how about applying for the town driver position? Minetta is leaving soon. We need someone responsible for that job. It's an important job."

"Um . . . let me think about it, Mr. Butorsky?"

"Sure, Kerman, you go right ahead and think about it."

On the one hand, being the town driver would mean the opportunity to rendezvous with Larry in gas station bathrooms in the outside world. On the other hand, the town driver was widely held to be the designated Camp snitch. I was no snitch, no way, and clearly no good could come from coziness with prison staff, which the town driver position required. The uncomfortable privilege and collaborator subtext was more than I could stomach. Plus, after my screwdriver misadventure, I didn't have the stomach for illicit activities, even assignations, no matter how much I lusted for Larry. The next week in Butorsky's office I quietly turned the job down, much to his surprise.

. . .

WHEN I first arrived at the Camp, Pop, the ruler of the kitchen, would watch the prison-screened movie-of-the-week flanked by Minetta and Nina, Pop's bunkie. They would sit in a prime spot in the back of the room and kibitz and enjoy contraband delicacies, courtesy of Pop. When Minetta left for the halfway house, her movie seat was briefly taken by a tall, imposing, and largely silent white girl who was a prolific crocheter and was also leaving soon. Nina was also preparing to depart, but she was going "down the hill" to a nine-month residential drug program. It was for prisoners with documented drug and alcohol addictions who had been fortunate enough to be flagged for the program by their sentencing judge. It was the only serious rehabilitative program at Danbury (other than the puppies), and it is currently the only way in the federal system to significantly reduce your sentence. Campers headed to the drug program were always scared, as it took place not in the Camp but in the "real" prison: high security, lockdown, and twelve hundred women serving serious time, some with life sentences.

Nina had the added concern of finding an acceptable replacement for herself at Pop's side. After my initial faux pas in the dining room, it didn't even occur to me that I was a candidate, but one Saturday night in the common room Nina beckoned to me. She and the quiet girl were sitting with Pop. "Piper, come have some food!" Contraband food was irresistible—one did not readily pass up the simple novelty of eating something other than institutional food, cooked with a measure of love. I was pretty damn shy, though, after Pop's veiled threat in the chow hall.

They had guacamole and chips. I knew the avocados had been purchased from commissary and were not really contraband. I took a little bite but didn't want to seem greedy. "It's soooooo good! Thank you!" Pop was looking at me sidelong.

"Go on, have some more!" Nina said.

"I'm okay, I'm kind of full, but thank you!" I started to edge away.

"C'mon, Piper, sit down for a minute."

Now I was nervous. But I trusted Nina. I pulled up an extra chair and perched on it, ready to flee at any sign of Pop's displeasure. I made small talk about the other woman's imminent return to the outside world, how great it would be for her to be reunited with her teenage son, and whether she would find work with the carpenter's union. When the movie started I excused myself.

They made the same advance the next week. That night they offered me burgers, fat and juicy compared to the ones in the dining hall. I wolfed one down without prodding, tasting oregano and thyme. Pop seemed entertained by my relish and leaned over to confide: "I use extra spices."

A day or two later Nina posed a question to me: "Whaddaya think about watching the movie with Pop when I go to the drug program?" she asked.

What?

"She needs someone to keep her company when I leave, and get her ice and soda for her, you know?"

Did Pop really want my company?

"Well . . . you're not a wacko, you know? That's why we're friends, 'cause I can really talk to you about things."

The invitation seemed like the ultimate endorsement . . . and not one to be turned down lightly. When I saw Pop, I tried to be charming, and perhaps I was somewhat successful. The nonwacko contingent must have been thin on the ground at that time in the Camp, because a week or so later Nina asked me if I wanted to take her place as Pop's bunkie in A Dorm, "the Suburbs."

I was perplexed. "But I'm already in B Dorm—I can't move."

Nina rolled her eyes. "Piper, Pop gets whatever bunkie she wants."

I was stunned by this revelation that a prisoner could get what she wanted. Of course, if that inmate is the prime reason that your institutional kitchen runs in an orderly fashion . . . "You mean, they'll move me?" More eye rolling. I frowned, lost between contradictory impulses.

B Dorm was certainly living up to its "Ghetto" moniker, with all the irritants of any ghetto. One B Dorm practice alone drove me to the tooth-grinding brink of sanity: people would hang their little headphones on the metal bunks and blast their pocket radios through the makeshift "speakers," foisting their staticky music on everyone at top, tinny volume. It wasn't the music I objected to, it was the terrible audio quality.

But A Dorm seemed populated by a disproportionate number of fussy old ladies, plus the Puppy Program dogs and their people, who were mostly nuts. And I didn't want anyone to think I was a racist—although nobody else in the Camp seemed to have the slightest compunction about expressing the broadest racial generalizations.

"Honey," another prisoner drawled to me, "everyone here is just trying to live up to the worst cultural stereotype possible."

In fact, that was part of the motivation of this new invitation. "Pop don't want any lesbians in there," said matter-of-fact Nina. "And you're a nice white girl."

On the one hand, Pop would certainly be an advantageous bunkie, as she clearly wielded a lot of influence in the Camp. On the other hand, I had a strong suspicion that she would be a high-maintenance cubemate—look at the hustle Nina was putting on for her.

Finally, I thought about Natalie: how kind she had been to me and how easy she was to live with—and she was just nine months from going home. If I bailed on her, who knew what kind of kook they would stick in Cube 18? "Nina, I don't think I can just ditch Miss Natalie," I said. "She has been really good to me. I hope Pop understands."

Nina looked surprised. "Well . . . help me think about who else we can get. What about Toni? She's Italian."

I said that sounded grand, they would be a perfect fit, and retreated to B Dorm, my Ghetto home.

CHAPTER 7

The Hours

||||

There were a host of religious opportunities at Danbury: a Friday Mass for Catholics, and sometimes a Sunday Mass as well (usually delivered by the "hot priest," a young padre who played guitar and spoke Italian and was thus adored by all the Italian-Americans); a Spanish Christian service on the weekends; a Buddhist meditation group and also rabbinical visits on Wednesdays; and a wacky weekly nondenominational be-in led by volunteers armed with acoustic guitars and scented candles. The biggie, though, was the "Christian" (aka fundamentalist) service held in the visiting room on Sunday evenings after visiting hours were over.

In March I asked Sister Rafferty, the German nun who was the head chaplain, whether there would be any provision for Episcopalians on Easter Sunday. She looked at me as if I had three heads, then replied that if I wanted to hunt down my own minister and put him or her on my (full) visitors' list, then we could use the chapel. Thanks for nothing, Sister!

I found the religious prostrations of my saber-rattling born-again neighbors tedious. Some of the faithful had a distinct aspect of roostering, loudly proclaiming that they were going to pray on any number of topics, how God was walking beside them through their incarceration, how Jesus loved sinners, and so on. Personally, I thought that one could thank the Lord at a lower volume and perhaps with less self-congratulation. You could worship loudly and still act pretty lousy, abundant evidence of which was running around the Dorms.

There were no new spring hats or dresses in prison, but the week before Easter someone erected a creepy giant wooden cross behind the Camp, right outside the dining hall. I was confronted with it at breakfast and could only ask "What the fuck?" of Mrs. Jones, the gruff old queen of the Puppy Program and one of the old ladies who always came to breakfast. I was surprised to learn that she was only fifty-five. Prison will age a gal prematurely.

"They always put it up," she reported. "Some clown from CMS came up and did it."

A few days later Nina and I were discussing the impending holidays over a cup of instant coffee. Levy and the one other Jew in residence, the decidedly more likable Gayle Greenman, had been given boxes of matzoh by the German nun for Passover. This excited the interest of the other prisoners. "How come they get them big crackers?" a neighbor from B Dorm asked me, probing the mysteries of faith. "Them crackers would be good with jelly."

Nina, her bangs in rollers, tilted her head as she reminisced about Passovers past. "One year I was in Rikers. Matzoh was the only edible thing they gave us," she mused, rolling her cigarette thoughtfully between her fingers. "It's a delicious with buttah." This year I would not be ferrying back and forth between Larry's family's seder and my own Easter traditions. Too bad—I love the ten plagues.

Pop and her crew pulled out all the stops for Easter dinner. It was positively lavish, a spring miracle. The menu: baked chicken and cabbage with astonishing dumplings, so dense you could have used them as weapons; mustardy deviled eggs; and real vegetables on the salad bar. For dessert, we had Natalie's very special bird's nest confection— a deep-fried tortilla cupping a mound of pudding, covered with lush green-dyed coconut "grass" strewn with jelly bean "eggs," and a gaily colored marshmallow Peep perched on top. I just stared at it, unable to believe my eyes, while everyone around me ate enthusiastically. I didn't want to eat this incredible diorama. I wanted to shellac it and save it forever.

RIGHT AFTER Easter, Nina left to go down the hill to the high-security prison for the drug program. I would miss her. She had been knitting a scarf for weeks and weeks, and I had been consulting on it. "What color do you think now?" she would say, pulling out a re-markable collection of little scraps of yarn she had scavenged. "Pur-ple!" I would point. "Green!"

The whole Camp was in the process of readying the eight women who were entering the strict nine-month drug program. This process included purging any contraband they might have, acquiring new stuff at commissary, and loading them up with snacks and mes-sages to carry to women who were doing time down the hill. It was a bit like sending them off to a scary summer camp.

Nina would be just a few hundred yards away behind that awful fence, but it might as well have been thousands of miles. I might never see her again.

Along with the seven other women, her duffel bag was loaded into the town driver's van, and I hugged her. "Thank you, Nina, for everything."

"The scarf's for you, Piper! I'm gonna finish it!" Pop was crying.

As Nina headed down the hill to the FCI, I felt a real sense of loss. She was the first real friend I had made, and I wouldn't have any contact with her at all. Prison is so much about the people who are missing from your life and who fill your imagination. Some of the missing were just across the prison grounds—I knew a half-dozen women who had sisters or cousins down the hill in the high-security prison. One day while walking back to work after lunch, I glimpsed Nina through the back gate of the FCI and went crazy jumping up and down and waving. She saw me and waved too. The truck that pa-trolled the prison perimeter screeched to a halt between us. "Cut that shit out!" came sharply from the guard inside.

Pop, who had spent many years "down on the compound" before being moved up to the Camp, had enlisted multiple messengers to deliver treats to her friends still behind the wire. Living in A Dorm, "the Suburbs," Pop had an enormous locker in her cube, twice the size of mine and Natalie's. It was crammed with a bounty of her favorite things—food items like SPAM that were no longer available on commissary, clothing from long ago that no one else had, and most important, perfume. She liked to mix her own—a little White Diamonds, a little Opium. *Eau de Pop.* "I'm almost done," said Pop as she selected a few precious contraband lace brassieres to send to a friend doing life down the hill. "What am I hanging on to these for? I go home in January; I'll get pretty new bras for my jewels!"

Pop was a source of wonder and mystery and revelation. I didn't know it at the time, but Nina had set me up with the woman who would help me do my time in every sense of the word, who would baby me when I needed it most and tell me to suck it up and get tough when there was no other option. She had cast a skeptical eye over me at first. But when I procured a wooden board from the CMS shop to put under her mattress for back support, her opinion of me improved significantly. My ability to write her furlough requests was also useful. But it was my voracious appetite for her cooking and her stories that won her over.

Pop had lived a crazy life on the outside, arriving in this country from Russia at the age of three. She was married out of her parents' house at eighteen, to a Russian gangster. Their life together had included all the excessive disco splendor of New York in the 1970s and 1980s, and several years on the run from the feds. "The feds tried to nail us every which way . . . my husband would just laugh. Well, if they want you bad enough, they're gonna get you. They don't ever give up." Her husband was in prison somewhere down south, and her children were grown now. She had lost everything, yet managed to take a dozen years in prison and hold it all together and make the best of it. Pop was cunning and exuberant. She was kind, but she could be ruthless. She knew how to work the system and also how not to let them break you. And they were always trying.

Pop's grown children came to visit her every week, along with several other family members, murmuring in Russian. The visiting room was the only place I ever saw her in regulation khaki uniform— otherwise she was always in her checked kitchen pants, burgundy smock with "Pop" embroidered on the breast in white yarn, and a hairnet. But for visits she would always fix her hair and put on makeup, so she would look ladylike, girlish almost.

Anyone who received visits on a regular basis usually maintained at least one uniform exclusively for these occasions—one that fit well, was kept pressed and stain-free, and in some instances was specially tailored. It was against prison rules to alter clothing in any way, but that never stopped anyone from trying to find ways to make the drab men's uniforms a bit more flattering, a bit more feminine. Some women would iron patterned folds into the backs of the boxy, billowy shirts. Everyone knew which inmates had sewing skills, and you could trade commissary goods for a better fit—the Spanish mamis particularly liked to wear their pants tight, tight, tight. I was thrilled when someone gave me a pair of the most desirable flat-front Dickies, which had been taken in at the waist and tapered narrow at the ankle. The inner thighs were threadbare, but my fellow prisoners clicked their tongues approvingly as I sashayed to my visits. "P-I Piper!" my neighbor Delicious shouted appreciatively. "Brick House!" Larry agreed, his eyes popping when he first saw me in the tight pants.

Hair was at least as important as unis. This was not an issue for a blond, straight-haired gal like me, but for the black and Spanish women, it was the source of endless preoccupation and countless woman-hours. You could generally tell who was expecting a visit by the state of their hair. There were frequent disputes about chair time in the salon room, played out against the overpowering smells of perm solution and burning hair. The electric supply for the room was insufficient for the demand, and the circuits tripped all the time. But reprehensible DeSimon refused to do anything about it. "They oughta close that so-called 'beauty salon' down," he snarled when the gals in the shop suggested that the electric crew might work on the wiring there. "It's not working on these convicts!"

Once a prisoner completed her coiffure, she could move on to makeup. Approximately a third of the population wore makeup almost every day—out of habit, as an effort to feel normal, or to be more alluring either to a staffer or another inmate. It was bought at the commissary or, in the case of one ex-stockbroker who was addicted to Borghese, smuggled in via a visitor. Before she left for the drug program, Nina gave me a little heart-shaped compact, the kind you might find at a dollar store, and I experimented with lurid eye shadow colors. A significant percentage of the Spanish women had tattooed eyeliner, lipliner, and eyebrows, an effect I found unnerving—I associated it with Meatpacking District transsexual hookers. The tattooed brows never matched the real brows, which then had to be plucked or shaved, and with time they would fade from black to blue.

Almost everyone expecting a visit would present themselves pressed, coiffed, and painted on the landing next to the pay phones, where you could see your loved ones approaching up the hill from the parking lot. Those who weren't expecting visits would plant themselves on the stairs anyway to observe the comings and goings, as a source of vicarious entertainment—they could generally identify any regulars on sight. "Oh, there's Ginger's kids! There's Angela's parents—he always drops her mom off before he parks, she's got a bad hip."

Visitors had to fill out a form stating that they had no firearms or narcotics on their person. The CO would then check the inmate's list to be sure that the visitor's name was on it. You had to hope that the list was up to date, something that was completely dependent on the inmate's counselor. Did he do his paperwork? Had he bothered to turn it in? If not, tough shit. It didn't matter who your visitor was or how far they had come to see you—they were not getting in. Larry told me how painful it was to watch every visitor—old or young, street punk or fancy yuppie—have to suck it up and kiss the prison guard's ass in the hope of culling some sort of favor. The power games that fueled so much of the prisoner-guard experience extended to the visiting room.

Larry came to see me every week, and I lived for those visits—
they were the highlight of my life in Danbury, a chest-filling affirma-
tion of how much I loved him. My mother drove six hours round-trip
until I begged her to come every other week. I saw more of her during the eleven months I was at Danbury than I had in all my previous
adult years.

Yoga Janet and Sister Platte always had lots of visitors, aging
counterculture hipsters and rosy-cheeked lefties in homespun Guate-
malan cottons, respectively. Sister Platte was frustrated by the BOP's
effective censorship of her visiting list—international peace figures
had tried to gain permission to visit her and had been denied.

Some women never got visits because they had effectively said
goodbye to the outside world. No children, no parents, no friends,
nobody. Some of them were halfway around the world from home,
and some of them didn't have a home. Some women stated flatly that
they did not want their people to see them in a place like this. In general, the longer you were down, the fewer and farther between were
your visits. I worried about my bunkie, Natalie, finishing her eight-
year bid; she spoke to her young son on the phone every night and
received many letters but didn't have a single visit in the year we lived
together. I observed the unspoken privacy wall we erected between
us in our seven-by-ten-foot space, and never asked.

ALTHOUGH EACH day often seemed endless, now each week came to
an end before I expected it, hastened by visiting hours. I was remarkably lucky to have a visit from someone on Thursday or Friday, and
also on Saturday or Sunday. This was a function of Larry and my
mother's commitment, plus that of a large stock of friends in New
York who were eager to come see me. Larry juggled my complex visiting schedule with cruise-director aplomb.

When my counselor Butorsky suddenly left, I feared another bu-
reaucratic nightmare. He reportedly preferred early retirement to
submitting to the will of Warden Deboo, a much younger non-

"northern" female, and he was replaced with another "lifer," Mr. Finn, who was also nearing the twenty-year mark at the prison. Finn immediately made enemies among the Camp prisoners and staff by demanding a private office and harassing the orderlies about the quality of their floor-waxing. When he moved into his fancy private office, he placed a brass nameplate on the door. Of course, the damn thing disappeared immediately, which resulted in an army of COs coming in to shake down the Camp. They would not rest until Officer Finn's nameplate was found!

"You out of the frying pan and into the fire, bunkie," said Natalie, who knew Finn from previous years down the hill. "That man is nothing nice. At least Butorsky did his paperwork. Finn hates paperwork."

This stressed me out, given the extensive visiting-list-juggling I was trying to perform. But my blond hair and blue eyes stood me in good stead, just as they had with Butorsky. Mr. Finn was automatically inclined to like me, and when I approached with a new visitor's form and a timid request that maybe he would grant a special visit or shift my list around as Mr. Butorsky had done, he snorted.

"Gimme that. I don't give a shit how many people you have on your visiting list. I'll put 'em all on."

"You will?"

"Sure." Finn looked me up and down. "What the fuck are you doing in here? We don't see women like you much."

"Ten-year-old drug offense, Mr. Finn."

"What a waste. It's a waste for half of you people up in this Camp. Most of you drug people shouldn't even be here. Not like those scumbags down the hill . . . there's one that killed her two kids. I think it's a waste to keep her alive."

I didn't know how to respond to that. "So you'll put that visitor on my list, Mr. Finn?"

"Sure."

And he did. My visiting list grew beyond twenty-five rapidly, another example of the mystifying way that no prison rule was ever really cast in stone.

. . .

LARRY AND my mother were my lifelines to the outside world, but I was also lucky enough to have friends who came to see me. Their visits were particularly refreshing because they weren't tinged with the guilty knowledge of what I was putting Larry and my family through. I could just relax and laugh my ass off as my friends brought news and questions and observations from their miraculously normal lives.

David, my San Francisco book club buddy and Larry's ex-roommate, was a visiting room regular. He lived in Brooklyn now and would schlep up to Connecticut on the train once a month. What was especially wonderful about his visits was that he acted as if everything were perfectly normal, surveying the landscape with both curiosity and acceptance. He loved the vending machines—"Let's stroll over there and get a nosh!" I wanted to weep at how my friends took my calamity in stride.

David excited much attention at the Camp. Perhaps it was his combination of red hair, blasé charm, and arty eyeglasses that attracted so much pointed comment. Or maybe they just weren't used to gay New York Jews in that neck of the woods. "That's quite a friend you've got there," commented one of the male COs after a visit. Leered Mr. Finn, "Just pretend I feel about women the way that buddy of yours from the visiting room does." But the other prisoners loved David, who was always chatty with them. "Did you have a good time today with your faggot friend?" Pop asked after one of David's visits; of course I had. "Faggots make the best friends," she said philosophically. "They're very loyal."

My dear friend Michael wrote to me every Tuesday on his beautiful Louis Vuitton writing paper; his letters seemed like artifacts of a distant and exotic culture. On his first visit to see me, he had the misfortune of arriving at the same time as the airlift transport bus, and he was treated to the sight of disheveled women in jumpsuits entering the FCI in full shackles, supervised by guards with high-gauge rifles. When I joined him at a card table, cheerful in my tidy khaki uniform, he looked shaken but relieved.

Friends also came from Pittsburgh, Wyoming, and California to visit. My best friend Kristen left her new business in Washington to come see me every month, peering worriedly at my face for signs of trouble that others might not have caught. We have been inseparable friends since the first week of college, an odd pair to be sure: she a fairly proper southerner, a straight arrow, an overachiever driven to please; I a not-so-straight arrow. But deep down she and I are very much the same—similar families, similar values, simpatico. She was going through a rough time; her marriage was ending as her company was being born; and to have a heart-to-heart talk with her best friend, she had to haul ass to a Connecticut prison. I noticed that every time Kristen came to see me, Officer Scott would materialize in the visiting room and gaze at her like a teenage boy.

Once a male friend came to visit me; a tall, curly-headed lawyer, he had been consulting with a pro bono client at a nearby men's prison, so he decided to stop by on his way home. Usually he and his wife came to see me together. On that quiet Thursday afternoon he and I had a grand old time, talking and laughing for hours.

Afterward Pop cornered me. "I saw you in the visiting room. You looked like you were having some good time. So who is that guy? Does Larry know he's visiting you?"

I tried to keep a straight face while I assured Pop that my visitor was an old college friend of Larry's and that yes, my fiancé knew about the visit. I wondered if Larry had any idea how many fans he had behind bars.

When visiting hours were over, the last inmate stragglers hugged and kissed their loved ones goodbye, and we were left together, sometimes lost in our own thoughts, hoping the CO would be lazy and skip the strip searches. If someone was crying, you smiled sympathetically or touched their shoulder. If someone was grinning, you asked, "How was your visit?" as you unlaced your shoes. Once you were finished with squatting naked and coughing, you could burst back through the double doors into the rest of the Camp building, onto the landing, where there were always lots of women loitering, waiting for the phones, and watching the visitors walk down the hill to the parking lots. If you were quick, you could dart to the window and catch one last glimpse of your visitor departing. Larry only told me later, when I was safe at home, how devastating it was for him to turn back and see me waving goodbye through the glass, and then to head back down the hill, leaving me alone.

CHAPTER 8

So Bitches Can Hate

||||

One hobby I did not pick up was crocheting, an obsession among prisoners throughout the system. Some of the handiwork was impressive. The inmate who ran the laundry was a surly rural white woman named Nancy whose dislike for anyone but "northerners" was hardly a secret. Her personality left a lot to be desired, but she was a remarkable crochet artist. One day in C Dorm I happened upon Nancy standing with my neighbor Allie B. and mopey Sally, all howling with laughter. "What?" I asked, innocently. "Show her, Nancy!" giggled Allie. Nancy opened her hand. Perched there in her palm was an astonishingly lifelike crochet penis. Average in size, it was erect, fashioned of pink cotton yarn, with balls and a smattering of brown cotton pubic hair, and a squirt of white yarn ejaculate at the tip.

"More sentimental than functional, I guess?" was all I could manage.

Allie B. lived several cubes down in B Dorm and was a tall, skinny woman with broad shoulders and a strong jaw, who teetered between odd-looking and good-looking. She loved candy bars and reminded me of Wimpy from *Popeye:* "I will gladly pay you Tuesday for a Snickers bar today!" A daffy horndog and an unrepentant junkie, she was counting the days out loud until she could go home, get laid, and score some junk, in that order. She was straightforward and unapologetic about her love of narcotics. Heroin was her drug of choice, but she was willing to get high on anything and often threatened to sniff the solvents at her job in the construction shop. I didn't think there was anything there worth huffing.

Allie's sidekick was a young woman from western Pennsylvania who proudly called herself a redneck. I called her Pennsatucky. One day Pennsatucky and I were standing at my cube in B Dorm when my next-door neighbor Colleen and her pal Carlotta Alvarado walked by. Colleen had a big, shit-eating grin on her face as she asked Carlotta, "So? What'd you think about that little toy I gave you last week? Pretty sweet, huh?" Carlotta laughed, a rich, satisfied laugh, and they kept walking.

I cocked an eye at Pennsatucky. "Diiiiildoooos," she drawled in her backwoods twang. I must have looked intrigued, because she hastened to explain: "Colleen prob'ly carved somethin' nutty out of a carrot or something. Different than the usual."

"Which is?"

"Pencil with an Ace bandage wrapped around it, with one a' them finger condoms from the infirmary over the whole deal."

"Doesn't sound that enjoyable."

"Huh. When I was locked up in county, they used to make dildos out of a spork, a maxipad, and a finger from a rubber glove!" Another use for maxipads revealed. The industrious hobbyists of the penal system would work with whatever materials they had.

"Desperate times, desperate measures, eh Pennsatucky?"

"Whatever *that* means."

JUST AS we had sent eight prisoners down the hill to the drug program, the FCI returned the favor in kind, with a fresh batch of hard-timers "graduating" up the hill. Sometimes these women were very close to release, and sometimes they still had a stretch of time to do. Regardless, they usually hung together for a time, quietly watching the situation—unless of course they had friends in the Camp, either from the street or from the inside.

One of the new arrivals from the FCI was Morena, a Spanish woman who looked like a deranged Mayan princess. Deranged, but not because she was unkempt or wild in her overall appearance. She had the clear air of someone who knows how to do time and was immaculately groomed, with "good" unis, pressed and sharp, and she was generally very composed. But Morena had unsettling eyes. She would stare at you; those crazy brown eyes were powerfully expressive, and you couldn't tell what the hell it was they were telegraphing. Whatever was going on in her head, it was taking a lot of effort for her to restrain it, and her eyes were giving her away. It wasn't just me who noticed her spooky eyes. "That one's not right," said Pop, tapping her temple. "Watch it."

Imagine my surprise when Morena asked if she could walk with me in the morning to work—she had been assigned to the safety shop in CMS. I always chose to walk the half-mile to work alone, a little freedom that I treasured. I had no idea what to talk to her about. I thought she was about my age, wasn't sure where she was from (her English was heavily accented and good), and I sure as hell wasn't going to start asking personal questions. "How do you like safety?" was pretty neutral. Crazy Eyes couldn't take offense at that.

"It's fine," she snorted. "I know the boss from the FCI. It's no problem. Where are you from, *chica*?"

I gave her the standard bare-minimum information—New York City, fifteen months.

"You have children?"

No children. Did she?

Morena laughed, a throaty, crazy laugh that said, *Oh, you naïve and innocent straight girl, you can't even tell that I am a bulldagger on the outs, not just up in this joint where one cannot get any dick . . . and how I will relish turning you out.* "No baby, I got no children."

Over the next week or two Morena was my companion on the walk to work, like it or not. I got an earful about her low opinion of the women in the Camp. "They are like little girls, they think this shit is a game," she opined, curling her lip. I was scrupulously polite and noncommittal, because Crazy Eyes made me nervous. In addition to many halting conversations on the way to work, her interactions with me in the Camp sharply increased. Morena would materialize at the entry of my cube and coo at me in a bizarre way, "Hello, babeeeeee!" I had decided when I moved into B Dorm that I did not want anyone visiting me in my cube; the space was tiny and shared with Natalie and was as close to privacy as I was going to get. I went out to socialize. If I was in my cube, I was either reading or writing letters or sleeping. Other women, especially the young ones, loved to have people pile into their cubes, sit on their beds and footstools, and stand around and jaw; this was not for me.

"Looks like you have a new friend, bunkie," Natalie observed drily.

One day while we were walking to work, Crazy Eyes cut to the chase. She was once again ranting about the immaturity and silliness of the women in the Camp. "They act like they are on vacation here or something, running around and acting silly. They need to act like women."

I said rather mildly that most of the women were really bored and perhaps not so well educated and that they did indeed divert themselves with foolish things.

This observation prompted a sudden and passionate declaration from Crazy Eyes: "Piper, they are like children, and I am looking for a real woman! I cannot be bothered with this bullshit, with these silly girls! On the street, I am a big-time drug dealer! I do serious business, big business! My life is serious! Even in here, I cannot waste my time with these silly bitches—I need a real woman!"

I opened my mouth and then closed it. I felt like I had been dropped into a telenovela. Morena's bosom was practically heaving under her prison khakis. Hey, I could understand what she was saying. Her life was indeed serious, her desires were serious, and I could understand why she didn't want to mess around with some trifling bimbo who was experimenting with lesbianism just to entertain herself in prison. But hell no, not me.

I tried to choose my words with delicacy. "Er, well, Morena, I'm certain that you'll find the right woman for you. It just might take a while for her to show up? Right?"

She looked at me with those unreadable crazy eyes. Was she pissed? Hurt? Vindictive? I couldn't tell.

I was vastly relieved when we got to work—the ten-minute walk never seemed so long. I kept the conversation to myself.

Morena made a few more attempts to express her need for a real woman, perhaps thinking that I was too dense to get her meaning, but my response remained the same—I was sure that the right woman was out there somewhere in the correctional system and that providence would deliver her to Danbury with all haste. It wouldn't be fast enough for me.

Once it was clear that I was not her future boo, Crazy Eyes quickly lost interest in me. The companionable walks stopped, and the cubicle drop-bys ceased. She still greeted me, but in a disinterested way. I felt that I had navigated the situation with as much grace as I had available, and no hideous repercussions to my tacit rejection seemed forthcoming. I breathed a little easier, hoping Crazy Eyes would spread the word to the other committed lesbians that I was not "like that," even though in some other lifetime I had been.

FOR THE first time in many years I was living a completely chemical-free existence—right down to going off birth control pills. My body was returning to its actual organic state. And after almost three months of enforced celibacy, I was feeling very warm under the collar. If you had spit on me, I might have sizzled.

Larry was clearly feeling the pressure of our separation too. His hello kisses in the visiting room grew more ardent, and he wanted to play footsie under the card tables. My own yearnings for footsie were severely tempered by my fear of the guards. I understood on a visceral level, as he did not, that they really could end a visit and take all my visiting privileges away. This point was demonstrated to Larry one day when Gay Pornstar (aka Officer Rotmensen) materialized during visiting hours. Gay Pornstar was a strutting sadist with a flattop hairdo, close-set eyes, and a bristling mustache who resembled nothing so much as a Village People tribute-band reject. He had come into the visiting room to see his little buddy, Officer Jesus-Is-My-Homeboy, who was filling in for the regular visitation CO and bor-

ing two prisoners who were helpers in the visiting room with pre-
dictions about the Rapture.

As I entered the visiting room, I kissed Larry hello, and then he
stole another kiss as we sat down at our assigned table.

Seeing this, Gay Pornstar bellowed across the room, pointing,
"*Hey!!!* One more time and you're *outta* here!!!" Every head turned
to stare silently.

Larry was rattled. "What the hell is wrong with that guy?" He
tried to grab my knee under the table.

"That's just what they're like, darling—*don't touch me!* He's *not*
fucking around!"

It killed me to snap at him like that, when all I wanted was for
him to touch me, but Larry didn't understand that pushing boundaries in prison can have dire consequences. These men had the power
not only to end our visits but to lock me up in solitary on a whim;
my word against theirs would count for little.

Afterward, still traumatized, I asked Elena, one of the prisoners
who worked in the visiting room, what the hell had happened. "Oh,
the little guy was watching you, and he was turning red," she said, "so
Rotmensen got pissed off when he saw that his buddy was embarrassed seeing you kiss."

The next week the regular CO was back on duty. "I heard you
were out of line last week," she said, patting me down before allowing me in to see Larry. "I'll be watching you."

In such a harsh, corrupt, and contradictory environment, one
walks a delicate balance between the prison's demands and your own
softness and sense of your own humanity. Sometimes at a visit with
Larry I would be overwhelmed, suddenly overcome with sadness
about my life at that moment. Could our relationship weather this insanity? Larry had been steadfast for all those years waiting for me to
go to prison; now that I was here, could we make it through the real
test? Our minutes in the visiting room were so precious, we could
never bear to discuss anything difficult or negative. We wanted every
second in that room to be sweet and perfect.

Different women had different ways of dealing with prison's impact on their relationships. On a sleepy weekend afternoon I stood by the microwave with my friend Rosemarie. She was in the midst of an elaborate cooking project, making gooey cheese and chicken enchiladas, and I was "helping." Although I could be counted on to chop an onion (tricky with a butter knife), mainly my help took the form of indulging her passion for talking about our future weddings. Rosemarie was engaged to a sweet, quiet guy who visited her faithfully every week, and she was obsessed with wedding planning. She had subscriptions to all the bridal rags, which piled up in her cubicle, and she loved to dream and scheme about her Big Day.

She also wanted to plan for my Big Day—Larry and I had been engaged for almost two years. But I was hardly interested in a traditional ceremony, plus I knew we weren't getting married anytime soon, and this colored my willingness to take wedding planning very seriously. Which drove Rosemarie nuts. When I told her I would wear a red bridal dress, she squealed with outrage.

On this particular day, Rosemarie was preoccupied with my headgear. If I was not going to wear a veil (a shame, she thought), then a tiara was most advisable. I snorted, "Rosemarie, do you really think I am putting a crown on my head to walk down the aisle?" In the heart of a budding wedding planner, anything is possible.

As Rosemarie filled tortillas and argued passionately in favor of seed pearls, Carlotta Alvarado approached: she wanted to know who was in line for the microwave. This was a strategic question. Carlotta, a committed system-gamer, was assessing who would let her cut the line, and Rosemarie was a definite possibility. The two of them worked together training seeing-eye dogs, and while Carlotta, an around-the-way girl from the Bronx, and Rosemarie, a preppy geek from New England, didn't seem to have a lot in common, they got along very well. Rosemarie agreed to put the enchiladas on pause so Carlotta could fry some onions with Sazón, the Latin seasoning that makes everything orange, salty, and spicy.

"Carlotta's engaged too!" said Rosemarie as the onions sizzled. Engagements were rare around the Camp.

"That's great, Carlotta. What's your man's name?"

Carlotta beamed. "Rick—he's my sweetie, he comes to visit me all the time. Yeah, I'm getting married. I can hardly wait."

"It's *so* exciting!" sang Rosemarie. Then she grinned. "Tell her what you told me, Carlotta."

Carlotta smiled triumphantly. "Yeah, I can't wait to get married. You know why?"

I didn't.

Carlotta stepped back, to better deliver the truth that, when she contemplated holy matrimony, made her heart beat faster. She pushed her palm toward me, index finger pointing skyward for emphasis. "So bitches can *hate*!"

Er . . . bitches?

"That's right. I'm going back to my neighborhood, and I'm going to get married, and that will show all those bitches who talk shit about me. I'll be married, with my man, and you know what they'll have? No man. A bunch of babies by a bunch of guys. I cannot *wait* to get married, so those bitches can just hate on me!"

I studied Carlotta, her pretty face bright and animated as she envisioned her future—one that included her man, some bitches, and a ring around her finger. I was fairly certain that she would get what she wanted. Among all the women at the Camp, she was one who could always figure out an angle. She had a primo prison job training the service dogs, she had all the contraband onions she needed, she ran a side business doing pedicures, and rumor was that she even had a cell phone secreted somewhere in the prison, so she could call her man on the outside without waiting in line and paying the prison's sky-high rates. She was a smart cookie, with an unsentimental eye on the world. Rick, I concluded, was a lucky guy.

As FOR me, I felt caught between the world I lived in now and the world to which I longed to return. I saw that those who couldn't come to terms with their imprisonment had a very difficult time with staff and with other prisoners. They were in constant conflict because they couldn't reconcile themselves with their fellow prisoners. I saw young women who had been running wild in poverty most of their lives rail against authority, and middle-aged, middle-class women who were aghast to find themselves living among people they thought were beneath them. I thought they were all unnecessarily unhappy. I hated the control the prison exercised over my life, but the only way to fight it was in my own head. And I knew I wasn't better than any other woman locked up in there, even the ones I didn't like.

On the other hand, some people were way too comfortable in prison. They seemed to have forgotten the world that exists on the outside. You try to adjust and acclimate, yet remain ready to go home every single day. It's not easy to do. The truth is, the prison and its residents fill your thoughts, and it's hard to remember what it's like to be free, even after a few short months. You spend a lot of time thinking about how awful prison is rather than envisioning your future. Nothing about the daily workings of the prison system focuses its inhabitants' attention on what life back on the outside, as a free citizen, will be like. The life of the institution dominates everything. This is one of the awful truths of incarceration, the fact that the horror and the struggle and the interest of your immediate life behind prison walls drives the "real world" out of your head. That makes returning to the outside difficult for many prisoners.

So I became obsessed with the almost daily departures and found myself asking *Who's going home this week?* I kept a running tally in my mind, and if I liked the person, I would head up to the front door of the visiting room after breakfast to wave them off, a ritual observed by a gaggle of prisoners for every departure. It was bittersweet to watch them leave, because I would have given anything to be going with them. People planned their going-home outfit, which someone from the outside would ship to Receiving and Discharge (R&D) for them; their friends would prepare a special meal; and they would start to give away all their stuff—commissary clothing and "good" uniforms and blankets and other things of value that they had accumulated while doing their time. I fantasized about giving all my stuff away.

Watching people arrive was less pleasant but also interesting. I certainly felt bad for them, but my regard was tinged with a funny little sense of superiority, because at least I knew more about the workings of the Camp than they did and thus had a leg up. This impulse was often proved wrong when someone turned out to be returning to Danbury after violating the terms of their probation—they would often march right into the counselors' office and ask for their old bunkie and job assignment back. I knew that as many as two-thirds of all released prisoners are locked up again, a fact that mystified me at first—there was no way they would get me back in prison. Ever. And yet . . . no one ever seemed surprised to see a familiar face return to Danbury.

"Self-surrenders" who came to the Camp were easy to spot. They were usually white and middle-class and looked totally overwhelmed and scared to death. I would ask myself, *Did I look that wigged out?* and then I'd go get them some of the extra shower shoes and toothpaste I now kept stashed in my locker for such occasions.

But most new arrivals had been in custody for a while, sometimes since their initial arrest if they had not been granted bail or couldn't make the bail payment, and they were coming from county jails or from federal jails, called MCCs or MDCs—metropolitan correctional centers or metropolitan detention centers. The county jails were described to me as universally nasty, full of drunks, prostitutes, and junkies—not up to the standards of us *federales*. No shock then that the women arriving at Danbury from county usually looked fried. They seemed happy to get to Danbury because the conditions were better—that depressed me.

Also intriguing were the women like Morena who had "earned" their way up the hill from the high-security FCI to the minimum-security Camp—in theory, the really hardened and potentially dangerous criminals. They were always very composed in terms of physical appearance—hair done and uniforms just so, with their own name and reg number embossed on the shirt pocket. (Campers didn't get that.) They never looked scared. But they were often freaked out because they were unaccustomed to as much "freedom" as we were afforded, and they reported that there was far less to do in the Camp in the way of programs and recreation. In fact many of them were miserable in the Camp and wanted to go back to max lockup. One woman, Coco, marched right into the counselors' office and explained that she couldn't handle the freedom, and would they please send her back down the hill, because she didn't want to lose her good time due to an escape attempt. I heard that the truth was she couldn't stand to be apart from her girlfriend, who was still down in the FCI. Coco was sent back the next day.

SPRING WAS coming slowly to the Connecticut hills, and we were starting to shake off the cold. Being cooped up with so many "wackos" was affecting my worldview, and I feared that I would return to the outside world a bit cracked too. But I was learning something every day, resolving some new subtlety or mystery through observation or instruction.

The track by the field house gym was now mush, but I slogged determinedly around it, encouraged by the fact that I kept getting thinner and thinner and every visitor who came to see me said with astonishment, "You look fantastic!" I was making those mucky circles in silence, because the commissary was still out of the damn crappy headset radios that cost $42. Every week I put the radio on my shopping list before I turned it in, and every week, no radio. The commissary CO, who was a real prick in public and friendly in private, just barked, "No radios!" when I asked when they would get some. All the other new arrivals were in the same boat, and we commiserated bitterly. Movie night was all about reading lips for me, and my time on the track or in the gym left me with my thoughts echoing noisily in my skull. I had to have that radio!

Lionnel, the inmate consigliere of the warehouse, was one of my closest neighbors in our cramped quarters. Her bunkie had been the target of Lili Cabrales's protest pee on my first morning in B Dorm, and it was she who had sopped up the puddle. Lionnel had a black name plaque like Natalie's, indicating that she had been down the hill in the FCI and probably had a long sentence. She was formidable but still friendly, a no-nonsense player when it came to doing time, and a cheerful Christian who was quick with a wry observation. Lionnel was vocal about what you might call "community issues"—not stealing, "acting right" during count, treating other prisoners with respect. She wasn't about to go out of her way to befriend a random white girl like me, but she would still say good morning and occasionally smile at my attempts at humor when we found ourselves side by side at the bathroom sinks.

One quiet afternoon as I was fixing lights in B Dorm, Lionnel materialized outside her cube. This was unusual, as she would normally be at work in the warehouse. I seized the opportunity to find out more about the mysterious radios.

"Lionnel, I hate to bother you, but I've got a question." I quickly explained my radio problem. "I'm going crazy with no music. I just can't get the CO to tell me when they're coming in. What do you think?"

Lionnel gave me a skeptical, sidelong look. "You *know* you're not supposed to ask warehouse folks about that, we're not allowed to talk about any goods in the warehouse?"

I was taken aback. "No, Lionnel, I didn't know that. I didn't mean to put you on the spot. I'm sorry."

"No problem."

May was a week away. The sun was really starting to make itself known now, drying up the mud. There were leaves on the trees, migratory birds, and tons of baby bunnies all over the track. I realized that it wasn't so bad to be listening to my own thoughts when there was so much to look at. I had made it three months, almost a quarter of my sentence. If I had to watch silent movies for the next ten, so be it. I almost didn't bother putting the radio on my commissary list that week; someone who had already shopped was complaining that they were still out. So when a new radio headset came flying past the register to land in my grocery pile, I just stared at it.

"Is there something wrong with you, Kerman?" shouted the CO. "It's true what they say about blondes, huh?"

I looked past him, into the glassed-in commissary, and spotted Lionnel. She didn't meet my eye. I just smiled to myself as I signed my receipt and handed it back to him. It was funny how things worked around here, how other prisoners could make things happen. I wasn't really sure what I had done right, but did it matter?

That week the entire population of the Camp was summoned into the main hallway for an impromptu meeting with the staff—a bunch of white men looking too bored to smirk. We were told:

1. Your sanitation is wanting! We will hold more inspections!
2. No smoking under the unit manager's window! You have been warned!
3. No sex in the Camp! No exceptions! Zero tolerance! This means you!!

We were collectively unimpressed. All of us prisoners knew that Finn, the senior counselor, was way too lazy to bother inspecting the Dorms beyond the bare minimum and didn't care enough to enforce most rules. The only thing Finn did appear to care about was hierarchy (as demonstrated to us by the nameplate fiasco). And the administrative unit manager didn't give a rat's ass about anything having to do with the Camp.

True to the staff's charges against us, though, there had been quite an uptick in "sexin'" among the ladies since Butorsky's departure, which led to some comical matchups. Big Mama was a cheerful leviathan who lived in A Dorm—quick with a play on words, generally benevolent, and prodigious in girth. She was slim on modesty, however, as was proven by her shameless sexin' with a series of much younger, much skinnier girls in her open cubicle. I liked Big Mama and was fascinated by her romantic success. How did she do it? What were her tricks? Were they the same as those employed by fat middle-aged men to get young nubile girls to sleep with them? The girls didn't then turn around and disrespect her, so was it curiosity on their part? I was curious, but I wasn't quite brave enough to ask.

There was a constant dance between the prisoners and the staff around the rules. With a new rotation of officers on detail in the Camp, the dance would start anew. I was washed in relief to be rid of Gay Pornstar; it was amazing how much more bearable it was around the Camp with him gone.

In Pornstar's place we now had Mr. Maple, who seemed to be his predecessor's exact opposite. Mr. Maple was young, recently out of the military after service in Afghanistan, and exaggeratedly courteous and friendly. He was instantly popular with the women of the Camp. I still considered all COs the enemy on principle, but I was beginning to understand a bit better why a prisoner might look at them with anything other than a baleful eye. Regardless of "gay for the stay," the vast majority of female prisoners are heterosexual, and they miss male companionship, male perspective, and male attention. A fortunate minority have a husband or a boyfriend who visits regularly, but most are not so lucky. The only men they come in contact with are prison guards, and if the CO is a half-decent human being, he will find himself the object of crushes. If he is a cocky bastard, even more so.

It is hard to conceive of any relationship between two adults in America being less equal than that of prisoner and prison guard. The formal relationship, enforced by the institution, is that one person's word means everything and the other's means almost nothing; one person can command the other to do just about anything, and refusal can result in total physical restraint. That fact is like a slap in the face. Even in relation to the people who are anointed with power in the outside world—cops, elected officials, soldiers—we have rights within our interactions. We have a right to speak to power, though we may not exercise it. But when you step behind the walls of a prison as an inmate, you lose that right. It evaporates, and it's terrifying. And pretty unsurprising when the extreme inequality of the daily relationship between prisoners and their jailers leads very naturally into abuses of many flavors, from small humiliations to hideous crimes. Every year guards at Danbury and other women's prisons around the country are caught sexually abusing prisoners. Several years after I came home, one of Danbury's lieutenants, a seventeen-year corrections veteran, was one of them. He was prosecuted and spent one month in jail.

When Mr. Maple was on duty in the evening, he constantly patrolled the Dorms. There was something unnerving to me about the male COs seeing me in nothing but my muu-muu, billowing though it was. It was more unnerving still when I would look up from changing after the gym, in shorts and a sports bra, to see the eyes of a prison guard. It wasn't so much the idea of them seeing my body, although the thought made me recoil. It was more the idea that my intimate moments—changing clothes, lying in bed, reading, crying— were all in fact public, available for observation by these strange men.

On one of his early days on duty, Maple was running through mail call. "Platte! Platte! Rivera! Montgomery! Platte! Esposito! Piper!"

I stepped up and he handed me my mail, and I turned back to the crowd to rejoin it. Some of the women were tittering and whispering. I stood next to Annette and looked at her quizzically.

"He called you Piper!" Other prisoners were looking at me with curiosity. It wasn't done. I felt embarrassed and showed it by flushing deeply, which provoked more tittering.

"He just doesn't know. He thinks it's my last name," I explained defensively. The next day at mail call, he did it again. "That's her *first* name," some wiseass said pointedly, as I blushed again.

"It is?" he asked. "That's unusual."

Still, he kept calling me Piper.

CHAPTER 9

Mothers and Daughters

||||

Mother's Day was off the chain at the Camp. From the moment we awoke, every woman wished another "Happy Mother's Day" . . . repeatedly. I quickly gave up explaining that I had no children and just said, "Happy Mother's Day to you!" About eighty percent of the women in U.S. prisons have children, so odds were I was right.

A lot of women had crocheted long-stem red roses for their "prison mamas" or friends. Some women organized themselves into somewhat formalized "family" relationships with other prisoners, especially mother-daughter pairs. There were a lot of little clans at Danbury. The younger women relied on their "moms" for advice, attention, food, commissary loans, affection, guidance, even discipline. If one of the young ones was misbehaving, she might get directed by another irritated prisoner, "Go talk to your mama and work your shit out!" Or if the kid was really out of control with her mouth or her radio or whatever, the mama might get the request, "You need to talk to your daughter, 'cause if she don't get some act-right, I'ma knock her out!"

My de facto prison "family" revolved around Pop. It exemplified the complex ways that family trees grow behind bars, like topiaries trained into very odd shapes. My immediate "sibling" was Toni, the new town driver who had replaced Nina as Pop's bunkie. By automatic extension Rosemarie, Toni's best buddy, was another sibling—

I thought of them as the Italian Twins. But Pop had many other "children," including Big Boo Clemmons, the even bigger Angelina Lewis, and Yvonne who worked with Pop in the kitchen. I took a particular liking to Yvonne; we called each other "the sister I never wanted." All of Pop's black "daughters" called her Mama. All of the white ones called her Pop. She didn't have any Spanish daughters, though she did have Spanish pals from her own peer group.

Motherhood in prison was revered but also complicated by separation, guilt, and shame. To my eye, my fellow prisoners were mostly ordinary poor or middle-class mommies, grandmas, and even great-grandmothers, and yet some of them were serving very long sentences—five years, seven years, twelve years, fifteen years. I knew that, by virtue of being in the minimum-security Camp, they were unlikely to have been convicted of violent crimes. As I watched my neighbors, young women who lacked even a high school education, with their children in the visiting room, I found myself asking again and again (in my head), *What could she possibly have done to warrant being locked up here for so long?* Criminal masterminds they were not.

In the three months since my arrival in Danbury I had seen a number of pregnant women become mothers; in February young Doris was the vessel of my first prison nativity. I had never seen a woman in labor before and was both mesmerized and horrified to watch Doris enter a zone in which her body and her baby were taking over, regardless of surroundings. To my fascination, the population of the Camp snapped to attention and stepped in to help her as much as anyone could. She had a half-dozen surrogate midwives hovering over her at any given moment, checking to see what she needed, coaching her on how to get more comfortable, relating stories of their own labors, and reporting on her progress to an anxious audience of prisoners. The staff certainly wasn't paying much attention to what was happening; prison births were no big deal to them.

It was Doris's first child, and all she wanted to do was curl up in her bunk, which apparently was not a good thing for her or the baby struggling to be born. Older women took turns walking with her up and down the long main hall of the Camp, talking to her gently, telling stories, and cracking jokes. Observing keenly was Doris's roommate, also heavy with her first child and due any day. They both looked scared.

The next morning, as the contractions were growing closer, Doris was taken off to the hospital in handcuffs. In many places in the United States pregnant female prisoners are kept chained in shackles during their deliveries, a brutal and barbaric practice, though this was not the case for poor Doris. After many hours of labor she gave birth to a nine-pound baby boy in Danbury Hospital and was brought back to prison immediately, pale and drawn and sad. Her mother took the baby back to the rural outpost where she lived, eight hours away. There wasn't much chance that the new arrival would see his father anytime soon—Doris told me that her baby's daddy had just been picked up on three outstanding warrants. Fortunately she was due to go home within the year.

I hadn't witnessed anything at Danbury to allay my fear of child-birth, but for the first time I had some tiny insight on the mother-child relationship. The single most reliable way to get another prisoner to smile was to ask her about her children. There were al-ways families in the visiting room; this was both the best and the worst thing about the many hours I spent there. Young children were growing up while their mothers did time, trying to have a relation-ship via fifteen-minute phone calls and the hours spent in visitation. I never saw these women look happier than when they were with their children, playing with the small collection of plastic toys kept in the corner and sharing Fritos and Raisinets from the vending ma-chine. When visiting hours were over, it was gut-wrenching to watch the goodbyes. In one year a child could change from a squirming baby to a boisterous talkative toddler and mothers would watch foot-ball championships and prom nights come and go from the distant sidelines, along with their children's graduations, wedding days, and funerals.

As tough as it could be for a prisoner to visit with her children, it was also hard for parents to see their babies locked up. There were so many young girls among us, eighteen and nineteen years old. Some of these kids had been heading to a place like Danbury for some time, but one bad decision could suddenly land a young woman in a merciless and inflexible system. A lack of priors and a history of general good conduct didn't matter at all—federal mandatory mini-mums dictated sentences, and if you were pleading guilty (the vast majority of us did), the only person with real leeway in determining what kind of time you would do was your prosecutor, not your judge. Consequently there were sad-looking parents visiting their kids—though not mine. My mother was like a ray of sunshine in that room.

For our visits every week my mother was always dressed immac-ulately in soft, cheerful colors, with her blond hair carefully styled, her makeup perfectly applied, wearing a piece of jewelry that I had given her for a distant Christmas or birthday. We would talk for hours about my brother, her students, my uncles and aunts, the family dog. I would fill her in on whatever new electrician's skill I'd learned that week. She always seemed perfectly comfortable in the visiting room, and every time she visited, I got comments from other prisoners af-terward. "Your mama is so nice, you're a lucky girl," or "That's your mother? Get out! I thought it was your sister!"

I had been hearing that one most of my adult life. People would often say it to her as well, and even though she had received that compliment approximately three thousand times before, it always made her glow. In the past, this familiar exchange made me feel re-sentful. *Do I look like I'm in my late forties or fifties?* But now I enjoyed watching her pleasure when people drew a close comparison be-tween us. Even with this disaster I had dragged us all into, she was still proud to be my mother. It occurred to me that I had never seen my mother defeated, even when life presented difficulties and disap-pointments. I hoped that our resemblance extended beyond our blue eyes.

My father, more than a thousand miles away, was able to come visit me when the academic year was over. His relief when he saw me was palpable. I have always been a daddy's girl, and I could tell how it pained him to see his baby, even a baby in her thirties, in a place like this. We still enjoyed our time, eating peanut M&Ms while I spun all the intrigues of the place out for him to absorb. The difference between our weekly phone calls and an actual in-person conversation was like a text message versus a weekend-long visit. If there was one silver lining to this whole mess, it was the reminder of my family's greatness.

I had a lovely visit with my mother that Mother's Day—although the visiting room was deranged. I had never seen it so crowded with large family groups. A lot of women in Danbury had families who lacked the resources to come and visit often, even though many of them lived in New York City. Tired grandmas and aunties, taking care of their daughter's or sister's children during their prison stays, had a very hard time marshaling toddlers and teenagers on the buses, trains, and taxis necessary to get to Danbury—the trip could take four hours each way from the city and cost money. But Mother's Day was special, and children of every age swarmed the place, and a cacophony of conversations flowed in many languages and accents. In the midst of all of it was my mother, smiling happily when she spotted me walking into the madness.

Two copies of *The New Yorker* arrived for me at mail call, to my horror. Someone out there had sent me a second subscription. Miss Esposito from C Dorm also got the magazine, and had been mad at me when my first copy showed up in March—she thought it was a waste of money for both of us to get it. The damn things were piling up all over the prison.

Esposito was an odd duck. A big, solid woman in her fifties, she wore her dark hair in a disconcertingly girlish Dutch boy bob. She was always part of the welcome wagon for any new prisoner, regardless of race—she herself was Italian-American. She volunteered that she had been a gang leader with the Latin Kings, a claim I was at first skeptical about—why would the Latin Kings have an Italian Queen?—but it turned out to be true. She was a former 1960s radical intellectual who'd gotten involved with gang activity at a pretty high regional level. Esposito was doing a long, long sentence.

I could tell pretty quickly that Esposito, although a needy person, wasn't after anything from me that I wasn't willing to give, and she was heartwarmingly appreciative of my magazines and books. One day she came to me, with a fan in her hand. It was a medium-size oscillating plastic table fan, like you might buy in Woolworth's. It looked just like the one Natalie had. "Bunkie, you going to be glad we got this when summer comes," she said. "You can't get these no more. They stopped selling them at commissary." The commissary now sold a much smaller fan, a crappy little one that cost $21.80. The old-school ones were prized, especially by the older ladies, who seemed to feel the heat most acutely.

Esposito's fan was broken. It wasn't even hot out yet, but she was stressed. "Can you maybe take a look at this, down in the electric shop? I'll do anything to get it fixed." No promises, but sure, was my reply. I toted the thing down to work on the bus the next morning and took it apart, with my coworkers observing keenly. It turned out to be an easy fix, and I was glad that my access to tools was helpful to another prisoner. Back in the Camp, when I triumphantly plugged the fan in and it whirred to life, Esposito almost fainted with joy. I refused to take any commissary payment, but Esposito paid me in reputation.

Almost immediately another old-timer approached me, hoping for a board to slide under the mattress to help ease her back pain. There were a handful of older ladies doing very long sentences— Pop, Esposito, Mrs. Jones—and if I did one of them a favor, they were sure to tell everyone. Soon I was besieged by women bearing broken radios and broken fans and seeking repair for things in their cubicles—hooks for their clothing, loose conduits, busted shoe racks, all sorts of things.

Little Janet thought this was over the line. "That stuff's not our job, Piper. It's not electric, so why should we fix it?"

"No one else is going to do it, babe. The feds aren't going to take care of us in this shithole. We have to do for each other. "

She could accept that logic, and besides she had other things on her mind at the moment. Little Janet had attracted an admirer, a tiny little white girl named Amy with a loud mouth. Amy was new among the always-present subset of prisoners I called "Eminemlettes," Caucasian girls from the wrong side of the tracks with big mouths and big attitudes, who weren't taking shit from anyone (except the men in their lives). They had thinly plucked eyebrows, corn-rowed hair, hip-hop vocabularies, and baby daddies, and they thought Paris Hilton was the *ne plus ultra* of feminine beauty. Amy was the tiniest and the most obnoxious of the new crop of Eminemlettes, and she was smitten with Little Janet, who despite her two-year tenure in prison seemed to have no idea how to handle a middle-school crush. Little Janet did not mess with girls, so Amy was barking up the wrong tree. Little Janet wasn't so mean that she'd ice Amy; she tolerated her puppyish worship.

When Amy got assigned to the electric shop, though, Janet had to lay down the law. If Amy didn't stop writing her mash notes and acting like a lovelorn cow, Little Janet would stop talking to her. Amy seemed dejected but resigned. My read on the situation was that Amy was not in fact a lesbian and that this was basically a schoolgirl crush. I took one for the team, taking pity on Janet by taking Amy away with me on some of the housekeeping errands. I would not deny a fix-it request, even from someone I didn't like. We must have hung a hundred extra cubicle hooks, which we would make out of C-clamps with a hammer, Amy spluttering and cursing the entire time.

Despite her foul little mouth and frequent tantrums, I found within myself a surprising reserve of patience for Amy and adopted a mild but firm approach. She was kind of like a SweeTart—sugary but also puckeringly sour. No one else was showing her any positive attention. Amy reacted with undying allegiance to me, loudly alternating between calling me her mom and her wife—both of which caused me to snort with mock outrage. "Amy, I am not old enough to be your mother, and as for the other—you're not my type!"

Being helpful did make us more popular, and I got a lot more smiles and nods around the Camp, which made me a little less shy. After almost four months in prison I was still cautious, supercautious, and kept most people at arm's length. Many times I fielded the sly question, "What is the All-American Girl doing in a place like this?" Everyone assumed I was doing time on a financial crime, but actually I was like the vast majority of the women there: a nonviolent drug offender. I did not make any secret of it, as I knew I had lots of company; in the federal system alone (a fraction of the U.S. prison population), there were over 90,000 prisoners locked up for drug offenses, compared with about 40,000 for violent crimes. A federal prisoner costs at least $30,000 a year to incarcerate, and females actually cost more.

Most of the women in the Camp were poor, poorly educated, and came from neighborhoods where the mainstream economy was barely present and the narcotics trade provided the most opportunities for employment. Their typical offenses were for things like low-level dealing, allowing their apartments to be used for drug activity, serving as couriers, and passing messages, all for low wages. Small involvement in the drug trade could land you in prison for many years, especially if you had a lousy court-appointed lawyer. Even if you had a great Legal Aid lawyer, he or she was guaranteed to have a staggering caseload and limited resources for your defense. It was hard for me to believe that the nature of our crimes was what accounted for my fifteen-month sentence versus some of my neighbors' much lengthier ones. I had a fantastic private attorney and a country-club suit to go with my blond bob.

Compared to the drug offenders, the "white-collar" criminals had often demonstrated a lot more avarice, though their crimes were rarely glamorous—bank fraud, insurance fraud, credit card scams, check kiting. One raspy-voiced fiftyish blonde was in for stock fraud (she liked to keep me up to speed on her children's misadventures in boarding school); a former investment banker had embezzled money to support her gambling habit; and marriage-minded Rosemarie was doing fifty-four months for Internet auction fraud.

I gleaned this information about people's crimes either because they'd volunteered it or because another prisoner told me. Some people would discuss their offense matter-of-factly, like Esposito or Rosemarie; others would never utter a word.

I still had absolutely no idea why Natalie had been sentenced to eight years in this snake pit. We got along well and some evenings would spend companionable time together in our cube. I would sit on my bunk, reading or writing letters, while Natalie listened to her radio below. She would announce, "Bunkie, I'm going to get in my bed, listen to my music, and relax!" Every Sunday we cleaned the cube together—we would use her irreplaceable plastic basin filled with warm water and laundry soap. She cleaned the floor with one of her special rags taken from the kitchen, while I did the walls and the ceiling with Maxipads from the box that sat in the bathroom, getting all the dust and grime off of the slanting metal I-beams and the sprinkler system that ran over my bed. Then we would fix my bed together. No one who has been down a long time will let the junior bunkie make the bed, as I had been schooled on my first day.

I grew powerfully attached to Natalie in just a short time—she was very kind to me. And I could tell that being her bunkie conferred on me an odd credibility among other prisoners. But despite, or because of, the fact that we lived in the closest of quarters, I knew virtually nothing about her—just that she was from Jamaica and that she had two children, a daughter and a young son. That was really it. When I asked Natalie whether she had started her time down the hill in the FCI, she just shook her head. "No, bunkie, back in the day things were a little different. I went down there for a little while—an' it was nothin' nice." That was all I was going to get. It was clear that where Natalie was concerned, personal subjects were off limits, and I had to respect that.

But in a world of women confined to such close quarters, juicy stories and secrets had a way of leaking out, either because the prisoner in question had at some point taken a blabberer into her confidence, or because the staff had done the blabbing. Of course, staff is not supposed to discuss personal information with other prisoners, but it happened all the time. Certain stories had a lot of currency. Francesca LaRue, a vicious and crazy Jesus freak in B Dorm, had been disfigured by extreme plastic surgery. A bizarre sight with balloonlike breasts, duck lips, and even ass implants, she was rumored to have performed illegitimate backroom cosmetic surgery procedures and to have "injected people with transmission fluid" to dissolve cellulite. I suspected the truth was plain old medical fraud. A clever and manipulative middle-aged blonde was rumored to have stolen tens of millions of dollars in an elaborate fraud scheme. One elderly lady had barely got her walker through the door before it spread like wildfire that she had embezzled big money from her synagogue. Most viewed this with disapproval. ("You can't steal from a church!")

Any story you heard from another prisoner had to be taken with about a pound of salt. Think about it: put this many women in a confined space, give them little to do and a lot of time—what else can you expect? Still, true or not, gossip helped pass the time. Pop had the best gossip, the most historical and revealing. It was from her that I found out why Natalie had been sent down to the FCI all those years ago: she had thrown scalding water on another prisoner in the kitchen. I was incredulous. "Bitch was fucking with her, and what you don't know, Piper, is your bunkie got a temper!" It was very difficult to reconcile that kind of rage and aggression with my quiet, dignified bunkie, who treated me so kindly. In Pop's words, though, "Natalie's no joke!"

Seeing how puzzled and disturbed I was by this new facet of Natalie, Pop tried to illuminate some prison realities for me.

"Look, Piper, things are pretty calm around here now, but that's not always the way. Sometimes shit jumps off. And down the hill— forget about it! Some of those bitches are animals. Plus you've got lifers down there. You've got your little year to do, and I know it seems hard to you, but when you're doing serious time, or life, things look different. You can't put up with shit from anyone, because this is your life, and if you ever take it from anyone, then you're always going to have problems.

"There was this woman down the hill I used to know—little woman, very quiet, kept to herself, didn't bother nobody. This woman was doing life. She did her work, she walked the track down there, she went to bed early, that's it. Then some young girl shows up down there, this girl was trouble. She starts in with this little woman—she's giving her shit, she's hassling her all the time, she's a fucking stupid kid. Well, that little woman, who never said boo to no one, put two locks in a sock, and she let that girl know what time it was. I never seen anything like it, this girl was a mess, blood everywhere, she was fucked up good. But you know what, Piper? That's where we are. And we're not all in the same boat. So just remember that."

When Pop told me a story like this one, I would hang on every word. I had no way of verifying whether it was gospel truth or not, like most things I heard in prison, but I understood that these stories held their own accuracy. They described our world as it was and as we experienced it. Their lessons always proved invaluable and inviolable.

Mercifully, the closest I got to fighting did not involve a slock (the formal name for a weapon made out of a combination lock inside a tube sock), but rather, roughage. Whenever something other than cauliflower and iceberg lettuce appeared on the salad bar, I went to town. One day there was a bunch of spinach mixed in with the iceberg, and I happily began to select dark green leaves for my dinner. I hummed a little melody under my breath, trying to tune out the din of the dining hall. But as I carefully plucked the spinach, avoiding the lettuce, words began to emerge out of the noise, near my ear.

"Hey! Hey! Hey you! Stop picking! Stop picking in that!"

I looked around to see where the shouting was coming from and at whom it was directed. To my surprise, a beefy young girl in a hairnet was glaring at me. I looked around, then gestured with the salad tongs. "Are you talking to me?"

"Hell, yeah. You can't be pickin' out the greens like that. Just fill up your plate and keep moving!"

I looked at my salad bar adversary, wondering who the fuck she thought she was. I vaguely recognized her as new, a reputed trouble-maker up in the Rooms. Just the other day Annette, who was still stuck up there, had been complaining about the disrespectful mouth on this eighteen-year-old kid. I knew from Pop that the salad bar was among the least desirable kitchen jobs, because so much washing and chopping was involved in the prep. So it was usually done by the low woman on the culinary totem pole.

I was furious that she had had the nerve to step to me. By now I felt like I was pretty firmly established in the Camp's social ecology. I didn't mess with other people, I was friendly but respectful, and hence other people treated me with respect. So to have some kid giving me shit in the dining hall was enraging. Not only that, but she was breaking a cardinal rule among prisoners: *Don't you tell me what to do—you have eight numbers after your name just like me.* To get into a public battle with a black woman was a profoundly loaded sit-uation, but it didn't even occur to me to back down from this punk kid.

I opened my mouth, mad enough to spit, and said loudly, "I *don't eat* iceberg lettuce!"

Really? I asked myself. *That's what you're going to throw down with?*

"I don't care *what* you eat, just don't be pickin' in there!"

Suddenly I realized that things had quieted down quite a bit in the dining hall and that this unusual conflict was being watched. All clashes between prisoners were sporting events, but for me to be in the mix was freakish. I was transported back to my middle school's parking lot, when Tanya Cateris had called me out and I knew that the only choice was to fight or prove to every person in school that I was chickenshit. In suburban Massachusetts, I went with chicken-shit; here that just wasn't an option.

But before I could even draw breath to assert myself with Big Mouth and raise the stakes, Jae, my friend from work and B Dorm, materialized at my side. Her normally smiling face was stern. I looked at her. She looked at Big Mouth, not saying a word. And just like that, Big Mouth turned and slunk away.

"You okay, Piper?" said Jae.

"I am totally okay, Jae!" I replied hotly, glaring after Big Mouth. Disappointed, everyone turned back to their food, and the volume went right back up to its usual level. I knew that Jae had just saved me many months of trouble.

Now THAT I had my headset radio, I couldn't believe how much easier it was to carve some enjoyment out of the day. With a pair of white sneakers purchased from commissary, I began jogging around the track every evening. I could tune out the pandemonium of B Dorm at will, and go much farther around the quarter-mile track now that I had music in my ear.

Rosemarie tipped me off to WXCI, 91.7, the radio station of Western Connecticut State University. I had forgotten about the pleasures of college radio, the exquisite randomness of what got played, the twenty-minute between-songs banter of nineteen-year-olds, the smack of music I'd never heard against my brain cavity. I was in heaven as I went around and around that track, giggling at sophomoric radio skits about Dick Cheney and listening to the new bands like the Kings of Leon that I'd been reading about in my copies of SPIN but had never actually heard in the endless repeat of classic rock vs. hip hop vs. Spanish radio that is the soundtrack of daily life in prison.

Best of all was a recurring weekly show, 90s Mixtape, which compiled the best songs from every year of the 1990s, one year every week. The 1991 top ten included Pavement, N.W.A., Naughty by Nature, Teenage Fanclub, Blur, Metallica, Nirvana, and LL Cool J. Those songs made me think of Larry and of the trouble-seeking girl I had been when they were first released. Running around the track, I relived every song I had heard in the background when I was running around the globe, a careless and ignorant young girl, launching myself into trouble so deep that it put me on this prison gravel eleven years later. No matter how stupid, how pointless, how painful my current situation was, as I listened to Mixtape every week I couldn't deny the love I still felt for that reckless, audacious fool who was still me, if only in my mind.

MAY 17 was Larry's and my anniversary. The wretched fact that we were separated and it was all my fault was impossible to deny, but when I found the right Hallmark greeting in the free collection handed out via the chapel, I felt a tiny bit better.

> *This is you, Baby,*
> *such a fine black man—*
> *Who knows who he is*
> *and knows where he stands.*
> *Who doesn't have time*
> *to play any games,*
> *Who's earned my respect*
> *and gives back the same.*
> *Who gives of himself*
> *to build up trust*
> *And commits his heart*
> *to big dreams for us.*
> *Who can heat me up*
> *and then love me down,*
> *And within his arms*
> *all my joy is found . . .*

And on the inside:

> *This is you Baby*
> *such a fine black man.*
> *This is me loving you—*
> *hard as I can.*

Joking aside, the sentiment was all true.

I spent an evening in my bunk composing what I would write on the card. It was our eighth anniversary of dating. I told him how quickly that time had passed, a quarter of our lives spent together. How all the risky choices we had taken together were the right ones, and how I couldn't wait to come home to him, the only man for me. I promised to keep counting sunrises until I could be where he was, anywhere that might be.

ONE DAY when we got to work, DeSimon stepped out of his office and locked the door. "Today we're going to practice with the lift," he announced. What the hell did that mean?

The lift turned out to be a mechanical hydraulic lift. I tried to figure out what it might be used for—all of the buildings were pretty low-lying, and the FCI itself was only a few stories tall. DeSimon shed some light on my question. There were a handful of area lights around the grounds that were hundreds of feet high. The lift was used when a bulb or fixture on one of them needed attention. "Oh, hell no!" said Jae, who was trying to get transferred to the warehouse. "No motherfuckin' way are you getting me up on that!" The rest of the crew were in agreement with her.

But we still had to go through the elaborate process of setting up the lift properly—essentially a metal platform a few feet square with a railing that went straight up in the sky when you pressed a button. If you screwed up one of the safety measures, it was easy to imagine the splat on concrete.

When we had finally done it properly, DeSimon said, "Who wants a ride?" A few intrepids—Amy, Little Janet, Levy—climbed onto the platform and pushed the button, each stopping long before the lift reached its full height, then coming down. "Scary!"

"I want to try!" I climbed onto the platform, and DeSimon handed me the control button. Up, up, up—my heart beat hard as I left the concrete behind, the faces of six women and a beard up-turned to watch me. Higher, higher. I could see everywhere, for miles farther than I had imagined beyond the confines of the prison. Maybe I could see my future from up here. The entire platform was swaying in the breeze, as I kept my finger on the button. I wanted to go all the way up, even though I was clutching the railing with white knuckles and the blood was pounding in my ears.

At its highest extension the lift stopped with a jerk, scaring me even more. A little half-cheer rose from my coworkers, who were shading their eyes to see me. Women were coming out of the other shops to have a look. "She crazy!" I heard someone say admiringly.

I peered over the railing that I was clinging to, grinning. Mr. DeSimon appeared to be trying to hide a smile in his beard. "Come on down, Kerman. No one wants to clean you off the concrete." I almost liked him that day.

THE PLACE was emptying out. Early in the month there was a rush of new faces, including a clique that had smuggled in marijuana via the cootchie express (squat and cough doesn't really seem to work) and brought a flurry of shakedowns onto the entire Camp. But then the flow of new prisoners seemed to stop abruptly. The prevailing rumor was that the BOP had "closed" the Camp, accepting only prisoners who were already doing time in other facilities, because they didn't want Martha Stewart designated to Danbury. Unclear was whether this was because the place was a broken-down dump, or for some other, more sinister reason. The moratorium on new prisoners seemed real, because the flow of new faces slowed to a feeble trickle. But people kept leaving to go home.

I wished that I was leaving. The adrenaline of the initial "Can I do this?" period was definitely over, and the rest of my time in Danbury stretched ahead of me. Larry and I had spent much time and energy hoping to get my sentence down to a year, feeling like that would be a victory. Now I was in the midst of it, and the months felt like they would never end.

Still, the novelties of prison socializing could distract me. Jae, like many of my favorite people, was a Taurus, a fact I learned when Big Boo Clemmons approached me in B Dorm to invite me to Jae's birthday party. Big Boo was a giant bulldyke. When I say giant, I mean at least three hundred pounds. She had skin like a Dove ice cream bar and was the most attractive three-hundred-pound woman I have ever seen. She used her massive bulk to intimidate, but her girth was less daunting than her wit. She had a lightning-sharp way with words—she was the resident rhymemaster, and her charisma and charm were undeniable. Her girlfriend Trina, at two hundred pounds, was pretty but a bitch on wheels and was commonly referred to by other prisoners as "Pieface"—but only behind her back. She loved to argue, was as disagreeable as Boo was smooth.

Boo told me the day and time when the party would take place, and that I could bring a cheesecake. "Where's the party?" I asked, and was surprised when she said, "Right here in B Dorm." Prison parties were usually held in the common rooms; otherwise you risked being hassled by the guards.

When Jae's birthday arrived, I wondered how she felt. This must have been her second or third birthday in prison, and she had seven more stretching in front of her like hurdles on a very long track. I turned up for the party promptly after dinner, cheesecake in hand (it was the only prison cuisine I knew how to make). The party guests gathered in the middle corridor of B Dorm outside Jae's cube, which she shared with her bunkie Sheena. B Dorm residents made up most of the guests, and we pulled up the folding chairs and stools from our cubes.

My neighbor bipolar Colleen was there, and so were Jae's buddy Bobbie, the biker mama from back in the Brooklyn MCC, Little Janet, Amy, and Lili Cabrales, who I had observed in action on my first morning in B Dorm. Lili almost drove me insane when I first moved in, as she would call out across the room again and again, "Pookie, what you doin'? Pookie, come over here! Pookie, do you got any noodle soups? I'm so hungry!" Pookie was her very quiet special friend, who lived two cubicles over from me. I would sit on my bunk and ask myself (and sometimes Natalie), "Will she ever shut up?" Lili was a loud-ass Bronx Puerto Rican gay-for-the-stay don't-fuck-with-me piece of work. But a funny thing happened, especially after Pookie went home and Lili quieted down a bit—she began to grow on me. I guess maybe I grew on her, until we got to the point where she nicknamed me "Dolphin" after my tattoo, and I could get a big smile out of her with a little joke.

Delicious the cheerful tittie-admirer was there—she played Spades with Jae. Delicious might have been my old friend Candace's doppelganger. This may seem surprising, as Candace is a North Carolinian, white Dartmouth grad who is a high-powered technology PR maven on the West Coast, mother of one and a clown enthusiast, whereas Delicious is a black D.C. native with a five o'clock shadow, a bunch of tattoos, and unusually long nails, who worked as a prison dishwasher while sharpening her excellent singing voice and off-the-cuff witticisms. But they had similar hair, similar stature, the identical button nose, and the same mellow-with-a-touch-of-hyper way of looking at the world. It gave me goosebumps. Delicious sang all the time. All. The. Time. She would rather sing than speak. As soon as I got to B Dorm, she asked me, "Y'all got any gangsta books?" When I told her about my friend Candace on the outside, and how they were like twins, Delicious looked at me as if I were the weirdest person she had ever met.

For the party, Boo had prepared a game for us to play. She made up a rhyme that was a riddle about every invitee, and the game was to guess the identity of the riddle's subject. This was an irresistible novelty, and soon we were laughing at each other, although Boo had refrained from being really mean at anyone's expense.

She lives right here
Between you and me,
And when you see her
You think of the sea.

When Boo read that rhyme, I had to bite my lip to hide my smile while I looked around quickly. Most people looked confused, but a few were smirking, pleased with themselves for getting it right away.

"Who is it?" asked Boo. A lot of shoulders were shrugged, which irked her.

"It's Piper!" shouted Sheena and Amy in triumphant unison.

"I don't get it," Trina pouted at her girlfriend. "That don't make no sense."

Boo was exasperated. " 'She lives right here between you and me'—that means she lives in B Dorm. 'And when you see her, you think of the sea,' that's her tattoo. Get it? *See, sea*? The fish?!"

"Oh yeah!" Lili Cabrales grinned, "That's my Dolphin!"

CHAPTER 10

Schooling the OG

||||

I had learned a lot since arriving in prison five months ago: how to clean house using maxipads, how to wire a light fixture, how to discern whether a duo were best friends or girlfriends, when to curse someone in Spanish, knowing the difference between "feelin' it" (good) and "feelin' some kinda way" (bad), the fastest way to calculate someone's good time, how to spot a commissary ho a mile away, and how to tell which guards were players and which guards were nothin' nice. I even mastered a recipe from the prison's culinary canon: cheesecake.

I made my first effort at cooking for someone's going-home party, preparing a prison cheesecake according to my coworker Yvette's Spanish-and-hand-gesture instructions. Unlike a lot of prison cookery, most of the necessary ingredients could be bought at the commissary.

Prison Cheesecake

1. Prepare a crust of crushed graham crackers mixed with four pats of margarine stolen from the dining hall. Bake it in a Tupperware bowl for about a minute in the microwave, and allow it to cool and harden.

2. Take one full round of Laughing Cow cheese, smash with a fork, and mix with a cup of vanilla pudding until smooth.

Gradually mix in one whole container of Cremora, even though it seems gross. Beat viciously until smooth. Add lemon juice from the squeeze bottle until the mixture starts to stiffen. Note: this will use most of the plastic lemon.

3. Pour into the bowl atop the crust, and put on ice in your bunkie's cleaning bucket to chill until ready to eat.

It was a little squishy the first time; I should have used more lemon juice. But it was a great success. Yvette raised her eyebrows when she tasted it. "*¡Buena!*" she proclaimed. I was very proud.

Prison cuisine and survival techniques were all well and good, but it was time to learn something more productive. Pleasantly but persistently, Yoga Janet had been inviting me to join her class, and when I wrenched my back, she iced it while I lay prone on my bunk. "You really should learn yoga with us," she gently chided me. "Running is too hard on the body."

I wasn't going to give up the track, but I started descending to the little gym for yoga class several times a week. Larry laughed when I told him. He had been trying to get me to try yoga at a fancy downtown studio for years, and he found it both entertaining and annoying that it had taken incarceration to get me into Downward Dog.

The field house gym had a rubber floor. At first we used undersize blue foam mats, but with great effort and persistence Yoga Janet got proper orange yoga mats donated to the Camp from the outside. Tall and calm and down to earth, Janet managed to create the sense that she was teaching us something important and valuable without taking herself too seriously.

Camila from B Dorm was always there. Alongside all the many misfit toys at Danbury, Camila was instantly noticeable. My friend Eric spotted her in the visiting room and declared her "the hottest woman in prison in America—no offense to you, Pipes." She glowed with health and radiated beauty; tall, slim, with a glossy black mane, tawny brown skin, a pointed chin, and huge dark eyes, she was always laughing, loudly. I was drawn to her willingness to laugh, but that very quality was the subject of derision among some of the white women.

"Those Puerto Ricans, it's like they don't even know they're in jail, they're always laughing and dancing like idiots!" sneered tall, mopey Sally, who wanted everyone to be as miserable as she was. And as ignorant—Camila was Colombian, not Puerto Rican. Camila was a natural at yoga, easily mastering warrior poses and backbends and giggling helplessly with me as we tried to balance on one leg while twisting the other around it.

On the mat next to Camila would be Ghada. Ghada was one of the handful of Muslim women I met in prison. It was difficult to guess her age—her face was deeply creased, but she had an air of tremendous vitality—she might be in her fifties or sixties. Her hair was salt-and-pepper, and she hid it under makeshift head scarves— sometimes a pillowcase, sometimes a contraband cloth napkin. I never quite got the story straight, but it seemed that the guards frequently confiscated her head scarves. We were not allowed to wear "doo-rags" when in uniform, only commissary-purchased baseball caps or prison-issue wool knit caps that itched like hell. I thought surely there should be some exception for Muslim women. I could never figure out if I was mistaken and the hijab was forbidden in the prison system, or if Ghada just couldn't get it together to obtain a prison-approved head scarf. She wasn't much for rules.

Ghada was from Lebanon but had lived in South America for many years and so was fluent in Spanish, with pretty tenuous English. Because of her long residence in Latin America, Ghada was an honorary Spanish mami. This was a good thing, because she was totally unaccepting of the authority of the staff and uninterested in the institution's rules, and only the monumental efforts of her friends to protect her from the consequences of that indifference kept her out of the SHU. This won her both annoyance and respect from her fellow prisoners. No one seemed to know what Ghada was down for, but we could all agree that she was another OG. Ghada loved Yoga Janet, which was the primary reason she came to class. She was not all that interested in doing the poses properly, but she brought great enthusiasm to the ritual.

The final member of our ragtag band of aspiring yogis was Sister Platte, who took proper form very seriously. Sister had tight hips, so twists and Pigeon Pose prompted a knitted brow, and if she had indulged in the greasy home fries at the midday meal, the forward bends would give her trouble. When I sank into a deep lunge, the tiny nun would study me, plaintively wondering, "What am I doing wrong?"

The five of us had a camaraderie that made those few hours among the most enjoyable of the week. Every class we would meet to claim the peace that, at Danbury, could only be found within one's own body. Each session ended with Janet's final relaxation, when she spoke soothingly to us of the work we had just completed, and the things we had to be grateful for every day, together in prison. And every single week Ghada would fall asleep within minutes during final relaxation, snoring loudly until someone woke her.

ONE EVENING Miss Mahoney, the cheerful education administrator from down the hill, made a lot of people very happy. Miss Mahoney was one of the few prison staffers who seemed to be on our side. As near as I could tell, she was one of the education department's few saving graces. She did have an annoying habit of trying to be "down on tha mic" when she was on the PA system. On this particular evening she announced that a gender awareness class would be offered in the dining hall. What exactly was going to be conveyed there was unclear.

Then she got to the important matters: "Would the following ladies please report to the CO's office for their GED test results . . ." And you could just tell from her voice that the news was good for every name called.

"Malcolm!" Mahoney called.

I jumped out of my bunk. Natalie had taken the GED test approximately a dozen times and was definitely way past due to pass it. She got nervous during the testing, and time and again the math section had proved her bête noir. Where was Natalie?

When I got to the main hall, there were already screams of joy, and women were pouring out of all of the Rooms and Dorms. When a woman of twenty-five, thirty-five, forty-five has struggled to earn her high school diploma in prison, taking pretest after pretest and trying to learn in a poorly run program and classes full of every imaginable delinquent student behavior, and then actually passes, it is a victory. Some of these women had dropped out of school thirty years before and were finally getting one of the only positive things—one of the only measures of achievement—one can earn in prison. Plus, it meant that these women could finally earn above the lowest pay grade at their prison jobs—if you didn't have your GED, you couldn't earn over fourteen cents an hour, which was barely enough to pay for toothpaste and soap. Everything came out of our prison accounts—hygiene items, phone calls, fines. If a prisoner didn't have her GED and didn't have money coming in from outside, she was screwed. Natalie had toiled for many years as a skilled baker in that prison kitchen, a treasured member of the cooking staff, and yet she could never be paid more than $5.60 a week for forty hours of work.

Where was Miss Natalie? Her name had been called five minutes ago, but I didn't see her in the throng of jubilant, shouting, laughing women in the hall. Where was my enigmatic bunkie, that supremely self-possessed woman? I knew how badly Natalie wanted that diploma, I suspected it hurt her that she had struggled for so long to pass that math section. With embarrassed dignity, she had declined my offers of study help. This was her moment! Could she possibly be hiding, ashamed to join the orgy of congratulations and illegal hugs taking place in the hallway?

No, wait, she was down at the track! I had watched her putting on her sneakers. In my flip-flops I took off down the hall, out the building, and down the stairs to the track at top speed. She didn't even know! Halfway down the stairs I was calling out to the others

on the track, "Is my bunkie down there?" I rounded the field house—
and there she was with her crazy friend Sheila.

"Bunkie! Your GED results are back!" I panted.

Natalie smiled nervously.

"Come up, bunkie, come up and see!"

"Okay, bunkie, I'm coming." Ladylike to the end, Natalie did not
rush.

I started up the stairs as a number of people came down. "Where's
Natalie? Where's Miss Malcolm? There she is! Come on, Natalie!"
My bunkie looked surprised, but she still didn't hurry. She had that
look of skepticism on her face, unwilling to give herself over to celebration until she saw its cause with her own eyes.

When she entered the Camp, an entourage traveling before and
behind her, the noise in the hall was deafening, and people were calling out, "Where's Miss Malcolm?" She was immediately enveloped
by people hugging and congratulating her. As she made slow progress up the hall, Natalie laughed and smiled and looked overwhelmed.

Down near the CO's office, someone was waving her test results
in the air. "Natalie, you did it!"

I suddenly thought I was going to lose it and start crying right
there, and I was not a crier. The release of so much collective happiness in that miserable place was almost too much for me. It was like
hot and cold air colliding, creating a tornado right inside the hall. I
took a deep breath, stepped back, and watched my bunkie be enveloped by well-wishers. When I congratulated her in the relative
privacy of our cube, she tried to downplay her triumph, but I could
tell that she was deeply satisfied.

THE FACT that I'd become used to life in prison shocked my friends
and family, but no one on the outside can really appreciate the galva-
nizing effect of all the regimented rituals, whether official or informal. It's the insidious, cruel paradox of lengthy sentences: for women

doing seven, twelve, twenty years, the only way to survive was to accept prison as their universe. But how on earth would they survive in the outside world when released? "Institutionalized" was one of the greatest insults one could throw at another prisoner, but when you resisted the systems of control, you suffered swift retribution. Where you fit in and how comfortable you were willing to get depended on the length of your sentence, the amount of contact you had with the outside world, and the quality of your life on the outside. And if you resisted finding a place in prison society, you were desperately lonely and miserable.

Mrs. Jones had been in the Camp longer than any other prisoner but would be going home next year. Her cubicle, a Puppy Program single in the corner of A Dorm next to the outside door, was so cozy we all feared what would happen when it came time for her to leave it. "I like this cube. I get all the fresh air I want, plus I can walk the puppies just like that!" she cackled. During the day I liked to drop by Mrs. Jones's cube to play with Inky, the Labrador retriever she was training as a service dog. I would sit on the floor and rub Inky's belly while Mrs. Jones fussed around the cube, showing me photographs of women with whom she had done time or her latest crochet project (she specialized in Christmas stockings), and asking me if I wanted random objects she had squirreled away during her fifteen years in prison.

Mrs. Jones spent a lot of time down on the track walking Inky, and she was impressed by my running. She was concerned that she was overweight, so she resolved to start running too. "You and me, we're going to compete!" she would crow, poking my shoulder hard. "We'll see what you're made of!" But Mrs. Jones was perilously top-heavy, and after wheezing her way around only one lap, she sat on a bench, heaving for breath. I suggested she try speedwalking instead. This she found manageable and would huff and puff around all morning at top speed, obsessively.

One day Mrs. Jones came to see me in my cube. I was writing letters up in my bunk. She peeked around the particleboard like a little girl, which I found disconcerting. "What's up, Mrs. Jones?"

"Are ya busy?"

"Not too busy for you, OG. Come on in."

She came closer to the bunk bed and whispered conspiratorially, "I got a favor to ask ya."

"Shoot."

"You know I'm in the college class, right?"

The class was a basic business course, taught by a pair of professors who came in from a nearby accredited college. It didn't mean much in terms of getting one closer to a college degree (for that you needed to pay for correspondence courses), but it did count toward "program" credit with an inmate's case manager. The case managers were tasked with managing the completion of our sentences, which meant recalculating our "good time" (we were supposed to serve only 85 percent of our sentences if we earned good time), collecting fines from our inmate accounts (if you couldn't pay fines, you wouldn't get good time), and assigning our "program" activity, including mandatory reentry classes. The "programs" available to Campers were feeble and few. The college class was one of the only options, but after reading over and helping to revise a number of women's homework assignments, I was skeptical about the class's usefulness. Camila's business plan for a Victoria's Secret competitor, for example, was entertaining but highly hypothetical and totally unrelated to what she might be doing when she got out of this human warehouse in five years.

"How's it going, Mrs. Jones?"

She explained that it was not going so well. She had received a bad grade on her business plan. The OG was worried. "I need a tutor. Will ya help me? We have a paper due on a movie we saw. I'll pay you."

"Mrs. Jones, you will not pay me anything. Of course I'll help you. Bring me your stuff, and let's look at it together."

When I agreed to help the OG, I had in mind a typical student-tutor relationship; I would talk to her about her assignments, ask thought-provoking questions, and review and correct her work. She came back with her notebook and papers and a book that she put on my bed: *Managing in the Next Society* by Peter Drucker.

"What's this?"

"Our textbook. Ya gotta read it."

"No, Mrs. Jones, *you* have to read it."

She looked at me, anguished and pleading. "It gives me a headache."

I remembered that in addition to being nutty from having been locked up for well over a decade, Mrs. Jones was reputed to have had a few screws knocked loose by her abusive husband.

I frowned. "Let's take a look at your paper that's due, the one about the movie."

This provoked another anguished look. "*You* need to write it, I can't do it! They didn't like my last paper," she said, pulling out her business plan, embarrassed. She had received a poor grade in big red pen.

I flipped through it. Mrs. Jones's handwriting was hard to read, but I realized that even if her penmanship had been flawless, the contents of the paper made little sense. I had a sinking feeling in my stomach. I might be a convicted felon, but as the daughter of teachers, I had a strong aversion to cheating on tests.

"Mrs. Jones, I shouldn't write your papers for you. And how am I going to write a paper about a movie I didn't see?"

"I took notes!" She thrust them at me, triumphantly. Oh, great. It appeared that the movie had had something to do with the Industrial Revolution.

Was it better to let Mrs. Jones fail on her own or to help her cheat? I knew I was not going to let her fail. "OG, why don't I ask you questions about the movie, and I'll help you do an outline, and then you can try writing the paper?"

Mrs. Jones shook her head, stubbornly. "Piper, look at my business plan. I can't write it. If ya won't help me, Joanie in A Dorm said she would do it, but you're smarter than her."

Joan Lombardi was hardly a rocket scientist, and I knew she would charge Mrs. Jones for her "tutoring." Plus my ego was involved.

I sighed. "Let me see your notes." After extracting a few context-free specifics about the movie from her, I set to work writing an incredibly generic three-page paper about the Industrial Revolution. When I was finished I walked the neatly handwritten paper over to the OG's cube in A Dorm.

She was ecstatic. "Mrs. Jones, you are going to recopy this paper so it's in your handwriting, right?"

"Nah, they'll never notice."

I wondered what would happen to me if her instructors caught this. I didn't think I'd be sent to the SHU or get expelled from prison.

"Mrs. Jones, I want you to at least read the paper so you know what it's about. Do you promise me?"

"I swear, Piper, on my honor."

Mrs. Jones was beside herself when she got her paper back in class. "An A!! We got an A!" She glowed with pride.

We got an A on the next film summary as well, and she was jubilant. I couldn't believe that her teachers had no comment or questions about the difference between these papers and her previous one—right down to the different handwriting.

Now she grew serious. "We gotta write the final paper. This is fifty percent of the grade, Piper!"

"What's the assignment, OG?"

"It needs to be a paper on innovation, and it has to be based on the textbook. And it has to be longer!"

I moaned. I desperately wanted to avoid reading the Peter Drucker book. I had spent my entire educational and professional career avoiding these types of business books, and now they'd caught up to me in prison. I didn't see any way around reading it if the OG were to pass her class.

"Innovation is a little broad, Mrs. Jones. Any ideas on a more specific topic?"

She looked at me helplessly.

"Okay, how about . . . fuel-efficient cars?" I suggested.

Mrs. Jones had been locked up since the mid-1980s. I tried to explain to her what a hybrid car was.

"Sounds good!" she said.

Larry was perplexed when I asked him to put in the mail some basic Web articles on hybrids. I tried to explain about the OG's term paper. He was totally swamped, having just started a new job as an editor at *Men's Journal*. Part of his job negotiations had included securing permission to work a half-day every Thursday or Friday, so that he could visit his girl in prison. I tried to imagine what exactly that conversation had been like. The lengths he went to for me were amazing. Soon I got a packet of information at mail call and started to slog through *Managing in the Next Society*.

AMONG THE last prisoners to show up in May, before the Camp was "closed" to deflect Martha Stewart to another facility, were three new political prisoners, pacifists like Sister Platte. They had been arrested and sent to prison for protesting at the School of the Americas, the U.S. Army training center for Latin American military personnel (read: secret police, torturers, and thugs) located in Georgia. These special newbies were pretty much central-casting leftists, earnest pale-faces who were willing and eager to sacrifice for their cause—and to discuss it ad nauseam. One of them looked like Mr. Burns from *The Simpsons*, all watery blue eyes, bad posture, and Adam's apple, and she seemed irritated by her situation; the other was like a young novice in a convent, with shorn hair and a perpetually surprised expression; then there was Alice, about five feet tall with the thickest Coke-bottle glasses I had seen in a long time. She was as friendly as the dogs in the Puppy Program, and as garrulous as her partners were withdrawn. Sometimes they would all join us for yoga class.

These three made a beeline for Sister Platte and followed her around like ducklings. I thought it was cool that Sister had a posse of pacifists in prison—yes, the government wasted millions of taxpayer dollars prosecuting and locking up nonviolent protesters, but here on the inside the political prisoners now had a community of like-minded folks. Sister certainly enjoyed their company, discussing theories and tactical strategy for bringing the military–industrial complex to its knees for hours on end in the dining hall. Alice and her co-defendants managed to get jobs teaching in the GED program, the gig I had previously longed for but that didn't interest me any longer.

I felt guilty about preferring CMS work, but I had been observing the unpleasant developments in the education department and was keeping my distance. Following the mold shutdown of the GED program in the winter, all the tainted books and curriculum materials had been thrown out and were not replaced. The prison had transferred a popular female staff teacher out of the Camp and down the hill—I guess she was too sympathetic to prisoners. In her place the new head of education in the Camp was a mullet-wearing, Trans-Am driving vulgarian—I called him Stumpy—who rumor held had basically flunked out of the postal service, only to be picked up by the BOP. He was an inadequate excuse for a teacher, who resorted to (and clearly enjoyed) threatening and verbally abusing his pupils. He was universally loathed by all Campers and most of all by the inmate tutors who worked for him. According to them, his attitude toward his pupils was simple: "I don't care if they never learn that one plus one equals two. I get paid for eight hours of work."

One day I returned from the electric shop to find the Camp in an uproar. Stumpy had been on a serious tear that day in the classroom, more abusive than usual, and Alice the pacifist had finally had it. She wanted to be released from her job as a tutor. Stumpy went ballistic, screaming and ranting and writing her up with a shot for defiance, or resisting a direct order, or something along those lines.

Pennsatucky, who had been in the classroom (and was probably the object of his initial abuse), said that his dumbass face had turned purple. He had gone storming out of the Camp and down the hill, but now rumor had it that he was trying to have Alice locked up in the SHU, and everyone was outraged.

Sure enough, after dinner and mail call, we heard the thud of heavy boots and the rattle of chains. Massive men, their boots making the most stereotypically ominous storm-trooper noise, entered the

Camp carrying restraints. They stomped by the phones, down the stairs, and down the hallway toward the Camp CO's office. Every prisoner picked up on those sounds no matter where they were in the building, and the front hall quickly and quietly filled with women, gathering to see it go down. Sometimes when someone was getting locked up for doing something shitty, or when the miscreant was widely disliked, there was an air of the tumbrels on the way to the guillotine. This was not one of those times.

The PA crackled as Mr. Scott called the condemned: "Gerard!" Little Alice Gerard came up to the office and stepped inside. The door closed, and she was in there with those three huge men, as the lieutenant read her the shot that had been filed against her.

A buzz was building among the women. "This is BULL-shit!!"

"This ain't no thing for the SHU . . . that little lady didn't do a damn thing that didn't need to be done."

Someone started to cry.

"I can't believe these pansy-ass cracker cops got nothing better to do with their time than lock up Alice!"

The door to the office swung open. Alice stepped out, followed by the three jailers. They loomed over her, making her look extra tiny as she gazed up at the assembled crowd. Blinking through her Coke-bottle glasses, she said brightly and clearly, "I'm going!" One of the lieutenant's goons cuffed her, not that gently, and the buzz among the women surged to a low roar. Then Sheena started to chant: "Al-ice, Al-ice, Al-ice, Al-ice, Al-ice!" as they led the little pacifist away. I had never seen prison guards look scared before.

ONE HOT afternoon found me under a tree, trying to stay out of the sun. Along came Mrs. Jones, with Inky, her constant companion. I had finished her final paper, a pretty straightforward essay I had pieced together about the role that hybrid cars might play in the future economy. I had tried to pull some big ideas from *Managing in the Next Society* into my argument about knowledge-based economies, globalization, and the ways in which demographics change society. But it was upsetting to think about what role the millions of Americans who were former prisoners might play in the next society—I knew from the Families Against Mandatory Minimums (FAMM) newsletters (which many prisoners received) that over 600,000 returned home from prison every year. The only markets most of them were accustomed to participating in were underground economies, and nothing about the prison system that I had seen showed them any other route to take when they hit the streets again. I could count on two hands the number of women in Danbury who had participated in a real vocational program—Pop, who had earned a food service certificate down at the FCI; Linda Vega, who worked as the Camp's dental hygienist; and the handful of women who worked in Unicor. For the rest, maybe their work scrubbing prison floors or in the plumbing shop might translate toward a real job, but I was skeptical. There was no continuity at all between the prison economy, including prison jobs, and the mainstream economy.

"Hey, Mrs. Jones! Did you get the paper back yet?"

"I was just coming to talk to ya about that. I'm mad as hell!"

I sat up, worried. Had she been busted? Maybe a disgruntled classmate had ratted her out? That wouldn't shock me. "What's wrong?"

"We got an A-minus!"

I laughed, which only made her more irritated.

"What was the problem?" she wailed. "It was a great paper! I read it, just like I said I would!" She was very indignant.

"Maybe he didn't want you getting too cocky, Mrs. J. I think an A-minus is just great."

"Hmph. I don't know what they're thinking. Well, anyway, I wanted to say thank you. You're a nice girl." And with that she jerked Inky's leash and marched off.

A COUPLE months later she was marching again; all of the women who had completed the GED or college classes were honored in a ceremony held in the visiting room. Miss Natalie, Pennsatucky,

Camila, and of course Mrs. Jones would be wearing mortarboards, along with a number of other women. Each graduate was allowed to invite a set number of guests from either the outside or the inside, and I would be attending as a guest of the OG.

The valedictorian was Bobbie, who had scored the highest on the GED exam. Over the weeks leading up to the ceremony she agonized over her address, writing and rewriting it. The day dawned scorching hot, and the room was set up with two banks of chairs facing each other, graduates vs. guests. The women filed in solemnly, looking sharp in their caps and gowns—black for the GED students, bright blue for the collegians. There was a podium, where Bobbie would give her speech, but first we would have to hear from Warden Deboo. This would be her swan song; she was getting a brand-new prison in California to supervise, and we were getting a new warden, a guy from Florida.

Bobbie gave a great speech. She had picked a theme—"We did IT!"—and was off and running, congratulating her fellow students for getting IT done, reminding all assembled that achieving a diploma was not easy in this setting but they had done IT, and proclaiming that now that everyone knew they could do IT, there was nothing else they couldn't do, if they stuck with IT. And they each had a diploma to prove IT to the world. I was impressed by the care Bobbie had put into her words and by how well she delivered them, with just the right edge of defiance. The speech was brief, lean and mean, but firmly asserted that it was the graduates' day to celebrate, not the institution's. She spoke forcefully, naturally, and with pride.

Afterward, the prisoners were allowed to have pictures taken. Against a fake cherry-tree backdrop in a corner of the visiting room, I stood with my friends, each of whom I was proud to know. Bobbie, posing with a group of us clustered around her in our khakis, looked stern and short in her robes and special gold-corded valedictorian's robe, but her hair was blown out and beautifully curled. In one snapshot Pennsatucky and another Eminemlette grin as widely as any high school senior in America on their last day; I look so old next to them, smiling in my khaki uniform. My favorite is the photo of me and Mrs. Jones: I stand happily behind her, and she is seated, radiant in her royal blue robe and cap, holding her diploma in front of her with pride. On the back of the picture, in her terrible handwriting, it says:

Thank you.
     To a dear friend. I made it. God bless you.

Mrs. Jones

CHAPTER 11

Ralph Kramden and the Marlboro Man

||||

I hit a groove, and the days and weeks seemed to go faster. I passed milestones—one-quarter of my sentence, one-third of my sentence—and prison seemed more manageable. The outdoors showed me the natural passage of time in a way that was new to a lifelong city girl. I went from trudging through ice, then mud, then grass (mowed by the ladies in grounds). Trees budded, and wildflowers and even peonies bloomed. Baby bunnies appeared at the side of the track and grew into saucy teenage rabbits right before my eyes as I ran around and around that quarter-mile loop thousands of times. Wild turkeys and deer freely roamed the federal reservation that the prison sat on. I developed a deep distaste for Canada geese, who shat dark green goose poop all over my track.

One sunny afternoon I was loitering on the bench in front of the electric shop in the sun, listlessly trying to read a slim volume of *Candide* that some wiseacre had sent me. Mr. DeSimon had not shown up to work, a mercifully common experience. That morning it had been difficult to read because of the thundering gunfire. Very close by the CMS shops, hidden about a quarter mile away in the woods, was the prison's rifle range. Correctional officers could spend quality time with their firearms down there, and the hammering of multiple rounds was typical background noise during our workdays. There was something unsettling about toiling away for a prison while listening to your jailers practice shooting you.

When we got back from lunch, the gunshots had ceased, and it was once again a placid rural Connecticut day. One of the institution's white pickup trucks pulled up next to me in front of the carpentry shop.

"What the hell are you doin', convict?"

It was Mr. Thomas, the boss of the shop. The carpentry and construction shops were housed in one building, to the left of the electric shop and on the other side of a shambling greenhouse. The electric shop did not have a bathroom, and we had to walk over to use the one in their building. The bathroom was for single use only, a spacious private room on whose walls someone had painted pretty blue designs. I loved that bathroom. Sometimes when my coworkers in electric were squabbling, or watching illicit trash television when DeSimon wasn't around, I would just flee to the bathroom for a few blessed minutes of privacy and quiet. It was the only door in the prison that I could lock.

The construction and carpentry shops were led by Mr. King and Mr. Thomas, respectively. Mr. Thomas was round and volcanic and inclined to noise, jokes, and occasional blue-streak outbursts, like a present-day Jackie Gleason. Mr. King was lean and lanky, taciturn and weathered, always with a cigarette dangling from his mouth. He looked like the Marlboro Man. They had been sharing this shop for many years and had a close working relationship. When I would walk into the shop to use the facilities, Mr. Thomas would usually note my presence with a shout: "Hey, criminal!"

Now he wanted to know what the hell I was doing. My fellow B-Dormer, Alicia Robbins, was in the seat of the truck next to him. Alicia was Jamaican and tight with Miss Natalie. She was giggling, so I doubted that I was in trouble.

"Um . . . nothing?"

"Nothing?! Well, do you want to work?"

"Sure?"

"Well g-e-e-e-e-e-e-t in!!!!"

I jumped up and climbed into the truck. Alicia scooted over to make room for me. I didn't think I could get in trouble if I was with a CO. Mr. Thomas pressed the gas and the truck took off. We veered past the plumbing and grounds shops, headed behind the FCI, and then abruptly plunged down a steep gravel road. I had no idea where it led. Almost immediately the buildings disappeared, and all I could see through the pickup's open windows was forest—trees and boulders and the occasional creek—all sloping sharply downward.

The truck radio was blasting classic rock. I looked at Alicia, who was still giggling. "Where is he taking us?" I asked her.

Mr. Thomas snorted.

"Boss crazy" was all Alicia would say.

The road plunged down, down, down. We had been driving for many minutes. It didn't feel like I was in prison anymore. I felt like a girl in a truck heading toward an adventure. Resting my bare forearm on the truck door, I fixed my gaze deep into the woods, so that when the trees flew by, all I saw was a blur of green and brown.

After several minutes the truck broke into a sort of clearing, and I saw signs of people. In front of us was a picnic area, and some of the women who worked in construction and carpentry were painting wooden picnic tables. But they didn't interest me at all, because what I saw beyond them filled me with so much excitement. The picnic area lay on the edge of an enormous lake, and the June sunlight was glinting off the water that lapped gently at the edge of a boat launch.

I gasped. My eyes widened, and I could not have cared less about maintaining my cool.

Mr. Thomas parked the truck, and I jumped out. "It's a lake! I can't believe how beautiful it is!"

Alicia laughed at me, grabbed her painting gear out of the back of the truck, and ambled over to a picnic table.

I turned to Mr. Thomas, who was also looking at the lake. "Can I go look at it? Please?"

He laughed at me too. "Sure, just don't jump in. Get me fired."

I rushed down to the edge, where there were floating docks and a number of small motorboats that belonged to prison staff were moored. I was trying to look everywhere at once. On the far bank I could see houses, beautiful houses with lawns that sloped down to the water. The lake appeared to be very long, disappearing out of sight on both my right and my left. I crouched down and stuck both my hands into the cool water. I looked at my two white hands through the brownish cast of lake water, palms down, and imagined myself submerged, holding my breath in with my eyes open underwater, and kicking as hard as I could to swim fast. I could almost feel the water swirling in currents around my body, and my hair rising like a halo around my head.

I edged along ten yards of the lake shore in one direction and back again, thinking that this would be the first summer of my life without swimming. I had always been a total water baby, never scared of the surf. Now I itched to rip off my clothes and throw myself in. But that wouldn't be prudent or fair to the guy nice enough to have brought me down here. The sunlight off the water made me crinkle my eyes. I looked for a long time, and no one said anything to me. Finally I turned and climbed back up the concrete embankment.

I went over to Gisela, who drove the bus and worked for Mr. King, and asked her if there were any extra paintbrushes.

She smiled. "Sure, let me show you."

And I spent the rest of the afternoon silently painting under the trees, listening to boats on the lake and the sounds of water birds.

When it was time to go, Mr. Thomas drove us back up to the shops. I got out and stood on the passenger side with my hands on the window frame and looked into the truck at him.

"It was really nice of you to bring me down there. Thank you so much, Mr. Thomas. It meant so much to me."

He looked away; he seemed embarrassed. "Yeah, well, I know that boss of yours won't bring you down there. So thanks for helping out." He drove away. From that moment forward, I was obsessed with getting back to the lake.

ARRIVING AT work one day, we were startled to discover that DeSimon had shaved off his beard and mustache and now looked a lot like a lost penis, wandering around in search of a body. My interactions with him had grown unpleasant, as I resented the fact that I worked for the nastiest man in construction services, and he seemed to take perverse pleasure in treating me in as degrading a manner as he could devise. At lunch I was complaining bitterly about him when Gisela stopped me. "Why don't you come work in construction? I'm going home in September. Mr. King will need somebody good. He's so nice, Piper."

It hadn't occurred to me that I could change jobs. A couple days later I sidled up to Mr. King in front of the shop, shy but desperate. I wasn't used to asking COs for anything.

"Mr. King? I know that Gisela is leaving soon, and I was wondering if maybe I could come work for you in construction?" I waited, hopefully. I knew I was a desirable prison employee: I had my prison license, was willing to work, never "idled" (faked being sick), was educated, and could read manuals, do math, and so forth. And I didn't have a big mouth.

Mr. King looked at me, chewing on his cigarette, flinty eyes unreadable. "Sure." My heart leaped, then crashed: "But DeSimon has to sign your cop-out."

I wrote up the cop-out, a simple one-page form the official title of which was BP-S148.055 INMATE REQUEST TO STAFF. The next morning I marched into DeSimon's office and handed it to him. He did not take it from me. After a while I got tired of thrusting it toward him and put it on the desk.

He looked at it with distaste. "What is that, Kermit?"

"It's a cop-out, asking you to let me go work in construction, Mr. DeSimon."

He didn't even read it. "The answer is no, Kermit."

I looked at him, his bulbous, shiny pink head, and smiled grimly. I wasn't surprised. I marched back out of the office.

"What did he say?" asked Amy. We were down to me, my young Eminemlette pal, Yvette, and a couple other women working in the dim, airless electric shop.

"What do you think?" I said.

Amy just laughed, with a hollow wisdom way beyond her years.

"Piper, that man is not going to let you go anywhere, so you might as well get used to him."

I was furious. Now that I knew there was a better way to live within the confines of the prison, that there were jobs where prisoners were not the constant object of insults, I was desperate to make the switch. Getting out of electric and escaping from DeSimon filled my thoughts.

Summer was getting hot, and for months we had been working on a new circuit for the visiting room air conditioners. The only rooms in the Camp that had air conditioners were the staff offices and the visiting room, but the existing power was insufficient, and they always tripped off. So we had hung and wired a new circuit panel, bent and run conduit around the visiting room, and wired new outlets. Now we were close to finished, and all that remained was to connect the circuit board to the building's main power source, a floor below in the boiler room.

This involved pulling new cables up from the boiler room power source to the new panel in the visiting room—physically yanking them up through the guts of the building. When the momentous day dawned, we all gathered the tools that DeSimon had directed us to bring and stood in the boiler room, waiting for direction. We didn't have any big girls in the electric shop, and so reinforcements had been called in from plumbing, which had a bunch of them.

DeSimon busied himself with the cables. They were big thick industrial cables, totally different from the wiring that I now worked with every day. He bundled several of them, then bound them together with black electrical tape, taping over and over until they were bound together for over a foot. At the end he strung a rope, the end of which was snaked up to the visiting room. The women from plumbing were all up there, waiting.

Down in the boiler room stood me, Amy, Yvette, and Vasquez. We looked at DeSimon.

"They're gonna pull, and you're gonna push. You're gonna feed it upward. But we're missing one thing. We need a greaser."

The way he said those words, I knew that it must be an unpleasant job. And I knew who it would be.

"Kermit. You'll be the greaser. Take these." He handed me elbow-length rubber gloves. "Now grab that tub of lube." He pointed at a vat of industrial lubricant next to his feet. I could see where this was going. My cheeks were beginning to burn. "You're going to need a lot, Kermit."

I grabbed the container. DeSimon shoved the bound cables toward me. They were rigid and inflexible, and I was rigid with humiliation. "That's gonna need a lot to squeeze in there, Kermit. Lube it up good."

I bent and scooped up two handfuls of the stuff. It was like bright blue jelly. I slapped it onto the huge, previously innocuous but now disgusting foot-long phallus.

DeSimon threw his head back and yelled "Pull!" The rope yanked, but not enough to move the cables. "C'mon, Kermit, do your duty!"

I was so angry, I could barely see. I concentrated on turning the blood in my veins into ice. I tried floating up to the ceiling in detachment, but the scene was so ugly that my usual technique didn't work. I scooped up more blue jelly and slapped it all over the bound cables.

"Oooh, horse cock. You like that horse cock, don't you, Kermit."

Horse cock? I dropped my hands to my sides, in their big gooey gloves. Amy was looking at her shoes, and Yvette was pretending she didn't understand any English.

DeSimon yelled "Pull!" again, and somewhere above us prison laborers heaved on the rope. The cables slid. "Pull!" They slid again. "Push!"

My coworkers pushed the cables upward. Seeing them strain, I bent my knees and helped them push up as hard as I could. The cables started to slither upward, and then it was all over but the pulling. I stalked out of the boiler room, stripped off the gloves, and threw them down.

I was blind, nuclear mad. And all I could do was throw the ladders, the tools, and the gear into the back of the truck as hard as I could. My coworkers were unnerved. I didn't speak to anyone for the rest of the afternoon, and DeSimon didn't speak to me. Back in the Camp, I tried to shower the slime and humiliation off me. Then I wrote another cop-out, this time to DeSimon's boss. It read something like this:

As I have discussed with you on previous occasions Mr. De-Simon, my work supervisor, sometimes speaks to us at work in ways that I find crude, disrespectful and sexually graphic.

On 6/23/04 while working in the boiler room on the new electric circuit for the visiting room, we were working with large electric wires bound together with electrical tape. Mr. DeSimon referred to these materials, which I had to grease to pull through pipes, as horse genitalia, which I found very offensive. He did not use the word "genitalia," but rather a vulgarity.

That was all the room there was to explain a request on a cop-out.

I was not going to spend the next seven months under the thumb of this pig, I vowed. And I hoped that, in the form of horse cock, he had handed me the trump card for my escape.

At my next opportunity I went to the office of DeSimon's boss. He was a horse of a different color, making a career of the BOP and moving from prison to prison, climbing the corporate ladder. He was from Texas, where they certainly know something about prisons, and a complete professional. Very tall, he always wore a tie and often cowboy boots, and was unfailingly polite. He was also even-handed, which won him the admiration of the prisoners. Pop called him "My Texas Ranger" and liked it when he would come up to the Camp to eat her cooking.

I knocked on his door, walked in, and handed him my cop-out.

He read through it silently, then looked up at me. "Miss Kerman, I'm not sure I understand what you're tryin' to say here. Will you please have a seat?"

I sat and took off my white baseball cap. I could feel my cheeks getting hot again. I chose a spot on his desk to stare at so I wouldn't have to make eye contact with him, so he couldn't see my shame and I wouldn't start crying in front of a police. Then I explained what my cop-out meant, in great detail. When I was finally finished, I took a deep breath. Then I raised my eyes and looked at Tex.

He was as red as I was. "I'll switch you out of there immediately," he said.

JULY DAWNED with a sour flavor. The entire Camp facility seemed to groan in the heat, overtaxed. The phones stopped working. The washing machines broke, a horror show. Suddenly all the hair dryers disappeared. Two hundred women, no phones, no washing machines, no hair dryers—it was like *Lord of the Flies* on estrogen. I sure as hell wasn't going to be Piggy.

To escape the Camp's simmering tensions, I liked to sit under the row of pine trees overlooking the track and the valley beyond, especially at sunset. Now that I knew what the lake looked like, I would imagine diving in, deep under the water, and swimming away. I would strain my ears to catch the sound of the motorboats far below. It was such a pretty spot here, why did they have to ruin it with a prison? I missed Larry terribly on those evenings, wishing that I were with him.

I checked the callout every day to see if my work assignment had changed. After a week I learned that my attempt to escape the electric shop had been thwarted because rotten DeSimon had gone on vacation unannounced, and Tex wouldn't transfer me out to construction until he returned. I couldn't understand this at all.

But when I pressed him, sounding as desperate as I was, the big Texan put his hands up as if to say stop. "You're going to have to trust me and be patient, Miss Kerman. I'll get you out of there."

. . .

MIRACULOUSLY, MY transfer from electric to construction finally happened, popping up on the callout at the end of July. Tex had been as good as his word. I did a little victory dance in the Camp's main hall.

My new coworkers included my buddy Allie B., the cheerful six-foot oddball from B Dorm, and Pennsatucky, who was in contention for white girl with the biggest mouth. The carpentry shop was largely made up of Spanish mamis, including Maria Carbon, the almost-catatonic girl I had greeted in Room 6 back in February. She had regained her equilibrium in the intervening months, and the difference between that terrified girl and this slightly macho, bravado-filled convict was striking. Everyone was welcoming to me, and there was no evidence of the downtrodden misery I was used to in electric. The construction and carpentry shops were housed together and smelled of wood and paint and sawdust. I now worked for Mr. King, the chain-smoking Marlboro Man.

I HAD a new neighbor in B Dorm, who I nicknamed Pom-Pom based on her hairdo. Pom-Pom was a bashful twenty-two-year-old who spent a lot of time sleeping and quickly got a rep for laziness. She probably slept so much because she was depressed, a normal enough response to prison. She had been assigned to work in the garage, where she pumped gas into the prison vehicles enthusiastically; she didn't seem lazy to me. If you looked at her and smiled, she would cast her eyes away but smile her own shy smile.

One day in the dinner line Pom-Pom abruptly turned to me and began to talk. I barely knew her and assumed she must be speaking to someone else, her coworker Angel perhaps, who was standing on my other side. No, she was speaking to me, and with some intensity.

"Boss called me into his office today, and he was asking me if I've had any relatives here before." Mr. Senecal was her boss in the garage. "So he was asking me, and it turns out my mother worked for him."

I looked at Pom-Pom. At present we had three sets of sisters locked up in the Camp, and another neighbor's mother had apparently been shipped out right before I arrived. At this point in my own prison stay, it was less surprising to me that she was a second-generation federal inmate than that she did not know her mom had worked in the garage.

"You didn't know she worked in the garage?" I asked.

"No, I knew she was here, my aunt told me, but she never told me nothing about it."

I had a terrible suspicion that Pom-Pom's mother might be dead.

Angel, her coworker, was of course listening in and gently asked the question: "Where's your mom?"

"I have no idea," replied Pom-Pom.

I felt even worse, but I was still curious. "How did Senecal know?"

"He just guessed. He thought it was my sister, but he just guessed."

"Do you look like your mom? He guessed from looking at you?"

"I guess so—he asked me, 'Tall and skinny, right?' " Pom-Pom laughed. "He said he just had a feeling, so he asked me. Then he asked me what I was doing here."

I wondered if the prison staff connected the miseries of their chosen profession with the miseries of their prisoners' children. Did it trouble Mike Senecal to find Pom-Pom in Danbury, and was he waiting for her children to show up? Maybe if her mother had been put in treatment for her addictions (which were implicit) rather than in the garage in Danbury, Pom-Pom wouldn't be standing in his office today.

"What did Senecal say about your mom?"

"He said she never gave him any trouble."

I didn't much care for Pom-Pom's boss, but I liked to hang out in the garage. I stopped in every morning to get the white construction pickup and shoot the breeze with the gals who worked there pumping gas and fixing trucks. There was a debate going on about what was the song of the summer.

Angel said it was the big crossover reggaeton hit with Daddy Yankee; I didn't know the name was "Oye Mi Canto," but we could all sing the refrain:

> Boricua, Morena, Dominicano, Colombiano,
> Boricua, Morena, Cubano, Mexicano
> Oye Mi Canto

Bonnie snorted. "Y'all are crazy," she said. "It's Fat Joe!"

We all replied, "Lean Back," and dropped one shoulder back in smooth unison.

Kenyatta said, "Well, I don't like her, but that song by Christina Milian—'Pop, Pop, Pop That Thang'? That song is blowing up."

This made me giggle. In yoga class the other day Yoga Janet had been trying to get us to loosen up our hips. "Okay, everyone, wiggle your hips. Shake them out. Now rotate them, circle left . . . now right. Okay, now I want you to pop your hips forward, your pelvis, in a smooth motion. I want you to Pop That Thing!" Sister Platte had been bemused: "Pop that thing?" Camila and I had died.

Pom-Pom spoke up. "I don't know where you think y'all are at, but there's just one song this summer. And that's 'Locked Up.' Look around you! End of discussion."

We had to admit, she was dead on. All summer long, anywhere there was a radio playing, you could hear the almost eerie, plaintive voice of Akon, a Senegalese rapper, singing about prison.

> Can't wait to get out and move forward with my life,
> Got a family that loves me and wants me to do right,
> But instead I'm here locked up.

Even if the song had not been a huge hit on the outs, it had to be the guiding anthem in a place like the Camp; you heard women who weren't even hip-hop fans humming it tunelessly under their breath as they folded laundry: "'I'm locked up, they won't let me out, nooooo, they won't let me out. I'm locked up.'"

CHAPTER 12

Naked

||||

I was a big fan of my coworker Allie B. She made me laugh all the time. She seemed lighthearted—that is, when she wasn't pissed off about something; her pendulum swung a little wildly. She didn't have the heavy hallmarks of incarceration on her, even though this was not her first time down—in fact she was a violator, which made sense because she was a junkie. But she wasn't locked up for a drug crime, so she wasn't getting any kind of treatment for her addictions.

I would ask her, "C'mon, you're clean, and you've been clean for the whole time you've been locked up, so why go back to it?"

She would just cock her head and smile. "You obviously have no idea what you're talking about, Piper," she said. "I cannot wait to get a taste, that and some dick."

This we knew: as much as Allie loved to get high, she also loved sex. She would run filthy and hilarious commentary under her breath about any man she saw who struck her fancy—prison guard, staffer in a tie, or the occasional unsuspecting delivery guy who wandered into our field of vision.

Allie would sometimes refer to me as her "wife," to which I would respond, "Fat fucking chance, Allie." She occasionally experienced bursts of (I think) mock-lust, during which she would chase me around B Dorm screaming filthy things and trying to yank down my gray running shorts while I screeched. Our neighbors quickly grew irritated by our roughhousing.

From her speech and her writing, and despite her passion for *Fear Factor,* I could tell that Allie was better educated than most prisoners. Without asking my pal the personal questions, *verboten* even between friends, I had to guess that her multiple stints in prison were due to her addiction. I worried about Allie; I certainly hoped that she would never see the inside of a prison again, but more than that, I was concerned that she could end up dead.

I had similar concerns for Allie's sidekick Pennsatucky, who had been a crack addict (I could tell from her blackened front teeth). Unlike Allie, Pennsatucky didn't want to get high as soon as she hit the streets. She wanted to get her daughter back. The child, an angelic-looking toddler, lived with her father. Pennsatucky had no parental rights. She was "not right," according to women around the Camp, which was something said about people who struggled with behavioral problems or sometimes outright mental illness. The conditions of the prison did not make these challenges easier.

Now that I had known Pennsatucky for a while and worked with her, I thought she had more on the ball than people gave her credit for. She was perceptive and sensitive but had great difficulty expressing herself in a way that was not off-putting to others, and she got loud and angry when she felt disrespected, which was often. There was nothing wrong with Pennsatucky that would have prevented her from living a perfectly happy life, but her problems made her vulnerable to drugs and to the men who had them on offer.

If your drug problem lands you on the wrong side of the law, you might end up detoxing on the floor of a county jail. Once you get to your long-term prison home, the first thing they'll want to do is assess your psychiatric state . . . and prescribe you some drugs. The twice-daily pill line in Danbury was always long, snaking out of the medical office into the hall. Some women were helped enormously by the medication they took, but some of them seemed zombified, doped to the gills. Those women scared me; what would happen when they hit the streets and no longer could go to pill line?

When I walked through the terrifying gates of the FCI seven months before, I certainly didn't look like a gangster, but I had a gangster mentality. Gangsters only care about themselves and theirs. My overwhelming regret over my actions was because of the trauma I had caused my loved ones and the consequences I was facing. Even when my clothes were taken away and replaced by prison khakis, I would have scoffed at the idea that the "War on Drugs" was anything but a joke. I would have argued that the government's drug laws were at best proven ineffectual every day and at worst were misguidedly focused on supply rather than demand, randomly conceived and un-evenly and unfairly enforced based on race and class, and thus intel-lectually and morally bankrupt. And those things all were true.

But now, when I looked in dismay at Allie, who was champing at the bit to get back to her oblivion; when I thought about whether Pennsatucky would be able to keep it together and prove herself the good mom that she aspired to be; when I worried about my many friends at Danbury whose health was crushed by hepatitis and HIV; and when I saw in the visiting room how addiction had torn apart the bonds between mothers and their children, I finally understood the true consequences of my own actions. I had helped these terrible things happen.

What made me finally recognize the indifferent cruelty of my own past wasn't the constraints put on me by the U.S. government, nor the debt I had amassed for legal fees, nor the fact that I could not be with the man I loved. It was sitting and talking and working with and knowing the people who suffered because of what people like me had done. None of these women rebuked me—most of them had been intimately involved in the drug business themselves. Yet for the first time I really understood how my choices made me complicit in their suffering. I was the accomplice to their addiction.

A lengthy term of community service working with addicts on the outside would probably have driven the same truth home and been a hell of a lot more productive for the community. But our cur-rent criminal justice system has no provision for restorative justice, in which an offender confronts the damage they have done and tries to make it right to the people they have harmed. (I was lucky to get there on my own, with the help of the women I met.) Instead, our system of "corrections" is about arm's-length revenge and retribution, all day and all night. Then its overseers wonder why people leave prison more broken than when they went in.

VANESSA ROBINSON was a male-to-female transsexual who had started her bid down the hill in the FCI. Within the confines of the Danbury plantation, her presence was notorious; the COs insisted on calling her "Richard," her birth name. One day the Camp was abuzz. "The he-she is coming up!!!"

There was great anticipation of Miss Robinson's arrival. Some women swore that they would not speak to her; others professed fascination. The West Indian women and some of the Spanish mamis expressed disgust; the born-agains made outraged noises; and the middle-class white women looked bemused or nervous. The old-timers were blasé. "Ah, we used to have a bunch of girls that were trying to go the other way. They were protesters," said Mrs. Jones.

"The other way?" I asked.

"Go from a girl to a boy, always bitching about their medication and bullshit," she said, with a dismissive wave of her hand.

I soon got my first glimpse of Vanessa—all six feet, four inches of blond, coffee-colored, balloon-breasted almost-all-woman that she was. An admiring crowd of young women had gathered around her, and she lapped up the attention. This was no unassuming "shim" unfortunately incarcerated and trying to get along; Vanessa was a full-blown diva. It was as if someone had shot Mariah Carey through a matter-disrupter and plunked her down in our midst.

Diva though she was, Vanessa had the intelligence and maturity to handle her new situation with some discretion. She began her time in the Camp almost demurely, with no histrionics. Several other women had come up from the FCI with her, including a startlingly beautiful young woman named Wainwright who was her bosom buddy—they both sang in the church choir. Wainwright was petite, with green cat eyes, an enigmatic smile, and a college education—most of the other black women worshipped her on sight. They were a visually hilarious pair, similar-looking in theory and yet so dramatically different.

For their first several weeks in the Camp they hung together most of the time. Vanessa was friendly if approached but more reserved than her reputation and appearance would suggest. She went to work in the kitchen. "*He* can't cook," scoffed Pop, who fell into the "disgusted" category and was disinclined to be kind, although there was some truth in her culinary assessment. There was a ketchup-in-the-marinara-sauce episode that had the whole Camp up in arms. Pop hissed into my ear who the culprit was, but I kept it to myself.

I liked Vanessa. Which was a good thing, because she moved in next door to me. She and Wainwright managed to finesse the housing assignments they wanted. Wainwright bunked with Lionnel, from the warehouse, who was the voice of reason/discipline when it came to unruly young black women. ("Girl, you better get some act-right, or I'm going to bust your head to the white meat!") And Vanessa moved in next door to me with Faith, a steel-haired Oxy-dealing granny who was straight out of the New Hampshire woods and had come up from the FCI with Vanessa and Wainwright. They got along great. Vanessa's arrival in B Dorm evoked some eye-rolling from Miss Natalie, but she was more tolerant than her friend Ginger Solomon, who demanded, "Is that what you want to see in the bathroom, Miss Piper? Well, is it?!" I meekly pointed out that Vanessa was post-op, but no, I wasn't necessarily looking for a free show.

Free shows were available. As Vanessa settled in, she got more boisterous, and she was thrilled to display her surgical glory at the merest suggestion. Soon half the Camp had seen what she'd got. Her D-cup breasts were her pride and joy, and given our height difference they were often the first things I saw in the morning. She was certainly better looking than many of the prisoners who had been born to our gender, but close quarters revealed some of her more masculine qualities. Her pits were positively bushy—she said that if she couldn't wax them, then fuck it—and in the hot, close quarters of B

Dorm in the summer, she smelled unmistakably like a sweaty man. Vanessa was deprived of her hormones in prison and thus retained several male characteristics that would have been less evident otherwise, most notably her voice. While she spoke in a high, little-girl voice most of the time, she could switch at will to a booming, masculine Richard-voice. She loved to sneak up behind people and scare the crap out of them this way, and she was very effective at quieting a noisy dining hall, roaring, "Y'all hush up!" Best of all were her Richardian encouragements on the softball field, where she was a most sought-after teammate. That bitch could hit.

Vanessa was an entertaining and considerate neighbor, cheerful and drag-queen funny, smart and observant and sensitive to what others were thinking and feeling. She was quick to pull out her scrapbook and share photos and stories of the men whose hearts she had broken, cutting up to make the time pass. ("This is the program from the Miss Gay Black America pageant—I was third runner-up!") All the born-female aspiring divas (most of whom lived in B Dorm) immediately recognized that here was a master at whose feet they could learn. And Vanessa was a good influence on the young girls who flocked around her. She admonished them gently when they were behaving badly, and exhorted them to educate themselves, get with God, and love themselves.

She had just one ritual that was hard to take. Every evening when she was finished with work in the kitchen, Vanessa would return to her cube, climb up in her bed, and bring out a contraband tape player, obtained somehow through the chapel. Her absolute favorite gospel song, detailing the fact that Jesus was loving, forgiving, and helping us to take every step, would soar over the cube walls, and Vanessa's voice would soar with it. This was when the need for her hormones really became most apparent—Vanessa simply could not hit the high notes. The first couple of nights she did this, I smiled to myself, entertained; by the tenth, I was burying my head under the pillow. However, considering some of the other songbirds we had in close quarters, I decided to grit my teeth and bear it. One hymn a night wouldn't kill me.

. . .

ONE OF the many contraband items I had in my possession was nail polish. There had been a time when it was sold on commissary, but now it was a banned item. Yoga Janet had given me a bottle of gorgeous bright magenta polish, which my pedicurist Rose Silva openly coveted. I promised that I would give it to her when I went home, but for now I kept it for myself and for Yoga Janet, who also loved beautiful toes. Any self-respecting New York woman has a good pedicure, even if she's in the clink.

I had been Rose's customer for a while now. That there were prison pedicurists was one of the few true things I had gleaned in my pre-prison research, along with the strong recommendation that if you were going to avail yourself of their services, you had better buy your own tools from the commissary. The prison population has a high incidence of blood-borne diseases like HIV and hepatitis, and you don't want to risk an infection of any kind.

When I first got to the Camp, I was far too shy to request a pedicure, though I admired Annette's gold toenails. "I only go to Rose," she explained. There was actually only one other option to Rose, and that was Carlotta Alvarado—Pop was among Carlotta's clients. Between the two of them they split the market. Prison pedis are strictly a word-of-mouth business, and in this case prisoners were fiercely loyal.

I had my first pedi back in the chilly early spring. Annette had given it to me as a gift. "I got you a pedicure with Rose Silva, I can't stand looking at your toes in those flip-flops anymore." A week later I dutifully reported to one of the Rooms' bathrooms off the main hall to rendezvous with Rose, armed with my own pedicure tools—cuticle clippers, orange sticks, foot file (all of these were sold by the commissary, but no colors of nail polish). Rose arrived with her own toolkit, including towels, a square plastic basin, and an array of polishes, some in decidedly odd colors. I felt very awkward, but Rose had the gift of gab and was businesslike.

Rose and I quickly established that we were both from New

York, she from Brooklyn and me from Manhattan, and that she was Italian–Puerto Rican, born-again, and serving thirty months after getting caught trying to bring two keys of coke through the Miami airport. She had a no-nonsense briskness and liked to clown. She also gave a meticulous pedicure and a damn good foot massage. No one is supposed to touch you in prison, so the intimacy of a languorous foot rub, intended to please, almost sent me into ecstatic tears the first time. "Whoa, honey. Take some deep breaths!" she advised. For all this Rose charged five dollars of commissary goods—she would let me know on shopping day what to buy her. I was hooked. I was a customer.

Rose's latest effort on my feet was definitely her masterpiece so far. It was a pale-pink French pedicure with magenta and white cherry blossoms added on my big toes. I couldn't stop looking at my toes in my flip-flops, they were so cotton-candy fabulous.

DESPITE THE groove that I had settled into, I still had flashes of irritation with my fellow prisoners, which troubled me. In the gym I nearly lost my temper with Yoga Janet during class when she insisted that yes, I could get my foot behind my head if I just tried a little harder.

"No, I can't," I snapped. "My foot is not going behind my head. Period."

Being among many people who very pointedly couldn't or wouldn't exercise much self-control was taxing, and I meditated a great deal more on self-control. Sitting there in prison, I heard a lot of horror stories, of women with many children they loved but couldn't handle, of families with both parents locked away for long years, and I thought about the millions of children who are put through terrible experiences because of their parents' poor choices. Coupled with the government's crap response to the drug trade, which perpetuated the damaging myth that they could control the supply of drugs when demand was so strong, it seemed an enormous amount of totally unproductive misery, which could only come back to hurt us all later. I thought about my own parents, about Larry, and about what I was putting them through right now. This was the penitence that sometimes happens in the penitentiary. It was emotionally overwhelming, and when I saw women still making bad choices day to day in the Camp, or simply acting objectionably, it upset me.

I was pretty staunch in maintaining an "us and them" attitude about the prison staff. Some of them seemed to like me, and I thought they treated me better than they did some other inmates, which I considered rotten. But when I saw other prisoners behaving in ways that challenged my sense of unity, for lack of a better term, behaving in petty or ignorant or just plain antisocial ways, I really had a hard time with it. It drove me a little nuts.

I took this all as a sign that I was too engrossed in prison life, that the "real world" was fading too much into the background, and I probably needed to read the paper more religiously and write more letters. Focusing on the positive was hard, but I knew that I had found the right women at Danbury to help me do it. A little voice in my head reminded me that I might never see anything quite like this again, and that immersing myself in my current situation, experiencing it, and learning everything there was to know might be the way to live life, now and always.

"You're thinking too hard," said Pop, who had managed to do over a decade on the inside and still stay sane.

Boy, was that a nice pedicure. Plus there were lightbulbs to change, term papers to ghostwrite, sugar packets and hardware to steal, puppies to play with, and gossip to gather and pass along. When I thought too much about my prison life, when I should have been thinking about Larry, I felt a little guilty. Still, certain things brought my absence from the outside world into sharp relief, like once-in-a-lifetime events that would happen without me. In July our old friend Mike would be wed in the meadow on his fifty-one-acre spread in Montana. I wanted to be there, among friends, in the gorgeous Montana summer, toasting Mike and his bride with tequila. The world kept going despite the fact that I had been removed to an alternate universe. I wanted to be home desperately, and when I said "home," that meant "wherever Larry is" more than Lower Manhattan, but the next seven months stretched out in front of me. I now knew I could do them, but it was still way too early to count the days.

On July 20 Martha Stewart was sentenced to five months in prison and five months of home confinement, a pretty typical "split sentence" for white-collar criminals but far below the maximum for her conviction. Some prisoners raised eyebrows over her sentence. About 90 percent of criminal defendants plead guilty. Usually, a defendant who does take a case all the way to court and loses a federal trial is hit hard by the judge, with the maximum sentence, not the minimum; this had happened to a number of women in the Camp who were doing very long bids. Regardless, most of the Camp was convinced that Stewart would be someone's new bunkie in Danbury, and that would certainly liven things up. If Martha were designated to Danbury I felt pretty sure they'd stick her in the A Dorm "Suburbs" with the OCD cases.

I had been hearing about Children's Day since I got to Danbury. Once a year the BOP held an event when kids could come to the prison and spend the day with their mothers. Activities were planned, including relays, face painting, piñatas, and a cookout, and the children got to walk around the Camp grounds with their moms, very vaguely like a regular family enjoying a day at the park. All the other prisoners were confined to their housing areas. For this reason, gals in the know had strongly suggested that I volunteer to help out, if only so that I would not be stuck in my cube for eight hours on a potentially hot day.

They needed a lot of hands, so in the first week of August I was summoned to a volunteer meeting. I would be manning the face-painting booth. When Saturday arrived, it was in fact hot as hell, but the Camp was humming with nervous energy. Pop and her crew were toiling to get the hot dogs and hamburgers ready. Volunteers were either milling around or getting our stations ready; there was a little pop-up canopy over the face-painting table, scattered with pots and pencils of rainbow-colored greasepaint. I was surprised at how nervous I was. What if the kids were badly behaved and I couldn't handle them? I certainly wasn't about to reprimand another pris-oner's kid—just imagine how that would go over. I anxiously ques-tioned the other face painter, who was an old hand. "It's easy. Just show them the designs and ask 'em what they want," she said, totally bored. There was a sheet with line drawings of rainbows and butter-flies and ladybugs.

The first children arrived for their big day. Kids had to be regis-tered ahead of time, and they had to be dropped off at the visiting room and picked up by the same adult, who could not come into the Camp—the kids had to come alone. Many families had managed to get the kids there from long distances—Maine, western Pennsylvania, Baltimore, and farther—and for some of them it might be the only time they saw their mother this year. Being processed in through the visiting room must have been scary for the kids, who then could go racing into their mother's arms. After hugs and kisses, they could take their mother's hand and walk down the stairs by the dining hall and out behind the Camp, to the track and the picnic tables and the out-doors and the whole day stretching in front of them.

Our first customer shyly approached the face-painting booth with her mother, a coworker from the carpentry shop. "Piper, she wants a face painting."

The girl was probably about five, with curly golden-brown ponytails and chubby cheeks. "Okay, sweetie, what do you want?" I pointed at the sheet with the designs. She looked at me. I looked at her. I looked at her mother. "What does she want?"

Mom rolled her eyes. "I don't know, a rainbow?"

The rainbow in the picture was coming out of a cloud. It looked kind of hard. "How about a heart with a cloud—in blue to match her dress?"

"Great, whatever."

I cupped her tiny chin in my hand and tried to keep my other hand steady. The final result was very big, and very . . . blue. Mom examined my handiwork and then gave me a look like *What the fuck?* But she cooed, "That's so cute, baby, *que linda!*" and off they went. This was harder than it looked.

But it got easier. After the kids' shyness around strangers wore off, everyone wanted their face painted. The children were well behaved, waiting patiently in line and smiling sweetly when it was finally their turn and they got to pick their design. We were busy for hours, until we all finally got a lunch break. I went and ate a hamburger with Pop and watched families dotting the grass and the picnic tables. The little kids were playing together. Gisela's teenage daughters were flirting with Trina Cox's teenage sons, who were frankly pretty fine. Some of the mothers looked overwhelmed—they were no longer accustomed to supervising their own kids in a normal, day-to-day way. But everyone was having fun. I got that feeling again, the feeling I had when Natalie's GED scores had come back, that tornado feeling inside. So much concentrated happiness, in such a sad place.

After lunch I went back to the face-painting booth. Now some of the older kids started to approach.

"Can you do a tattoo? Of a tiger, or a lightning bolt?"

"Only if it's okay with your mom." Once I had secured maternal permission, I went to work "inking" thunderbolts and anchors and panthers on forearms and shoulders and calves, much to the delight of the postpubescent set. I showed off my own tattoo, which got gratifying oohs and aahs.

The younger of Trina Cox's two boys approached me. He was wearing an immaculate white New York Jets jersey, with matching new hat and green shorts.

"That's my team," I said, as he took a seat in my tattoo parlor.

He looked at me seriously. "Can you do Olde English?"

"Olde English? You mean, like fancy lettering?"

"Yeah, like the rappers have?"

I looked around for his mother, but I didn't see her. "I've never done that before, but I can try. What do you want it to say?"

"Um . . . my nickname, John-John."

"Okay, John-John." We sat knee to knee, and I held his forearm. I guessed he was about fourteen. "You want it lengthwise, or stacked?"

He thought about it a little harder. "Maybe it should be just 'John'?"

"That sounds good. 'John.' I'm going to do it lengthwise, big."

"Okay."

Neither of us talked while I worked, bent over his arm. I was very careful, and tried to make it as cool-looking as I could, as if it really were going to be permanent. He was quiet, watching me and maybe imagining what it might feel like to get a real tattoo. Finally I sat up, satisfied. But was he?

I got a big smile. He admired his arm. "Thank you!" John-John was a sweet kid. He ran off to show his older brother, the football star.

In the afternoon, near the end of the scheduled activities, it was time for the prison-made piñatas stuffed with candy and little trinkets. Breaking them open was supervised by the jerk from the commissary, who was uncharacteristically nice to all of the kids. John-John, blindfolded, whaled on the Pokémon piñata I had decorated until it burst, giving up its goodies to the throng of children. Now the moment we had all been trying to put out of our minds was drawing very close: the end of the day and the goodbyes. Kids who had traveled from far away, gotten closer to their moms than they had been all year, and then eaten a bunch of candy could hardly be blamed for shedding tears when they had to leave, even if they were "too big for that." At dinner the mothers appeared subdued and exhausted, if they came to the chow hall at all. I am just glad that I was too busy to think all day because afterward, curled up in a ball in my bunk, I also cried and cried.

ONE MORNING I checked the callout and saw that I had OBGYN next to my name.

"Oof, girl, the annual gynecologist! You can refuse the exam," commented Angel, who was also checking the callout and always had something to say.

Why should I refuse it? I asked.

"It's a *man*. Almost everyone refuses it because of that," Angel explained.

I was horrified. "That's ridiculous. It's probably the most important exam most of these women could have all year! I mean, of course a prison for fourteen hundred women should bring in a female gynecologist, but still!"

Angel shrugged. "Whatever. I'm not having no man do that shit."

"Well, I don't care if it's a man or not," I announced. "I'm getting a checkup."

I reported to the medical office at my appointed time, feeling smug about getting my money's worth out of the system. My smugness evaporated when the doctor called me into the room that served as his exam room. He was a white man who looked to be in his eighties and whose voice quavered. He commanded me, irritated, to "take off all of your clothes, wrap yourself in the paper sheet, and climb up on the examining table. Put your feet in the stirrups and slide all the way down. I'll be right back!"

In a minute I was stripped down to my sports bra, cold and freaked out. The paper sheet was inadequate covering for my body. I should have had a robe on, or at least my T-shirt. The doctor knocked, then entered. I blinked at the ceiling, trying to pretend that this was not happening.

"Slide down," he barked, getting his instruments ready. "Relax, I need you to relax!"

Let me just say, it was horrible. And it hurt. When it was over, and the old man gone, departed with a bang of the door, I was left clutching that paper sheet around me, feeling just like this prison system wanted me to—utterly powerless, vulnerable, alone.

THE WORK in construction was a lot more physically challenging than being an electrician. I got stronger and stronger, lifting extension ladders and paint cans and two-by-fours, loading and unloading the pickup. By the end of August we were almost finished with our work preparing the warden's house for its new resident, painting the garage door bright red and cleaning up the postconstruction debris. It was an old New England house that had been expanded a couple of times, with low ceilings and tiny upstairs bedrooms, but it was comfortable enough. It was nice to spend time in a house, after months of living in a barracks. At the far edge of the prison grounds, my coworkers and I would scatter around the empty house to finish various projects.

One afternoon, alone in the upstairs bathroom, I caught my reflection in the big mirror with surprise. I looked as though years had fallen away from me, shed like dry old snakeskin. I took off my white baseball cap and pulled my hair out of its ponytail and looked at myself again. I locked the bathroom door. Then I took off my khaki shirt and my white T-shirt and shucked off my pants. I was standing in my white sports bra, granny panties, and steel-toes. I took those off. I looked at my own body in the mirror, seeing myself naked for the first time in seven months. In the Dorms there was never a moment or a place where a woman could stand and stretch and regard herself and confront who she was physically.

Standing there naked in the warden's bathroom, I could see that prison had changed me. Most of the accumulated varnish of the five unhappy years spent on pretrial was gone. Except for a decade's worth of crinkly smile lines around my eyes, I resembled the girl who had jumped off that waterfall more closely than I had in years.

CHAPTER 13

Thirty-five and Still Alive

||||

The red maple and sourwood trees were already starting to change color, which thrilled me with the promise of an early fall and the speedy arrival of winter. In Danbury I had learned to hasten the days by chasing the enjoyment in them, no matter how elusive. Some people on the outside look for what is amiss in every interaction, every relationship, and every meal; they are always trying to hang their mortality on improvement. It was incredibly liberating to instead tackle the trick of making each day fly more quickly.

"Time, be my friend," I repeated every day. Soon I would go down to the track and try to chase the day away by running in circles. Even under very bad circumstances life still held its pleasures, like running and Natalie's homemade cookies and Pop's stories. It was these simple things that were within your grasp in the degraded circumstances of life in prison; the things you could do yourself, or the small kindnesses one prisoner could extend to another.

I needed some track time after a long day of painting the lobby down the hill. It was the new warden's first day on the job, and to celebrate, I overheard that they shook down the whole FCI, a tremendous and rare undertaking encompassing twelve units of twelve hundred women and every one of their lockers. I was pretty sure the Camp's turn would come quickly. The feds were looking for cigarettes.

The Bureau of Prisons had decreed that all of its institutions were

to go smoke-free by 2008. It put financial incentives in place for prisons to do it even before the deadline. Warden Deboo's parting shot to
the women of Danbury was to impose the ban, to officially take hold
on September 1. The preceding months had seen extensive communications about the ban. First of all, the commissary ginned up the
demand for cigarettes in July, trying to get rid of their stock. Then in
August everyone had one month in which to smoke their brains out
before going cold turkey on one of the most addictive drugs known
to man.

Truthfully, I didn't much care about the smoking ban. I would
never have admitted it to Larry or my mother in the visiting room,
but I'd have a social cigarette now and then with Allie B. or Little
Janet or Jae. A pal from the electric shop had taught me how to make
a lighter out of a scrap of tinsel, two AA batteries, bits of copper wire,
and some black electricians' tape. But I could do without it all easily.
Cigarettes were killing the "real" smokers, though, and the long
twice-daily pill line included not just the people getting psych meds
but also women who desperately needed their heart or diabetes medication to stay standing. According to the CDC, cigarettes kill over
435,000 people a year in the United States. Most of us in Danbury
were locked away for trading in illegal drugs. The annual death toll of
illegal drug addicts, according to the same government study? Seventeen thousand. Heroin or coffin nails, you be the judge.

When September rolled around, a lot of prisoners were flat-out
depressed. They sneaked smokes in absurd spots, practically begging
to be caught. Every time I rounded the track, I'd surprise a new
group rustling in the bushes. Then the shakedowns began in earnest,
and they started hauling people off to the SHU. The ever-canny Pop
had negotiated with her work supervisor that she'd be allowed one
protected smoke at the end of her shift and a safe hidey-hole in the
kitchen.

The Camp population continued to dwindle, with many empty
beds. The place felt quiet, which was nice, but I missed my loud
friends and neighbors who had departed: Allie B., Colleen, and Lili
Cabrales. As soon as the "Martha moratorium" was lifted, the Camp

would get dozens of freaks rushed in, ruining our temporarily placid prison lives. Per Larry's instructions, I had been watching more television but not the news. The presidential campaign was barely noted on the inside. Instead, I joined the crowd for the much-anticipated Video Music Awards in August. "What up, B?" asked Jay-Z, and the visiting room filled with squeals. In prison, everyone sings along.

SEPTEMBER 16 was the day of the prison Job Fair, an annual Danbury FCI event that paid lip service to the fact that its prisoners would rejoin the world. So far I had witnessed no meaningful effort to prepare inmates for successful reentry into society, other than the handful of women who had gone through the intensive drug treatment program. Maybe the Job Fair would impart some useful information to the crowd.

I was lucky to have a job waiting for me when I went home: a generous friend had created a position for me at the company he ran. Every time he came to visit me, Dan would say, "Would you hurry up and get out of here? The marketing department needs you!"

Hardly any of the women I knew in Danbury were as fortunate. The top three worries for women getting released from prison are usually: reuniting with their children (if they are a single mother, they have often lost their parental rights); housing (a huge problem for people with a record); and employment. I had written enough jailhouse résumés by now to know that a lot of the ladies had only worked in the (enormous) underground economy. Outside the mainstream, they didn't have the first notion of how to break into it. So far, nothing about prison was changing that reality.

A bald guy from the central BOP office in Washington, who seemed nervous, opened the Fair and welcomed us. Programs were handed out, folded photocopies with a drawing of an owl on the cover. Below the owl it read: BE WISE—Women In Secured Employment. On the back of the program were Andy Rooney quotes.

Various companies had committed to participating in the event, many of them nonprofits. The day would include a panel discussion on "Emerging Jobs in the Workforce & How to Land One," mock job interviews, and Mary Wilson, the legendary Motown singer from the Supremes, was going to deliver a motivational speech. That I had to see. But first, Professional Appareling!

Professional Appareling was run by Dress for Success, the nonprofit that helps disadvantaged women get business-appropriate clothes. A jovial middle-aged woman briefed us on the dos and don'ts of outfits for job interviews, then asked for volunteers. Vanessa almost broke her seatmate's nose waving her arm madly, so the woman had no choice but to pick her. And then in the blink of an eye I found myself standing at the front of the room with my Amazonian neighbor, Delicious, and Pom-Pom. "These lovely ladies are going to help us to demonstrate the dos and don'ts," said the volunteer brightly.

She herded us into the bathroom, then passed out togs. She gave Delicious a sharp, almost Japanese-looking black suit; Pom-Pom, a pink suit that looked like she was going to church in the South. I got a hideously dowdy and itchy burgundy outfit. And for Vanessa? A fuchsia silk cocktail dress with beading on the chest. "Hurry up ladies!"

We were like schoolgirls getting into costume for the senior show, giggling and fussing with the unfamiliar street clothes. "Is this right?" asked Delicious, and we fixed the long asymmetrical skirt on her. Pom-Pom looked pretty in pink—who knew?

But Vanessa was in a state of distress. "Piper, I can't zip this, help me!" My neighbor's pride and joy were busting out of the too-small cocktail dress. She looked like she was going to cry if she didn't get to wear it.

"Oh, man, Vanessa, I don't know. Okay, hold still . . . now suck it in!" I inched the zipper up. "Suck it *in,* bitch, it's almost there!" She arched her back, sucked wind, and I got the back of the dress closed over the broad V of her shoulders. "Just don't breathe, and you'll be fine."

The four of us looked each other over. "P-I Piper, put your hair up. Be more professional and shit," advised Delicious. I scraped my hair back into a quick bun. Now it was time to show off.

We each got a turn on the catwalk, much to the glee of our fellow prisoners, who whooped and whistled. They went bananas when they caught sight of Vanessa, who basked in the glory, tossing her curls. Then we were lined up, and the volunteer explained who was a job-interview do, and who was a don't. Delicious's outfit was deemed too "edgy"; Pom-Pom's was too "sweet." Vanessa looked crestfallen when she heard that she was wearing "the last kind of thing you would want for an interview."

"What kind of job are we talking about?" she asked plaintively.

My ugly tweed librarian outfit was lauded as the most work-appropriate.

After the dress-up fun, a panel of businesswomen spoke seriously about growing sectors of the economy that had entry-level jobs for workers, like home health care. But there was nervous rumbling among the audience. When the Q&A time came, hands shot up.

"How do we get trained for these kinds of jobs?"

"How do we know the jobs that are open out there?"

"How do we find out who will hire women with a record?"

One of the panelists tried to answer several things at once. "I recommend you spend quite a bit of time on the computer researching these companies and industries, looking at online job listings, and trying to locate training opportunities. I hope you have some access to the Internet?"

This caused a mild rumble. "We don't even have any computers!"

The panelists looked at each other and frowned. "I'm surprised to hear that. You don't have a computer lab, or any kind of computer training here?"

The bald BOP representative spoke up nervously. "Of course they do, all units are supposed to—"

This elicited outright shouts from the ladies. Rochelle from B Dorm stood up. "We do not have any computers up in that Camp! No sir!"

Sensing that he might have a situation on his hands, the BOP suit tried to be conciliatory. "I'm not sure why that would be, miss, but I promise I'll look into it!"

Mary Wilson turned out to be a lovely petite woman in an immaculate soft brown pantsuit. Right from the jump she held the room in the palm of her hand. She didn't really talk about work. She talked about life, and a couple times she burst into snippets of song. She mostly told stories of trials and tribulations and battling adversity and Diana Ross. But what was striking about Ms. Wilson, and was also true of the other outsiders who volunteered their time that day, was that she spoke to us prisoners with great respect, as if our lives ahead had hope and meaning and possibility. After all these months at Danbury, this was a shocking novelty.

MARTHA STEWART was still on everyone's mind. Hysteria had been building on the outside and the inside as to where she would serve her short sentence, and what would happen to her. She had asked her judge to be sent to Danbury, so that her ninety-year-old mother in Connecticut could easily visit her. Her judge had no say over it at all, however. The Danbury (or Washington) powers-that-be in the Bureau of Prisons didn't want her here, perhaps because they didn't want close media scrutiny on the facility. The Camp had been "closed" to new inmates since her conviction, allegedly "full," although we had more empty beds as every week passed.

A lot of nasty things had been written in the press about us. I wasn't in the least bit surprised, but the women around me were upset, especially the middle-class ones. An article came out in *People* calling us "the scum of the earth" and speculating about the beat-downs and abuse Martha might suffer.

Annette turned to me after mail call, anguished by her copy. "I have been subscribing to *People* magazine for over thirty-five years. And now I'm the scum of the earth? Are you the scum of the earth, Piper?"

I said I didn't think so. But the angst over *People* was nothing compared to the shock waves that rocked the Camp on September 20. I came up from the track in the early evening to find a cluster of A Dorm residents around Pop, cursing and shaking their heads over a newspaper. "What's up?" I asked.

"You're not going to believe this, Piper," said Pop. "You remember that crazy French bitch?"

On September 19 the Sunday *Hartford Courant* had published a front-page story—we always got newspapers a day behind, so the institution could "control the flow of information." Staff writer Lynne Tuohy had gotten an exclusive with a recently released Camper, "Barbara," whom Martha had contacted for the inside scoop on life in the Danbury Camp. And "Barbara" had some interesting things to say.

> "Once the shock of being in jail was over, it became a holiday," Barbara said in an interview after her talk with Stewart. "I didn't have to cook. I didn't have to clean. I didn't have to shop. I didn't have to drive. I didn't have to buy gas. They have an ice machine, ironing boards. It was like a big hotel."

It was Levy, all right. After being whisked away to testify against her chiseler ex-boyfriend, she had reappeared in the Camp for one short week in June, and then she was released, her six-month sentence over. Apparently her stay had been far more enjoyable than she had let on when we had the pleasure of her company. She was singing the prison's praises in the paper, going on about how much she had enjoyed the "wide range of classes" on offer plus:

> "two libraries with a wide array of books and magazines, including *Town and Country* and *People*." The food, Barbara said, was nothing short of "amazing."
>
> "This is a place that is so magnificent," she said.

I pictured Levy, swollen with hives, looking like the Elephant Man, crying every single day over her six-month sentence and sneering at anyone she thought was not "classy."

> "I had my hair done every week," Barbara said. "At home I don't take care of me. I take care of my kids. I take care of my

house. I had time there to take care of me. When I came home, I raised my standard of living a little bit."

She hastened to add that the massages "are on the up-and-up," and laughs when friends ask whether she was "at-tacked"—sexually assaulted—during her stay. "I'd say, 'Are you kidding? Most people there were so classy.' "

The reporter got many minor facts wrong, such as that there were four nuns resident, and that we could buy CD players at the commissary. Women were outraged by the false claim that we could buy Häagen-Dazs ice cream. The Camp freaked out, issuing loud threats against the now-free Levy. Boo Clemmons was beside herself.

"Häagen-motherfuckin-Dazs! Hotel! That lying little bitch better hope she don't violate, because if I get hold of her, she's going to think she checked into Motel Hell!"

"I think Martha will be assigned to the kitchen and she will cook and she will be happy," Barbara ventured.

I imagined Martha Stewart trying to take over Pop's kitchen. That would be better than Godzilla vs. Mothra.

Pop was really upset, but not about the prospect of Martha in the mess hall. "Piper, I just don't understand it. Why would she lie? You have the opportunity to get the truth out there about this place, and instead she makes up these lies? We have nothing here, and she makes it sound like a picnic, with her fucking six-month sentence. Try living here ten years!"

I thought I knew why Levy had lied. She didn't want to admit to herself, let alone to the outside world, that she had been placed in a ghetto, just as ghetto as they had once had in Poland. Prison is quite literally a ghetto in the most classic sense of the world, a place where the U.S. government now puts not only the dangerous but also the inconvenient—people who are mentally ill, people who are addicts, people who are poor and uneducated and unskilled. Meanwhile the ghetto in the outside world is a prison as well, and a much more difficult one to escape from than this correctional compound. In fact, there is basically a revolving door between our urban and rural ghettos and the formal ghetto of our prison system.

It was too painful, I thought, for Levy and others (especially the middle-class prisoners) to admit that they had been classed as undesirables, compelled against their will into containment, and forced into scarcity without even the dignity of chosen austerity. So instead she said it was Club Fed.

MY NEIGHBOR Vanessa had given me an in-depth account of how, as young Richard, she had been banned from her high school prom for planning to wear a dress (she whipped up some sequined palazzo pants, found a sympathetic PTA mom to approve them, and attended in triumph). But I never knew what had landed her in federal prison, or why she'd first been designated to a high-security facility. I was pretty sure she wasn't in prison for a drug crime, and I had a suspicion or intimation that she'd given the feds a bit of a chase before being taken into custody, which is probably why she'd ended up down the hill. She reminded me of the gay males and freshly females I had known in San Francisco and New York—smart, snappy, witty, curious about the world.

I was more curious about Vanessa's history than about most of my fellow inmates, particularly after she made an unusual appearance in the visiting room one weekend. There she was, hair and makeup perfect, uniform pressed, towering over her visitor, a tiny, beautifully dressed white woman with snow-white hair. They stood together at the vending machines, their backs to me, the old lady in soft periwinkle blue, Vanessa displaying broad shoulders and narrow hips that any man would have envied.

"Did you have a nice visit?" I asked afterward, not hiding my curiosity.

"Oh yes! That was my grandmother!" she replied, lighting up. I was further intrigued, but not enlightened.

I was definitely going to miss her—she was going home in a few weeks. As her release date neared, Vanessa got increasingly anxious, with a decided uptick in religious observance. Many women grow very, very nervous before they go back to the outside world—they face uncertain futures. I think that Vanessa felt this way. But her nerves did nothing to stop our enthusiastic planning for her surprise going-home party, spearheaded by Wainwright and Lionnel.

It was a grand affair. Many cooks contributed microwave treats, and it resembled a church picnic, with all of the attendant food rivalries over who prepared the best dishes. There were chilaquiles, fried noodles, and prison cheesecake—my specialty. Best of all, there was a platter of deviled eggs—a really challenging contraband item to produce.

We all huddled in one of the empty classrooms, waiting for the Diva. "Shhhhhhhhh!! I hear her!" someone said, dousing the light. When we all shouted "Surprise!" she feigned astonishment graciously, although her fresh makeup had been applied with extra care. At this point the entire prison choir launched into song, led by Wainwright, who soloed beautifully on "Take Me to the Rock." Tops in the singing department was Delicious, who had shaved for the occasion—Delicious had a voice that could really give you goosebumps, in a good way. She had to turn and face the wall while she sang for Vanessa so she wouldn't break down and cry. After the singing and the eating, the guest of honor got up and called out to each person by name, cheerfully reminding us that Jesus was watching over everyone and had brought her to us. She said thank you, with beautiful sincerity, for helping her through her time at Danbury.

"I had to come here," she said, drawing herself up to her full height, "to become a real woman."

SATURDAY NIGHT, movie night, was special, in an old-fashioned let's-go-to-the-picture-show way. But this particular Saturday was extra, extra special. Tonight the lucky ladies of Danbury were going to get a tremendous treat. The institutional movie this week was the remake of *Walking Tall,* the classic vigilante revenge fantasy, starring Dwayne Johnson, aka The Rock.

I am confident that someday in the future The Rock, who was once a professional wrestler, will run for president of the United States, and I think that he will win. I have seen with my own eyes the power of The Rock. The Rock is a uniter, not a divider. When the BOP showed *Walking Tall,* the turnout for every screening all weekend long was unprecedented. The Rock has an effect on women that transcends divisions of race, age, cultural background—even social class, the most impenetrable barrier in America. Black, white, Spanish, old, young, all women are hot for The Rock. Even the lesbians agreed that he was mighty easy on the eyes.

In preparation for The Rock, we observed our usual Saturday-night rituals. After visiting hours and chow were over, Pop and her crew finished cleanup in the dining hall, and I was handed our special movie snacks—nachos tonight, my favorite. Then it was on me, the runner, to whisk the food out of the kitchen to safety without getting busted by a CO. I usually slipped through C Dorm, dropped my Tupperware bowl and Pop's in my cube, and delivered bowls to Toni and Rosemarie, our movie companions.

It was Rosemarie who set up all the chairs in the visiting room for movie night. This meant that she controlled the setup of the special "reserved" chairs for certain people, including our four at the back of the room. Next to our reserved chairs was one of those random pieces of prison furniture, a tall narrow table, which served as our sideboard. I had the job of setting up another Tupperware bowl filled with ice for Pop's sodas and bringing up the food and napkins when it was time for the movie. Pop, who reported for work in the kitchen at five A.M. and worked all day long through the evening meal, was rarely seen in anything but a hairnet and kitchen scrubs. But on movie nights, just before the screening was to begin, Pop would sweep into the room, freshly showered and clad in pale blue men's pajamas.

The pajamas were one of those elusive items that had once been sold by the commissary but then were discontinued. They were the plainest men's pajamas, of a semisheer white cotton-poly. (Pop's had somehow been dyed for her.) I had wanted a pair desperately for months after arriving in prison. So when Pop presented me with a specially procured pair, I did an ecstatic dance around her cube, hopping madly until I beaned myself on the metal bunk bed frame. Now Toni and Rosemarie would say, "Do the pajama dance, Piper!" and I would dance around in my PJs, as ecstatic as Snoopy doing the Suppertime Dance. The pajamas were not for sleeping. I only wore them on the weekends, to movie night or other special occasions, when I wanted to look pretty. I felt so damn good in those pajamas.

Pop loved *Walking Tall*. She preferred a straightforward movie storyline, with maybe a little romance thrown in. If the movie was sappy, she would cry, and I would make fun of her, and she would tell me to shut up. She wept at *Radio*, while I rolled my eyes at the Italian Twins.

After *House of Sand and Fog*, she turned to me. "Did you like that?"

I shrugged. "Eh? It was okay."

"I thought that was your kind of movie."

I would never live down the shame of having enthusiastically recommended *Lost in Translation* when it had screened earlier in the year. The ladies of Danbury widely and loudly declared it "the worst movie *ever*." Boo Clemmons laughed, shaking her head. "All that talking, and Bill Murray doesn't even get to fuck her."

Movie night was as much about eating as anything else. Pop would prepare a special Saturday movie meal that was a respite from the endless march of starch in the dining hall dictated by the BOP. The competitive tension of the salad bar on a rare day when broccoli or spinach or—miracle of miracles—*sliced onions* appeared was a welcome change from the monotony of cucumbers and raw cauliflower—I refused to live on potatoes and white rice. I would wield the plastic tongs with a smile, eyeing Carlotta Alvarado across the salad bar as we both tried to fill our little bowls with the good vegetables faster than the other—me to wolf down immediately with oil and vinegar, she to smuggle out in her pants to cook later.

Chicken day was pandemonium. First of all, everyone wanted to get as much chicken as the kitchen line workers would give them. This is where it came in handy to be in tight with Pop. The rules of scarcity govern prison life: accumulate when the opportunity presents itself, figure out what to do with your loot later.

Sometimes, however, there were plans for that chicken. Often on a chicken day Rosemarie would plan to cook us a special meal. Toni and I would be asked to abstain from chicken-eating in the chow hall and to instead stick the bird in our pants, to be smuggled out for use in some elaborate, quasi-Tex-Mex creation later that evening. This required a plastic Baggie or a clean hair net, procured from a kitchen worker or an orderly. Slip the foodstuffs into the appropriate wrapping at the table, shove it down the front of your pants, and stroll out as nonchalantly as you could with contraband chicken riding on your hip bone.

The list of important things a prisoner has to lose is very short: good time, visiting privileges, phone access, housing assignment, work assignment, participation in programs. That's basically it. If they catch you stealing onions, a warden can take one of those things away, or can give you extra work. Other than that, the only other option is the SHU. So will a warden be willing to lock up onion thieves and chicken smugglers in Seg?

Let's put it another way: room in the SHU is a finite resource, and the warden and his staff have to use it judiciously. Fill the SHU up with chickenshit offenders, and then what are you going to do with someone who's actually done something serious?

BIRTHDAYS WERE a true oddity in prison. Many people refused to reveal theirs, whether out of paranoia or simply because they didn't want it observed by others. I was not one of these holdouts and was trying hard to be upbeat about celebrating my birthday in Danbury, telling myself things like "At least it's only one," and "At least it's not forty."

In a peculiar Camp ritual, a prisoner's pals sneak in the dark of night to decorate her cube with handmade "Happy Birthday" signs, magazine collages, and candy bars, all of which they would tape to the outside of her living quarters while she slept. These illegal decorations were tolerated by the guards for the day but then had to be taken down by the birthday girl. I hoped I would get a Dove chocolate bar.

The day before my birthday found me doing my laps after the dinner meal, when Amy materialized by the side of the track. "Pop wants you, Piper."

"Can't it wait?" This was highly irregular.

"She says it's important!"

I trotted up the steps and started toward the kitchen.

"No, she's up in the visiting room." I followed Amy up through the double doors.

"Surprise!"

I was really stunned. Card tables had been pushed together to make a long banquet, and around the table were an odd assortment of prisoners, my friends. Jae, Toni, Rosemarie, Amy, Pennsatucky, Doris, Camila, Yoga Janet, Little Janet, Mrs. Jones, Annette. Black, white, Spanish, old, young.

And of course there was Pop, beaming and gleeful. "You were really surprised, weren't you?"

"I'm shocked, Pop, not just surprised. Thank you!"

"Don't thank me. Rosemarie and Toni planned the whole thing."

So I thanked the Italian Twins, proclaiming the effectiveness of their surprise strategy and thanking everyone profusely. There were lots of Tupperware bowls filled with goodies. Rosemarie had worked "like a Hebrew slave" to produce a prison banquet. Chilaquiles, chicken enchiladas, cheesecake, banana pudding. Everybody ate and chatted, and I was presented with a big birthday card hand-drawn on a manila folder featuring a celebrating Pooh Bear winking lecherously. Jae slipped me her own handmade card, featuring leaping dolphins, the cousins of my tattoo. What she said in that card was echoed by the notes the others had written in the group card: "I never thought I would find a friend like you here."

After the party had broken up, Pop summoned me to her cube. "I got something for you." I sat down on her footstool and looked at her eagerly. What could it be? Pop wouldn't have gotten me anything from commissary—she knew I could get anything I wanted myself. Maybe it was some treat from the depths of her giant locker—SPAM, perhaps?

With great ceremony she presented me with my gift—a beautiful pair of slippers that she had commissioned from one of the skilled crocheters, a Spanish mami. They were ingeniously constructed: double soles from shower shoes were bound together and then completely covered in pink and white cotton yarn crocheted into intricate designs. I held them in my hands, so moved I couldn't speak.

"Do you like them?" Pop asked. She was smiling, a little nervously, as if maybe I wouldn't appreciate the gift.

"My god, Pop, they're so beautiful, I can't believe it. I can't even wear them to walk around in, they're so beautiful I don't want to ruin them. I love them so much." I hugged her hard, then put my new handmade slippers on.

"I wanted to get you something special. You understand I couldn't give to you in front of that whole crew? Ah, they look nice on you. They'll look nice with your pajamas. Don't let a CO catch you with them!"

That night, not long after lights out, I heard whispering and tittering immediately outside my cube. Amy was the ringleader of the decoration team, and her couple of shadowy helpmates sounded suspiciously like Doris and Pennsatucky.

In typical form she was soon cursing her accomplices under her breath. "Don't stick that picture there. What are you, stupid? Put it over here!"

I kept my eyes shut and breathed deeply, pretending to be asleep. It must have been my dreams that were making me smile.

The next morning I stepped out of my cube to survey their work. Glossy photos of models and bottles of liquor decorated my cube, along with "Happy Birthday Piper!!!" I had my Dove bar taped to the wall, plus more candy than I would ever eat. I felt great. All day I received birthday wishes. "Thirty-five and still alive!" said my boss in construction, laughing when I made a face.

In the afternoon I found a delicate little white paper box perched on my locker, hand cut into lacy designs, with a card from Little Janet.

Piper, on your birthday I'm wishing you the best of everything good—health, strength, security, peace of mind. You are an extremely beautiful person inside and out and on this day you are not forgotten. You have been such a good friend I never thought I'd find that here. Thank you crazy girl just for being you. Stay strong and don't ever feel weak, you will soon be home with the people who love & adore you. I hope you like the little box I made for you :) I made it thinking about you, of course it's not much but it's something that should make you smile and it's different. I will have you in my heart from now and always.

Happy B-Day Piper, may you have many more to come.

Love, Janet

CHAPTER 14

October Surprises

||||

The more friends I had, the more people wanted to feed me; it was like having a half-dozen Jewish mothers. I was not one to turn down a second dinner, as you could never be quite sure when the next good one would be served. But despite my high-calorie diet, I was getting pretty competent at yoga, I was lifting eighty-pound bags of cement at work, and running at least thirty miles a week, so I wasn't getting fat. Detoxed, drug- and alcohol-free, I figured the minute I hit the streets I would either go wild or become a true health nut like Yoga Janet.

I was going to lose Yoga Janet very soon. She was going to be a free woman, so I'd do yoga with her every chance I got, trying to listen carefully and follow her guidance on my postures. I had never had mixed feelings about anyone going home before, it was such a happy thing, but now the prospect of her leaving felt like a terrible personal loss. I would never have admitted this to anyone, it made me feel ashamed. But I still had more than four months to go and couldn't imagine getting by without her comforting and inspiring presence. Yoga Janet was my guide on how to do my time without abandoning myself. I learned from her example how to operate in such adverse conditions with grace and charm, with patience and kindness. She had a generosity that I could only hope to achieve someday. But she was tough too: she wasn't a sucker.

Janet's "10 percent date," the point in one's federal sentence when a prisoner is eligible to go to a halfway house, had come and gone, and she was wigging out because they had still not given her an out date. Everyone got edgy before they went home. These numbers and dates were something to cling to.

But Yoga Janet finally got to go home, or rather, to a halfway house in the Bronx. On the morning of her release, I headed up to the visiting room during the breakfast hour, where all Campers depart through the front door. For some reason, custom demanded that the town driver would pull up her white minivan to this door, where a small crowd gathered to say goodbye, and then Toni would drive the soon-to-be-free woman fifty yards down the hill. Most women just walked out the door with nothing more than a small box of personal items, letters, and photographs. Janet's friends had gathered to wave goodbye to her—Sister, Camila, Maria, Esposito, Ghada. Ghada was sobbing and carrying on—she always went bananas when anyone she liked went home. "No mami! No!" she would wail, tears streaming down her face. I still didn't have any idea how long Ghada's sentence was; long was a fair assumption.

Usually I loved saying goodbye. Someone going home was a victory for us all. I would even go up there in the morning to say goodbye to people I didn't know very well—it made me that happy. But this morning, for the first time, I understood what Ghada felt. I wasn't about to throw my arms around Yoga Janet's legs and sob, but the impulse was there. I tried to focus very hard on how happy I was for Janet, for her nice boyfriend, for anyone who was getting their freedom. Yoga Janet was wearing a pink crocheted vest that someone had made her as a going-away present (another tradition that flew in the face of the rules). She wanted to be gone so badly that it was obviously taking all of her considerable patience to bid each one of us goodbye.

When it was my turn, I threw my arms around her shoulders and hugged her hard, pressing my nose against her neck. "Thank you, Janet! Thank you so much! You helped me so much!" I couldn't say anything else, and I started to cry. And then she was gone.

Bereft, I went down to the gym in the afternoon. There were some VHS exercise tapes and a TV/VCR down there, and a couple of yoga tapes among them. In particular, there was one that Janet liked to do by herself. "Just me and Rodney," she would sigh. The tape was by a popular yogi named Rodney Yee—"my prison fantasy object!" she would laugh. I looked at the cover, at a guy with a long ponytail in the chair pose. He looked familiar. I popped it in.

A beautiful Hawaiian beach appeared on the screen. The waves of the Pacific were lapping on the shore, and there was Rodney, a smoothly handsome Chinese guy in a black banana hammock. I had a flash of recognition. This was the yoga guy who had been on the in-hotel channel in Chicago where Larry and I and my family had stayed when I was sentenced to this human warehouse! I took this as a sign, a powerful sign . . . of something. I thought it meant that I'd better stick with the yoga, and if Rodney was good enough for Janet, he was good enough for me. I fetched a yoga mat and got into Downward Dog.

ON OCTOBER 8 Martha Stewart was finally headed up the river. A week before, it had been announced in the press that she'd been designated to Alderson, the large federal prison camp in the mountains of West Virginia. Built in 1927 under the auspices of Eleanor Roosevelt, it was the first federal women's prison, intended as a reformatory. Alderson was an entirely minimum-security facility for about a thousand prisoners and according to the BOP grapevine by far the best facility for women. The ladies of Danbury were deflated by this news. Everyone had been hoping that against all odds she'd be sent to live with us, either because they believed that her presence would somehow raise all our boats or just for the entertainment value.

As we headed to work that day, news helicopters hovered over the federal plantation. We gave them the finger. No one appreciates being treated like an animal in the zoo. The staff was irritable too. Allegedly the perimeter guards had caught a photographer trying to infiltrate the grounds, crawling commando style on his belly. This was amusing, but overall the collective mood was dejected—we were missing out.

Homegrown drama quickly erupted to distract Campers from their disappointment. Finn, who cared so little about enforcing most of the prison rules, had been waging a somewhat covert war against Officer Scott and Cormorant.

As soon as I arrived in the Camp, I had noticed something odd that happened when Scott was on duty. A skinny white chick would materialize at the door of the CO's office, where she would remain, talking and laughing with him for hours on end. She had a job as an orderly and would spend several hours cleaning the tiny office whenever he was on duty. "What gives?" I asked Annette.

"Oh, that's Cormorant. She's got a thing with Scott."

"A thing? What exactly do you mean, Annette?"

"I don't know for sure. No one's ever seen them do anything but talk. But she's in that doorway every time he's on duty."

Other prisoners complained about this curious situation, out of spite, jealousy, or genuine discomfort. Even if the relationship was platonic, it was still totally against prison rules. But Scott was widely understood to be Butorsky's buddy, so nothing had ever been done about the odd, perhaps unrequited affair taking place in plain view. No one had ever caught them doing anything but talking, and everyone watched them like hawks. Amy was Cormorant's bunkie, and she said they passed love notes, but Cormorant was never missing from her bed.

Whatever the weird relationship entailed, Finn didn't like it, so he did the only thing he could within the reality of how prisons work: he went after Cormorant. Rumor had it that he had warned her that if he caught her hanging around Officer Scott, he was going to give her a shot (an incident report) for disobeying a direct order. All summer long they had been playing a cat-and-mouse game; when Finn was off duty and Scott was on, Cormorant was still a permanent fixture at the CO's office. Finn would probably never confront another prison staffer, and when he wasn't present, it was business as usual.

Until now. Quite suddenly Cormorant had been taken to the SHU, at Finn's behest.

This was shocking to all. Butorsky had retired in the spring, and it was rumored that Scott and Finn couldn't stand each other. Cormorant now seemed to be a pawn in a disturbing power play, and as soon as word spread throughout the Camp that she was gone, everyone wondered what Scott would do.

He quit. This was far more shocking. No one ever quit the BOP. They were all doing twenty years until their pensions kicked in, although some staffers daydreamed loudly of transferring to other federal agencies, like Forestry. No one quite knew how to take the dramatic Officer Scott development, but when we learned that Cormorant would not be coming back from the SHU, the prisoners who had been around for a long time were not surprised. The BOP had changed her security level, and she'd be down in the high-security FCI for the rest of her sentence.

Pop said she had seen much worse. "Down on the compound I had a friend, very pretty girl, she was with an officer. So one night he's on duty, he comes to get her, he takes her in the staff bathroom, he's doing her. Something happens, he's gotta rush out, he locks her in the bathroom. She's in there, and another officer walks in, so she starts to scream."

They kept her in the SHU for months during the internal investigation. They shot her full of psych drugs—she blew up like a balloon. When they finally let her out, she was a zombie. "It took a long time for her to get back to herself," Pop said. "They do not play here."

THE RIGHTS of a prisoner are so few, so unprotected, and so unenforced that a small minority of prisoners have an urgent need to fight for them at every opportunity. Or they see a way to make some commissary as a jailhouse lawyer. One way or the other. There were only a couple self-appointed legal experts in the Camp. But one was a totally untrustworthy wacko, and the other just wasn't that bright, and they both charged for their services. When other prisoners approached me for help writing legal documents, it made me uneasy.

I flat-out refused to help anyone with anything but a letter. I wasn't interested in learning how to draft a motion or a writ of habeas corpus or other common jailhouse documents. And I wasn't going to charge for my help. Very often the people who were seeking some remedy around their sentences were serving the most time, and to me their prospects seemed dismal without a real lawyer. Plus, the stories behind these efforts were often heartbreakingly awful—full of abuse and violence and personal failure.

When Pennsatucky came to me to ask for help writing a letter to her judge, I was relieved. She had a relatively short sentence of a couple of years but was trying to get an earlier release based on assistance she'd given to the prosecutor. Pennsatucky, like most of the Eminemlettes, always seemed to be looking for a fight. But she was like a lost girl. She talked about her baby's daddy and her boyfriend but not her family. She had shown me a picture of her sister, but I'd never heard a word about parents. Pennsatucky's boyfriend visited a couple of times, and her child's father brought the toddler to see her twice. I wondered what awaited her in the outside world. Pennsatucky drove me crazier than Amy, but I worried about her more.

She was one of the only people I knew who'd gotten anything positive out of her prison stay: new teeth. When she first showed up from county jail, her front teeth bore the hallmark of crack addiction—they were brown and damaged, and she rarely smiled. But recently, after several sessions with the cheerful little dentist (the only prison medic I liked and thought was competent) and Linda Vega, prisoner hygienist par excellence, she had undergone an amazing transformation. Usually they pulled teeth, but not this time. With sparkling white choppers, Pennsatucky was a very pretty girl, and her Jessica Simpson imitation was even better now that she would plaster a giant fake smile on while she was doing it.

Pennsatucky and I met in the converted closet that served as the

Camp law library, where there was an old beat-up typewriter. "Tell me again what you think this letter needs to say, Pennsatucky?" I asked. She explained the facts of her cooperation, and then said, "And throw some other stuff in there, about how I've learned my lesson and shit. You know what to say, Piper!"

So I wrote about the cooperation, and then I wrote about how she had used the two years she had been incarcerated to think seriously about the consequences of her actions, and how much she regretted them; I wrote about her love for her daughter and what her hopes and dreams were for being a better mother, a good mother; I wrote about how hard she had been working to be a better person; and I wrote about how cocaine had taken away all the things that were most important to her, had hurt her health, her judgment, her most important relationships, and wiped out years of her youth; I wrote about how she was ready to change her life.

When I handed Pennsatucky the letter, she read it right there. She looked at me, with big wet brown eyes. All she said was: "How did you know all this?"

I stood on line for twenty-five minutes to call Larry, just to hear his voice. He almost always picked up.

"Hey babe, I'm so glad you called. I miss you. Listen, my parents want to come see you this Friday."

"That's fantastic!" His parents, Carol and Lou, had come up to see me once before, but they had gotten stuck behind a highway accident for hours, and had arrived fifteen minutes before visiting hours were over, with Larry overheated and them flustered.

"Yeah, they're going to do some foliage stuff too, so I actually told them to go ahead and book the inn where they want to stay. I can't come then—I've got a big meeting."

Panic. "What? What do you mean? You're not going to come with them?"

"I can't, baby. It doesn't matter—it's you they want to see."

In no time at all, the infuriating click on the line was telling me my fifteen minutes were up and the prison system was going to end the call.

I went to see the Italian Twins. "My future in-laws are coming to see me . . . without Larry!"

This cracked them up. "They're going to make you an offer you can't refuse!"

Pop didn't think it was funny. "You should feel lucky they want to see you. They're good people. What's wrong with you girls?"

I loved visits with my family. My mother, my father—each provided a calm, loving, reassuring presence at the folding card tables that reinforced the fact that this would all be over eventually and I would be able to resume my life. My kid brother, the artist, showed up for his first visit in an Italian suit he'd bought in a thrift store. "I didn't know what to wear to prison!" he said. When my aunt brought my three young cousins to see me, little Elizabeth wrapped her arms around my neck and her skinny little legs around my waist, and a lump rose in my throat, and I almost lost it as I hugged her back. They were all blood relatives. They had to love me, right?

I had always gotten along well with Larry's parents. But I was still really nervous about a three-hour prison visit. So nervous that I let someone talk me into a haircut in the prison salon, which looked sort of choppy and uneven. It's a miracle I didn't end up with bangs, that week's jailhouse beauty trend.

On Friday I made myself as presentable as humanly possible, short of setting my hair in rollers. And then there they were, looking mildly nervous themselves. Once we had settled in at our card table, I was relieved to have them there. Carol had millions of questions, and Lou needed a tour of the vending machines. I think he was trying to gauge the likelihood of his own survival if he were standing in my shoes, and for Lou that means food. If that was true, his prospects were dim, as we peered at the anemic-looking chicken wings in the old-fashioned automat-style vending machine. The time flew by, and we didn't even miss Larry. Carol and Lou were cheery, and so normal, it felt almost like we were chatting in their kitchen in New Jersey. I was grateful that they had taken the time to see me, and at the end of the visit I waved until they disappeared from sight.

That night I thought about my own mother. I worried about Mom. She was supportive, positive, dedicated, but the stress of my imprisonment must have been terrible for her, and I knew that she worried about me all the time. Her forthrightness in the face of the disaster into which I had dragged my family had been impressive— she had informed her coworkers and her friends about my situation. I knew intellectually that she had a support system out there, but a great deal of the weight of helping me get through prison was clearly falling on her shoulders. How could she look so happy to see me every week? I searched her face at our next visit and saw only that maternal classic: unconditional love.

Afterward Pop asked me, "How was your visit with your mom?"

I told her I was worried about the strain my mess was causing.

Pop listened, and then asked me, "So your mother—is she like you?"

"What do you mean, Pop?"

"I mean is she outgoing, is she funny, does she have friends?"

"Well, sure. I mean, she's the reason I am the way I am."

"Sweetie, if you two are the same, then she's going to be okay."

As soon as Martha Stewart was dispatched to West Virginia, the Danbury Camp was suddenly "open" and a rush of new inmates arrived to fill all the empty beds. Any influx of new prisoners means problems, as new personalities are injected into the mix, and scarcity places more demand on both staff and inmates. It meant longer chow lines, longer laundry lines, more noise, more intrigue, and more chaos.

"Say what you will about Butorsky, bunkie, at least he was all about the rules," said Natalie. "Finn, he ain't about nothing." Over the summer daily discipline in the Camp had been largely nonexistent, and the low population had counteracted this in a pleasant "Go about your business and don't bother anyone" vibe. But now, with the place suddenly full of new "wackos" and lax oversight plus the ongoing contraband cigarette drama, the Camp was off the chain.

The cigarette situation was particularly irritating. Far more people were trying to get contraband from the outside now, with occasionally comic results. There were only a handful of ways to get outside contraband. A visitor could bring it in, or rumor had it, the warehouse was a source. Or someone from the outside could drop it on the edge of the prison property where there was a public road; the recipient had to either work for the grounds department or have an accomplice in grounds who would grab the package. Contraband included things like cigarettes, drugs, cell phones, and lingerie.

I was surprised to hear one day that Bianca and Lump-Lump had been taken to the SHU. Bianca was a pretty young girl with blue-black hair and wide eyes—she looked like a voluptuous World War II pinup. She was not the sharpest tool in the shed (it was a standing joke around the Camp), but she was a good girl, her family and boyfriend came to see her every week, and everyone liked her. Lump-Lump, her friend, was pretty much as you would expect given her nickname, in both appearance and personality. They both worked for the safety department in CMS, which was a do-nothing job.

"You're not going to believe this story," Toni told Rosemarie and me. The town driver usually had the inside scoop early on. "These two dumb bunnies had somebody outside drop a package for them. They go pick it up during CMS work hours, and then they've got the stuff with them, and they're walking by the FCI lobby, and they remember that they're supposed to do the monthly safety inspection in there. So they go into the lobby with their contraband, probably looking like the guilty idiots they are, and Officer Reilly for some reason decides to pat them down. So of course, she finds the contraband. Get this—cartons of cigarettes and vibrators! They were smuggling dildos!"

This was generally taken as hilarious, but it would be the last we saw of Bianca and Lump-Lump. Smuggling contraband was a very serious shot, a breach of security, and whenever they got out of the SHU, they would stay down on the Compound.

October 19, 2004

Piper Kerman
Reg. No. 11187–424
Federal Prison Camp
Danbury, Connecticut 06811

Dear Ms. Kerman,

I would like to thank you for your assistance in preparing the Warden's house for my arrival. Your eagerness to please and enthusiasm for the project made my arrival to Danbury a pleasant one. Your good workmanship was evident and is to be commended.

    Your efforts are greatly appreciated.

Sincerely,

W. S. Willingham
Warden

"Huh! Maybe this one's going to be better," said Pop. "The best ones are the ones who are for the inmates. The last one, Deboo, she was just a politician. Smile in your face, acts like she feels your pain, but she's not gonna do shit for you. When they come from a men's institution, like Willingham, they're usually better. Less bullshit. We'll see."

I was sitting on a footstool in her cube where I had brought the typewritten note from the new warden—I'd just received it at mail call. Pop had been through a lot of wardens, and I knew she'd be able to tell me if this was as surprising as I found it.

"Piper?"

I knew that tone of voice. Pop was never at mail call because she was still in the kitchen, cleaning up after dinner. She worked harder than any other person in the Camp. She was up and in the kitchen at five most mornings, and she usually worked serving all three meals, in addition to the cooking. Her fifty-year-old body was riddled with aches and pains, and the institution periodically sent her out to Danbury Hospital for epidural shots in her back. I nagged her to take days off—she wasn't required to work so many hours.

"Yes, Pop?" I smiled from the footstool. I was going to make her ask.

"How about just a little foot rub?" I don't remember exactly how Pop had first gotten me to give her a foot massage. But it had become a regular ritual several times a week. She would sit on her bed post-shower in her sweats, and I would sit facing her with a clean towel across my lap. I would get a handful of commissary lotion and firmly grasp a foot. I gave a very firm foot massage, and she would occasionally yelp when I dug a knuckle in hard. My services were a source of great amusement in A Dorm—women would come by and chit-chat with Pop while I worked on her feet, occasionally asking, "How do I get one of those?"

I was, of course, out of bounds and also breaking the prohibition against inmates touching each other. But the regular Camp officers extended special considerations to Pop. One evening while I was rubbing her feet, a substitute officer, up from the FCI, stopped dead in his tracks at the doorway of Pop's cube. He was a shaggy, craggy-looking white guy, with a mustache.

"Popovich?" It sounded more like a question than a warning.

I ducked my head, making no eye contact.

"Mr. Ryan! It's this foot of mine, I hurt it. She's just helping get the cramp out. Happens all the time since I'm on my feet all day. Officer Maple allows it. Is it okay?" Pop was all charm when it came to interacting with COs.

"Whatever. I'm gonna keep walking." He thudded away.

I looked at Pop. "Maybe I better beat it?"

"Him? I known him for years, from down the compound. He's all right. Don't stop!"

. . .

THE AMERICAN League Championship was so hotly contentious that year, I could barely stand to watch the games. The tension of being a Red Sox fan as they battled back from 0–3 made my stomach hurt, and my surroundings didn't make it any easier. The running joke in the Camp was that half the population of the Bronx was residing in Danbury, and of course they were all ferocious Yankees fans. But the Red Sox had plenty of partisans too; a significant percentage of the white women were from Massachusetts, Maine, New Hampshire, and the always-suspect border state of Connecticut. Daily life was usually racially peaceful in the Camp, but the very obvious racial divide between Yankees and Sox fans made me nervous. I remembered the riot at UMass in 1986 after the Mets defeated the Sox in the World Series, when black Mets fans were horribly beaten.

I'm not sure what kind of a brawl we could have come up with, though. The most hard-core Sox fans in the joint were a clique of middle-aged, middle-class white ladies, whose ringleader was nicknamed Bunny. For some reason most of them worked for the grounds department in CMS. During all of pennant fever, they went about their work cutting lawns and raking leaves serenading each other:

> John-ny Damon, how I love him.
> He's got something I can't resist,
> but he doesn't even know that I exist.

> John-ny Damon, how I want him.
> How I tingle when he passes by.
> Every time he says "Hello" my heart begins to fly.

> Other fellas call me up for a date,
> but I just sit and wait, I'd rather concentrate . . .

> . . . on John-ny Damon.

Carmen DeLeon, the biggest Yankees fan of all, straight from Hunts Point, gave me the hairy eyeball. "Those are *your* peoples," she pointed out acidly.

I glared, but I was too nervous even to talk smack, not because I was scared of Carmen but because I was worried about jinxing the Sox. The year before, Larry and I had gathered a roughneck band of Sox fans in our apartment in the East Village for game seven, and based on our lead in the sixth inning, we felt confident enough to venture out to a local bar, in the hopes that we could celebrate our victory loudly and publicly there, in the face of the vile, overbearing Yanks fans who had made our lives miserable for . . . our entire lives. Instead, we sat wretchedly nursing overpriced beers through extra innings as Martinez inexplicably stayed in and Red Sox Nation's hopes and dreams collapsed with the team.

"I tell you what," said Carmen, puffing out her already-considerable chest like a peacock. "If the Red Sox are in the World Series, I'm gonna root for them. That's a promise." *When pigs fly,* I thought gloomily.

When the Yankees went down in flames after a seven-game series, and the Red Sox were facing the St. Louis Cardinals in the World Series, the crowds in the TV room were actually smaller. But Carmen DeLeon was there front and center, grinning and rooting for the Sox. And the series was surreally easy, a four-game sweep. I couldn't trust it—after each victory I felt my anxiety mount. At the end of game four, after the final out by the Cards, I started to shake uncontrollably. Rosemarie, also a lifelong Sox fan, grabbed my knee. "Are you okay?"

Carmen looked at me in amazement. "Piper's crying!"

I was amazed too. I do love the Red Sox, but my reaction shocked even me.

I calmed down enough to watch the postgame celebration dry-eyed, but alone in the bathroom between B and C Dorms, I started to cry again. I went outside to stare at the half-cloaked moon and cry alone, out loud. Huge, shuddering sobs. I wasn't crying because I wished I was home celebrating, but I was completely taken aback at the level of my own emotion. I had joked that I had to do hard time in order to break the Curse so the Red Sox could win, and now I felt that there was some strange truth to that. The world I knew had changed right there in the bottom of the ninth.

CHAPTER 15

Some Kinda Way

||||

The garage girls liked to hang out in the visiting room together in the evenings during the week. I was chilling with them, surrounded by prisoners who were crocheting industriously, watching *Fear Factor* with their headsets on, or just talking. Pom-Pom was doing some sort of art project with colored pencils, probably a birthday card. Suddenly a woman rushed into the room, wild-eyed.

"The CO is destroying A Dorm!"

We followed her out into the hall, where a crowd was gathering. The new CO on duty that night was a pleasant, seemingly mild-mannered, and very big young guy. He, like a huge number of the prison guards, was former military. These folks would finish their commitment to the armed services and have several years in on a federal pension, so they'd end up working for the BOP. Sometimes they'd tell us about their military careers. Mr. Maple had been a medic in Afghanistan.

The CO on duty that night was fresh from Iraq and had just started work at the prison. It was rumored that he had been stationed in Fallujah, where the fighting had been brutal all spring. That night someone from A Dorm had been giving him trouble—some sort of backtalk. And something snapped. Before anyone really knew what was going on, he was down in A Dorm pulling the contents of the cubicles apart, yanking things off the walls, and ripping bedding off mattresses and turning them over.

We were scared—two hundred prisoners alone with one guard having a psychotic break. Someone went outside and flagged down the perimeter truck, which got help from down the hill. The young soldier left the building, and A Dorm residents started to put their cubes back together. Everyone was rattled. The next day one of the lieutenants came up from the FCI and apologized to A Dorm, which was unprecedented. We did not see the young CO again.

NEWLY ZEN thanks to Yoga Janet, well fed by Pop, and now proficient in concrete-mixing as well as rudimentary electrical work, I felt as if I were making the most of this prison thing. If this was the worst the feds were going to throw at me, no problem. Then when I called my father on the prison pay phone to talk about the Red Sox, he told me, "Piper, your grandmother is not doing well."

Southern-proper and birdlike but possessing a stern, formidable personality, my grandmother had been a constant figure in my life. A child of West Virginia who grew up in the Depression with two brothers and then raised four sons, she had little idea what to do with a young girl, her eldest grandchild, and I was scared of her. I remained in awe of her, although as I got older, we developed an easier rapport. She spoke frankly to me in private about sex, feminism, and power. She and my grandfather were dumbstruck and horrified by my criminal misadventures, and yet they never let me forget that they loved me and worried about me. The one thing that I feared most about prison was that one of them would die while I was there.

I pleaded with my father on the pay phone—she would be fine, she would get better, she would be there when I came home. He didn't argue back, just said, "Write her." I was on a regular schedule of writing short, cheery updates to my grandparents, reassuring them that I was fine and couldn't wait to see them when I got home. Now I sat down to write a different kind of letter, one that tried to convey how much she meant to me, how much she had taught me, how I wanted to emulate her rigor and rectitude, how much I loved her and missed her. I couldn't believe that I had screwed up so badly, to be in this place when she needed me, when she was sick and maybe dying.

Immediately after posting the letter, I asked the Camp secretary for a furlough request form. "Were you raised by your grandma?" she asked brusquely. When I said no, she told me there was no point in giving me the form—I would never be granted a furlough for a grandparent. I sharply said that I was furlough-eligible and would make the request anyway. "Suit yourself," she snapped.

Pop gently counseled me that in fact I had no chance of getting furloughed, even for a funeral, unless it was my parent, my child, or maybe my sibling, and that she did not want me to get my hopes up. "I know it's not right, honey. That's just how they do things."

I had seen many other prisoners suffer through the illnesses of their loved ones and had felt helpless watching them when the worst would come—when they had to confront not only their grief, but also the personal failure of being in prison and not with their families.

I was not festive that Halloween. I was feeling some kinda way, like I had been walloped in the gut with a sledgehammer. But there was no escape from the festivities of the two hundred-plus women I was living with cheek by jowl every day. The women love their holidays.

Halloween in prison was odd, I had been told. Could it be odder than anything else here? How would one create a costume with such limited and colorless resources as we had at our disposal? Earlier that day I had seen some idiotic cat masks made from manila folders. Besides, I was in no mood for anything, let alone handing out candy.

The faithful could be heard from halfway across B Dorm. "Trick or treat!"

Trying to focus on my book, I stayed in my bunk. Then Delicious spoke to me from the doorway of my cube. "Trick or treat, P-I Piper!"

I had to smile. Delicious was dressed as a pimp, clad in an all-white outfit she had put together somehow using her kitchen uniform and inside-out sweatpants. She had a "cigar" and a cluster of hoes around her. This included a bunch of the Eminemlettes but also Fran, the motormouthed Italian grandma, at seventy-eight the oldest woman in the Camp. The hoes had tried to sexy themselves up, hiking sweatshorts high and T-shirt necklines low, but mostly relying on makeup that was garish even by prison standards. Fran had a long "cigarette holder" and headband she had made from paper, and heavy rouge; she looked like an ancient flapper.

"C'mon, Piper, trick or treat?" Delicious demanded. "Smell my feet. Gimme something sweet to eat, y'know?"

I never kept candy in my cube. I tried to muster up a big smile to let them know I appreciated their creativity.

"I guess Trick, Delicious. I am flat out of sweetness."

I BEGAN to stalk the prison officials who might have some say in whether I ever saw my grandmother again. One was the always-absent temporary unit manager, Bubba, who could tell you to go fuck yourself in the most pleasant possible way. My counselor Finn, another BOP lifer, was an indifferent jokester who was quick with an insult and never did his paperwork, but he liked me because I was blond and blue-eyed and had "a tight ass," as he would mutter under his breath. He very kindly offered to let me call my grandmother from his office—the hospice number was not on the approved list in the prison phone system, so I could not call from the pay phones. She sounded exhausted and astonished to hear my voice on the line. When I hung up the phone, I dissolved in sobs. I rushed out of his office and down to the track.

I returned to my old, lonely ways. I shut myself off and kept quiet, determined to gut out this worst-case scenario alone. Anything else would be an admission to the world that the feds had succeeded in bringing me down, lower than my knees, flat on my face; that I couldn't survive my imprisonment unscathed. How could I admit that the All-American Girl's force field of stoicism and self-reliance and do-unto-others-and-keep-smiling wasn't working, wasn't keeping pain and shame and powerlessness away?

From a young age I had learned to get over—to cover my tracks emotionally, to hide or ignore my problems in the belief that they were mine alone to solve. So when exhilarating transgressions required getting over on authority figures, I knew how to do it. I was a great bluffer. And when common, everyday survival in prison required getting over, I could do that too. This is what was approvingly described by my fellow prisoners as "street-smarts," as in "You wouldn't think it to look at her, but Piper's got street-smarts."

It wasn't just my peers who applauded this trait; the prison system mandates stoicism and tries to crush any genuine emotion, but everyone, jailers and prisoners alike, is still crossing boundaries left and right. My deep contempt for Levy was not only because I didn't like the way she put herself above others but also because she was the opposite of stoic. Nobody likes a crybaby.

In the following weeks I walked around in a state of tightly leashed fury and despair. I kept to myself, civil within the requirements of prison society but unwilling to chat or joke. Fellow prisoners, offended, sniffed that I must be feeling "some kind of way," as I was not my usual optimistic self. Then someone in the know would whisper to them that my grandmother was very ill. Suddenly I was the recipient of kind words, sympathetic advice, and prayer cards. And all those things did indeed remind me that I was not alone, that every woman living in that building was in the same rotten boat.

I thought about one woman whose face had been a mask of pain upon the news of her mother's death—she had rocked silently, her face frozen in a howl as her friend wrapped her arms around her shoulders and rocked with her (in violation of the physical contact rules). I also remembered Roland, an upright Caribbean woman whose staunchness I admired. Roland would tell you straight up that prison saved her life. "I would be dead in a ditch for sure, the way I was living," she told me. She had done her bid with grace. She worked hard, didn't mess with other people, had a smile for the occasion, and asked no one for anything. A short while before Roland was to go home, her brother died. She was stoic and quiet and received permission for a half-day furlough to attend his funeral.

But when her family members arrived at Danbury to pick her up, they drove a different car than the one registered in her paperwork. And that was it—she was sent back up to the Camp from R&D, and her family was sent away. A few weeks later she was released. The heartlessness, the pettiness, the foolishness of the situation was the talk of the Camp. Contrarians pointed out that you had to assume that the feds would thwart you brutally given the chance, and that such mistakes were avoidable, but everyone's hearts ached collectively for her.

Pop sat me down for a talk. "Look, honey, you are eating yourself up. I am gonna tell you, when my father was dying, I was out of my head, so I know how you feel. But listen to me: these bastards—as far as they're concerned, you got nothing coming to you. You think if you were getting a furlough, you wouldn't know it by now? Sweetie, you need to call your grandma on the phone, you need to write her, you need to think about her a lot. But you cannot let these fuckers make you bitter. You're not a bitter person, Piper; it's not your nature. Don't let them do it to you. Come here, honey." Pop hugged me hard, squashing me to her big, scented "jewels."

I knew she was right. I felt a tiny bit better.

Still, I haunted the administrative offices, which were almost always empty. (God knows what those people were doing.) I wrote letters home and sat in my bunk with my photo album, staring at my grandmother's smile and her hairdo, the same Babe Paley set she had worn since the 1950s. The Eminemlettes would come by to see me in my cube, then wander away, frustrated that they couldn't cheer me up. As the air got colder and Veterans Day passed, I checked in with my father every other day by pay phone (she was holding stable, would I be able to get the furlough?), nervous that I would run out of phone minutes. I thought about praying, something I was certainly not practiced at doing. Fortunately several people offered to do it for me, including Sister. That had to count extra, right?

I wasn't inclined to formal prayer, but I was less skeptical about faith than I had been when I entered prison. On a late September day I had been sitting behind A Dorm at the picnic table with Gisela. She was my coworker in the construction shop, as well as the bus driver, and was one of the sweetest, kindest, gentlest women I've ever met, delicate and ladylike, and yet no simp, no Pollyanna. I can't remember ever hearing Gisela raise her voice, and given that she was the CMS bus driver, this was pretty amazing. Gisela was also graceful and lovely, her face a perfect, pale-brown oval, big brown eyes, long wavy hair. She was from the Dominican Republic but had lived in Massachusetts for years—not in neighborhoods I knew well, but we shared some common ground. Her two kids were waiting for her there, in the care of an elderly woman named Noni Delgado, whom Gisela called her angel.

On this particular day Gisela and I were talking about her upcoming release. Of course she was nervous. She was nervous about finding work. She was nervous about what her husband would do when she got out—he was in the DR, and they had what sounded like a tempestuous and tortured relationship. Gisela said she didn't want to reunite with him, but he sounded like a person who was difficult to resist, and of course they had children together. I knew that Gisela had no money, and many responsibilities, and that she faced a massive number of unknown but looming challenges. But while she was quick to acknowledge that she was nervous, she also exhibited the peacefulness at her core, the loving calmness that made her the kind of person to whom everyone was drawn. And then she started to talk about God.

Normally, professions of faith or discussions of religion in prison would win eye-rolling and a quick exit from me. I believed that everyone should be able to practice according to their own preferences and beliefs, but an awful lot of pilgrims in prison seem to be making it up as they go along, in silly ways—wearing a contraband napkin on their head one month when they're practicing Islam, and then appearing in the Buddhist meditation circle the next—after realizing that they could duck out of work for this new brand of religious observance. Couple that with a pretty reliable volume of ignorance about the rest of the world's faiths ("Well, the Jews did kill

Jesus . . . everyone knows that!"), and I generally didn't want any part of it.

Gisela wasn't talking about religion or church or even Jesus, though. She was talking about God. And when she talked about God, she looked so happy. She spoke so freely, and so easily, about how God had helped her through all the struggles in her life, and especially the years she had spent in prison; how she knew that God loved her completely, and watched over her, and gave her the peace of mind, the good sense, the clarity to be a good person, even in a bad place. She said that she trusted God to help her, by sending her angels like Noni Delgado to care for her children, and good friends when she most needed them to help her survive prison. She glowed while she talked calmly and quietly about God and how much His love had given her.

I was startled to feel so moved by what Gisela had to say, and I listened quietly. Some of her beliefs weren't stated all that differently from the scuttlebutt I had heard from the holy rollers in the Camp, but their protestations of faith were imbued with the need for redemption—*Jesus loves me even if I'm a bad person, even if no one else does.* Gisela already knew about love. She was talking about an unshakable faith that gave her real strength and that she had carried for a long time. She wasn't talking about repentance or forgiveness, only love. What Gisela was describing to me was an exquisitely intimate and happy love. I thought it was the most compelling description of faith that I had ever heard. I wasn't about to grab a Bible; nor was our conversation about me or my choices in any way. It was food for thought.

I had long recognized that faith helped people understand their relationship to their community. In the best cases it helped women in Danbury focus on what they had to give instead of what they wanted. And that was a good thing. So for all my scoffing at "holy rollers," was it such a bad thing if faith helped someone understand what others needed from them, rather than just thinking about themselves?

In prison, for the first time, I understood that faith could help people see beyond themselves, not into the abyss but into the street, into the mix, to offer what was best about themselves to others. I grew to this understanding by way of knowing people like Sister, Yoga Janet, Gisela, and even my holy-roller pedicurist Rose.

Rose, chatting in the midst of a pedicure one day, told me what she had learned from her faith; I thought later that hers were the most powerful words a person could utter: "I've got a lot to give."

I HAD added frustrations, and my methods for dealing with them met with obstacles at every turn. The track was now closed after the four P.M. count. After work I would race back to the Camp, change into my sneakers, and run furiously until count time, cutting it closer and closer and stressing out most of B Dorm. I would look up from the far side of the track and see Jae frantically beckoning me, and I would run at top speed up the rickety steps and through C Dorm to my cube, other prisoners urging me to hurry.

"Pipes, you going to fuck up the four o'clock count, get your ass sent to the SHU!" Delicious admonished from the other side of B Dorm.

"Bunkie, you cutting it close." Natalie would shake her head.

Best case, I was only getting in about six miles on a weekday. I tried to make it up on the weekend, running ten miles around the quarter-mile track on Saturdays and Sundays, but that didn't help with my daily tides of stress and anxiety about things and people I could not control.

So I started doing more yoga. Initial interest in keeping the yoga class going had surged a bit, but a number of the new adherents (Amy, cursing and squealing with every pose) didn't last long. Ghada still appeared occasionally to stretch beside me, crooning at me affectionately, but I didn't have any decent Spanish or Janet's soothing yogi presence, and she never dozed off with me. Camila would come and do a tape with me sometimes on the weekend, and she was still radiant good company (and could arch into a backbend next to mine), but she was preoccupied with her impending departure to the drug program down the hill. It was mainly me and Rodney Yee.

I got into the habit of rising at five, checking carefully to be sure that the morning count was complete—boots thudding, flashlight beams bobbing, keys sometimes jangling if the CO didn't care enough to hold them still. I'd stand silently in my cube, hoping to startle them and make them jump. Natalie would already be gone to the kitchen to bake. I would revel in the complete darkness of B Dorm, listening to forty-eight other women breathe in a polyrhythm of deep sleep as I prepared the right measures of instant coffee, sugar, and Cremora. It was warm and peaceful in B Dorm, as I slithered through the warren of cubicles to the hot water dispenser. Occasionally I would see someone else awake—we would nod or sometimes murmur to each other. Steaming mug in hand, I would slip out of the building into the bracing cold and down to the gym to commune with the VCR and Rodney. In the perfect privacy of the empty gym, my body would slowly awaken and warm on the cold rubber floor, my head and heart stayed calmer longer, and the value of Yoga Janet's teaching became clearer every day. I missed her terribly, and yet she had given me a gift that allowed me to cope without her.

In the last ten months I had found ways to carve out some sense of control of my world, seize some personal power within a setting in which I was supposed to have none. But my grandmother's illness sent that sense spinning away, showed me how much my choices eleven years earlier and their consequences had put me in the power of a system that would be relentless in its efforts to take things away. I could choose to assign very little value to the physical comforts I had lost; I could find the juice and flair in who and what was precious in my current surroundings. But nothing here could substitute for my grandmother, and I was losing her.

On a gray afternoon I was whipping around the track, pushing myself to keep at a seven-minute-mile speed. Mrs. Jones had given me a digital wristwatch that she never used, and I paced myself relentlessly with it. The weather was crap, it was going to rain. Jae appeared at the top of the hill, gesturing to me urgently. I looked at the watch and saw that it was only 3:25, thirty-five minutes until count time. What did she want?

I pulled off my earphones, annoyed. "What's up?" I shouted into the wind.

"Piper! Little Janet wants you!" She beckoned me up again.

If Little Janet wanted something she should bring her young ass down here to the track to talk to me . . . unless something was wrong?

Sudden panic pushed me up the stairs to Jae. "What is it? Where is she?"

"She's in her cube. Come on." I strode along with Jae, tense. She didn't look like disaster had struck, but Jae was so used to disaster that you couldn't always tell. We got to A Dorm quickly.

Little Janet was sitting on her bunkie's bottom bed, and she looked okay. I looked around her cube. It was bare, and there was a box on the floor.

"Are you okay?" I wanted to shake her for scaring me.

"Piper? I'm going home."

I blinked. What the hell was she talking about?

"What are you talking about, baby?" I sat down on the bed, pushing a pile of paper aside. I thought she might have lost her rabbit-ass mind.

She grabbed my hand. "I got immediate release."

"What?" I looked at her, afraid to believe what she was saying. Nobody got immediate release. Prisoners put in motions that took months and months to wend their way through the legal system, and they always lost. Immediate release was like the Easter Bunny.

"Are you sure, sweetie?" I grabbed both of her hands. "Did they confirm, did they say for you to pack out?" I looked at her pile of stuff, and I looked at Jae, who was smiling a huge smile.

Toni appeared in the doorway of the now-crowded cube with her coat on, jingling the town driver keys in her hand. "Are you ready, Janet? Piper, can you believe this! It's incredible!"

I whooped, not a scream but more like a war whoop. And then I crushed Little Janet in a bear hug, squeezing her as hard as I could and laughing. She was laughing too, in joy and disbelief. When I finally let her go, I put both hands on my head to try to steady myself. I was staggered, as if it were me who was leaving. I stood up and sat down.

"Tell me everything! But hurry, you have to go! Toni, are they waiting for her in R&D?"

"Yeah, but we gotta get her down there before the count, or she's gonna be stuck behind it."

Little Janet hadn't told a soul that she had a motion entered in court—typical jailhouse circumspection. But she had won, and her sixty-month sentence had been cut to the time served, two years. Her parents were on their way to pick up their little girl and bring her home to New York. We hustled her out of her cube and out the back door to where the white van was parked next to the chow hall. It was almost dusk. There were just a few of us, everything was happening so fast no one else knew what was up.

"Janet, I am so happy for you."

She hugged me, hugged Jae, and kissed her bunkie Miss Mimi, a tiny old Spanish mami. Then she climbed in next to Toni, and the van pulled away, up the incline to the main road that circled the FCI. We waved wildly. Little Janet was turned around in her seat, calling good-bye to us out the window, until the van crested the hill and turned right, out of sight.

I kept watching for what seemed like many minutes after she had disappeared. Then I looked at Jae—Jae who had seven more years to do of a ten-year sentence. She put her arm around my shoulders and squeezed. "You okay?" she said. I nodded. I was more than okay. Then we turned back and helped Miss Mimi into the Camp.

I TRIED to share the indescribable miracle of Little Janet's freedom with Larry, and he tried to cheer me up with news of our new home in Brooklyn. Larry had been house-hunting while I was away, and many people on the outside found it astonishing that I was comfortable with him picking out a new home for me sight unseen. But not only was I grateful, I also trusted completely that he would find a great place for us to live. He bought an apartment for us in a lovely, tree-shaded neighborhood.

Still, at the moment it was a little difficult for either of us to grasp the other's good news. I was having trouble imagining owning anything more than a bottle of shampoo, or living anywhere other than B Dorm, and I stared rather stupidly at the floor plan and paint chips he brought with him. I assured Larry that when I came home to him, I would be Ms. Fixit in our new apartment with all my prison-acquired skills.

On the way out I scowled at the guard on duty; he was a pig, all hands. Before you could enter the visiting room, the guard stepped out to frisk you, to ensure that you were not bringing anything out with you to pass to your visitor. (In fact, a guard could pat you down at any time if they suspected you had contraband on you.) These pat-downs were delivered by both male and female guards and ran the gamut from perfunctory to full-out inappropriate.

Most of the male guards made a great show of performing the absolute minimal frisk necessary, skimming their fingertips along your arms, legs, and waist in such a way that said "Not touching! Not touching! Not really touching!" They didn't want any suggestion of impropriety raised against them. But a handful of the male guards apparently felt no fear about grabbing whatever they wanted. They were allowed to touch the lower edge of our bras, to make sure we weren't smuggling goodies in there—but were they really allowed to squeeze our breasts? Sometimes it was shocking who would grope you—like polite, fair, and otherwise upstanding Mr. Black, who did it in a businesslike way. Other male COs were brazen, like the short, red-faced young bigmouth who asked me loudly and repeatedly, "Where are the weapons of mass destruction?" while he fondled my ass and I gritted my teeth.

There was absolutely no payoff for filing a complaint. A female prisoner who alleges sexual misconduct on the part of a guard is invariably locked in the SHU in "protective custody," losing her housing assignment, program activities (if there are any), work assignment, and a host of other prison privileges, not to mention the comfort of her routine and friends.

Guards were not supposed to ask us personal questions, but this rule got broken all the time. Some of them were completely matter-of-fact about it. One day, while I was learning how to solder in the greenhouse with one of the cheerful plumbing officers, he posited a friendly "What the hell are you here for?"

But for the guards who knew me better, I could tell, this was a more disturbing question, one that some of them brooded over. One afternoon alone in a pickup truck, another CMS officer turned to me intensely and said, "I just don't understand it, Piper. What is a woman like you doing here? This is crazy." I had already told him that I was doing time on a ten-year-old drug charge. He wanted the story badly, but it was more than clear to me that intimacy with a guard would be ruinous for me—or for any prisoner. It made no sense to share any of my secrets with him.

ON THE weekend when the New York Marathon took place, I completed thirteen miles on the quarter-mile track, my own private prison half-marathon. The following weekend was unusually warm, beautiful really, and I was enjoying my sabbath ritual, *Little Steven's Underground Garage,* a two-hour radio program devoted to garage rock and hosted by Steven Van Zandt from the E Street Band and *The Sopranos* that was broadcast on a local radio station at eight every Sunday morning.

Best of all was listening to Little Steven, whether he was riffing on film noir, women, religion, rock rebellion, or the fate of the legendary CBGB's back home in New York. I never missed the show. I felt like it was keeping a part of my brain alive that would otherwise lie completely dormant—even in prison you had to work at being a nonconformist. I was a freak and an outcast, but in the Underground Garage I always had a home out in the ether. Unless the weather was awful, I would usually listen while chugging around the track for the full two hours, often laughing out loud. It was like a lifeline that went straight into my ears.

Just one thing marred my ritual today, and that was LaRue, the nasty plastic surgery casualty from B Dorm. LaRue was the only woman in the Camp whom I flat-out loathed. I did not hide my revulsion well, which was considered odd by my friends. "She's a freak for sure, Piper, but no more so than some of these other wackos. It's weird how she gets to you."

She was getting to me now. She was walking around the track in the center of the path, listening to what I assumed must be one of her fundamentalist radio shows, with her arms extended, Christ-like, and singing tunelessly in her high-pitched squeak about Jesus. Every time I lapped her, she remained smack in the middle of the gravel strip, arms spread wide. She was doing it on purpose, I was sure, to aggravate me and to force me off of the path. By the tenth time I passed her, my vision had stained red and I was boiling with focused fury. She was ruining Little Steven, she was ruining my run. I ground my teeth with hatred.

On my eleventh circuit, I watched her from across the oval, fantasizing her own crucifixion. I zoomed around the curve into the straightaway, gaining on her quickly. Her weird ass, fat with implants, remained in the center of the track; her arms stayed pinned to her imaginary cross. And as I closed the distance between us, I raised my own hand and smacked one of hers down as I passed her.

LaRue squawked in surprise and dove to the edge of the track, dropping her radio headset. A stream of Spanish invective followed me around the track. My heart soared for one moment and then immediately crashed. What the hell was wrong with me? What had I allowed this place to do to me? I couldn't believe I had raised my hand in aggression against another prisoner, especially this pathetic nutjob. Shame washed over me. I stopped running, sick to my stomach.

When I got around the track, LaRue was by the gym, with one of the Spanish mamis I knew from work.

I apologized awkwardly. "Francesca, I'm sorry. I'm really sorry. I didn't mean to scare you. Are you all right?"

This was answered with another stream of irate Spanish. I got the gist.

"Francesca, she said she was sorry. Let it go, mami," advised my coworker. "She's fine. Just keep running, Piper."

IF YOU are a relatively small woman, and a man at least twice your size is bellowing at you in anger, and you're wearing a prisoner's uniform, and he has a pair of handcuffs on his belt, I don't care how much of a badass you think you are, you'll be fucking scared.

One of the lieutenants was doing the bellowing, his mouth grim under his bristling mustache and crew cut. It had nothing to do with my smacking LaRue's imaginary stigmata on the track. I had been caught out of bounds in A Dorm by a renegade, off-duty Mr. Finn, who turned up out of the blue on a night he wasn't even working and wrote shots for me and seven other out-of-bounds women, lining us up outside his office. This, in turn, earned each of us private face time with the senior officer, who demanded to know if I disputed the charge, shot number 316 in the prison rule book. I said quietly that I did not and offered no excuse.

This did not make him happy, and he growled. "Do you think this is funny, Kerman?"

I sat perfectly still, not smiling. No, I didn't think any of this was the least bit funny; nor was I interested in jailhouse irony anymore. In the back of my mind I knew he wasn't going to do shit to me. He wasn't going to put me in the SHU, he wasn't going to lay a hand on me, I wasn't going to lose my good time. It wasn't worth it to them to do the paperwork that that would require. And he knew that I knew. Which was why he was screaming at me, and scaring me, even though we both knew it was a totally pointless exercise. No, I didn't think it was funny.

My out-of-bounds infraction was a minor one, a 300-series shot, along the same lines of: refusing to obey a direct order, participating in an unauthorized meeting or gathering, failing to stand for count, giving or accepting anything of value to or from another inmate, possession of nonhazardous contraband; and indecent exposure. Even lower on the list were the 400-series: faking sick, tattooing or self-mutilation, conducting a business, or unauthorized physical contact (like hugging someone who was crying).

More serious by far were the 200-series shots: fighting; extortion, blackmail, protection rackets; wearing a disguise; engaging in or encouraging a group demonstration; work stoppage; bribery; stealing; demonstrating, practicing, or using martial arts, boxing, wrestling, or other forms of physical encounters, military exercises or drills; and the best-known of all shots, the 205—engaging in sexual acts.

The 100-series were the worst of all; you could catch another charge for them. Murder, assault, escape, possession of a weapon, inciting a riot, drug possession, and one perfect catch-all: "conduct which disrupts or interferes with the orderly running of the institution or the BOP."

Eventually the lieutenant stopped glaring at me and cast his eyes over to the bald man in the corner of the room. "Is there anything you'd like to add, Mr. Richards?"

Certain prison guards relish the power and control that they wield over other human beings. It oozes from their pores. They believe it is their privilege, their right, and their duty to make prison as miserable as possible by threatening, withholding, or abusing at every opportunity. In my experience, these creatures weren't the sleazeballs who'd act sexually toward prisoners; in fact, they would never fraternize with lower life-forms like us, and they reserved their most withering scorn for their colleagues who treated us humanely.

Richards, also an enormous man, was a permanent shade of florid pink and kept his shaved head shiny. He looked like Mr. Clean's evil twin.

"Yeah. There is." Richards leaned forward. "I don't know what the hell has been going on up there, but we all know that the Camp is off the chain. Well, you go back up there and you tell your friends that I'm headed up there this new quarter, and things are going to be completely different. You make sure you pass the word." He leaned back in his chair, satisfied.

All eight of us got the same speech—of course we compared notes. My punishment was ten hours of extra duty.

I volunteered to work on the special overnight kitchen crew that was needed to produce Thanksgiving dinner. That way I would get all ten hours over in one fell swoop. Pop and the prison foreman she worked for, a well-liked guy whose office was full of plants, took holiday meals seriously. An extra-large team of women prepared turkey, sweet potatoes, collard greens, mashed potatoes, and stuffing, plus Natalie's pies. I was on pots detail, clad in a rubber apron, giant rubber gloves, and a hairnet. We played the radio, I got a few tastes as we went, and everything was finished despite Pop's nervousness. (She had only done it for ten years in a row.)

We worked all night until the sun came up, and I felt pleasantly exhausted. This was the best way to be penitent, to pour my energy into the communal meal that we would all be sharing soon, even though most of us would rather be someplace else. Thanksgiving Day I slept, had a visit with Larry and our friend David, and then ate my fill with Toni and Rosemarie—it was easily the best meal of the year. The feast was somewhat marred when the quiet Spanish mami sitting next to me burst into tears in the middle of dinner and proved inconsolable.

I ALWAYS thought I was an Episcopalian. I didn't realize it, but I had really been raised to follow the ethos of Stoicism—the Greco-Roman answer to Zen. Many people on the outside (especially men) had admired my stoicism when I was on my way to prison. According to Bertrand Russell, the virtuous stoic was one whose will was in agreement with the natural order. He described the basic idea like this:

In the life of the individual man, virtue is the sole good; such things as health, happiness, possessions, are of no account. Since virtue resides in the will, everything really good or bad in a man's life depends only upon himself. He may become poor, but what of it? He can still be virtuous. A tyrant may put him in prison, but he can still persevere in living in harmony with Nature. He may be sentenced to death, but he can die nobly, like Socrates. Therefore every man has perfect freedom, provided he emancipates himself from mundane desires.

Stoicism sure comes in handy when they take away your underpants. But how to reconcile it with one's insatiable need for other people? Surely my desire for connection, for intimacy, for human touch was not "mundane"? The very worst punishment that we can come up with short of death is total isolation from other humans, the Supermax, Seg, solitary, the Hole, the SHU.

The truth is, I was having trouble being a good stoic. I couldn't resist life's emotional flow and pulse, or the imperfect people I found so vital. I kept on throwing myself into the current, although once in I could usually stay calm and keep my head above water.

Still I had to wonder, why had my need to transgress taken me so far, to a prison camp? Perhaps I was just dense, unable to understand these things from a distance but instead intent on scorching myself face to the fire, burning off my eyelashes. Do you have to find the evil in yourself in order to truly recognize it in the world? The vilest thing I had located, within myself and within the system that held me prisoner, was an indifference to the suffering of others. And when I understood how rotten I had been, what would I do with myself, now that I was revealed as wretched, not just in private but in public, in a court of law?

If there was one thing that I had learned in the Camp, it was that I was in fact good. I wasn't so good with chickenshit rules, but I was more than capable of helping other people. I was eager to offer what I had, which was more than I had realized. Judging others held little appeal to me now, and when I did it, I regretted it. Best of all, I had found other women here in prison who could teach me how to be better. It seemed to me that my total demonstrated failure at being a good girl was more than matched by the urgency of being a good person. And that was something of which I hoped my grandmother would approve, and maybe forgive me, when I could not attend to her suffering.

THE DAY after Thanksgiving my grandmother died. I mourned quietly and with the sympathy of my friends. I felt like a wrung-out rag. I stared for many hours over the valley, lost in the past, and slowed to a walk on the track. I had never received a response to my furlough request. As Pop said, I had had nothing coming.

About a year later, when I was home on the street, I got a letter from Danbury. Formal, a little stilted, it was from Rosemarie, and folded in it were two photographs of my grandmother. My cousin had sent them to me in prison, and I had looked at them hundreds of times when I needed to smile. In the first, my grandmother has just opened a festively wrapped present, an oversize black Harley-Davidson T-shirt. Her face shows undisguised horror. In the second, the gag gift is clasped in her lap, and she beams at the camera, her eyes bright with laughter. Rosemarie wrote that she hoped I was doing well on the outs, and that she had found these photos in a book in the library and recognized who it was. Rosemarie said she knew how much I loved my grandmother, and also that she was thinking of me.

CHAPTER 16

Good Time

||||

The free world was getting closer. Despite my incident report in November, I was on course to serve thirteen months of my fifteen-month sentence and be released in March with "good time," the standard federal sentence reduction for good behavior. In January I would be eligible to go to a halfway house in deep Brooklyn on Myrtle Avenue (known as "Murder Avenue" in the Camp). Prison scuttlebutt was that as soon as you passed a few drug tests and found a job, the halfway house would send you home—as long as they could claim your paycheck.

Natalie would be waiting for me on Murder Avenue. I said goodbye to my bunkie the first week of December. The night before she left I was practically jumping out of my skin, asking her questions, leaning over from the top bunk to look at her lying below me for the last night. Natalie seemed to have willed herself into a state of calm. The next morning as she said goodbye to the assembled crowd of well-wishers, I was hopping nervously around the front door like a little kid. I wanted to be last. I was trying to keep my cool, even more than when Yoga Janet left.

"Natalie, I don't know what I would have done without you. I love you." This was probably the most direct thing I'd ever said to the proud woman I had lived with so intimately for nine months. I was going to lose the battle with tears again. In the last month I had become the freaking waterworks queen.

Natalie hugged me gently. "Bunkie, it's okay, I'll see you soon. I'm gonna be waiting for you in Brooklyn."

"That's right, Natalie. Hold it down till I get there."

She smiled and walked tall out the door for the last time.

Pop was also supposed to go to a halfway house in January. One reason she and I grew so close was that we were going home at the same time. For Pop, as well as Natalie, going home meant something very different than it did for me. Pop had been down for more than twelve years, since the early 1990s. She remembered a world with no cell phones, no Internet, and no probation officer to report to. She was nervous as hell. We spent many hours talking about what it would be like when she was released, first to a halfway house for six months and then to the house that she would share with her family. Her husband was in prison down south, due for release in three years. She planned to work in a restaurant and confided that she would like to buy and run a hot dog cart someday. She was nervous about computers, nervous about the halfway house, nervous about her kids, and nervous about leaving the place that, for better or worse, had been her home for more than a decade.

I was nervous too, but not about going home. In the second week of December I received a letter from my lawyer, Pat Cotter in Chicago, that informed me that one of my codefendants, a man named Jonathan Bibby, was going on trial, and I might be called to testify as a witness. He reminded me that under the terms of my plea agreement, I was required to provide complete and truthful testimony if called upon by the government. Pat advised me that the feds could choose to transport me to Chicago to appear in court and were in fact planning to do so. He wrote:

It is not that I would not enjoy the opportunity to see you again, of course, but it is my understanding based on comments of prior clients that travel courtesy of the Bureau of Prisons can be an uncomfortable and tiring experience for the inmate involved. I would like to spare you that experience, if possible.

I was horrified. Jonathan Bibby was a stranger to me. I didn't want to go to Chicago, and I certainly didn't want to be a government witness—a rat. I wanted to stay right here in the Camp and do headstands and go to movie night with Pop. I called my lawyer and explained that I had never even met Jonathan Bibby, that I couldn't pick him out of a lineup. If I were moved to Chicago for his trial, it might screw up my halfway house date in January. Could he please make some calls on my behalf and let the U.S. Attorney know that I had no personal experience with the defendant and couldn't possibly be a valuable witness?

"Of course." he said.

I sensed I shouldn't count on staying in Danbury.

I kept it all to myself, telling only Pop about the letter.

"Oh, baby," she said. "The airlift." She was talking about the federal transport system, Con Air. "The airlift is nothing nice."

WITH NATALIE gone, I lived solo in my cube for several days. The naked ticking stripe of her mattress made me feel lonely. I had been down long enough to know that just waiting passively for the prison gods to give me a wonderful new bunkie was a losing strategy. Faith, my next-door neighbor, was a good egg, and so a switch of cubes was engineered, and I got permission to move next door. I was now sleeping in the bunk that Vanessa had occupied, and Colleen before her. Faith was very different from Natalie, though happily not much more talkative. She was very glad to have me as a bunkie and would tell me about her pretty teenage daughter back in New Hampshire while she knitted—she had a special knitting permit.

Faith was doing a long drug sentence, and I vaguely gathered that she had taken the fall for someone else. She worried constantly about her daughter, whom she hadn't seen in over a year. She was making her a green sweater for Christmas. There never seemed to be more than three or four colors of acrylic yarn at the commissary—gray, white, burgundy, and green—and they would run out of the burgundy and green all the time, frustrating the hobbyists. Jae was crocheting Christmas toys for her kids—she had started months in advance. I couldn't see anything harder in prison than being a mom, especially at the holidays.

I GOT a letter from Pom-Pom, formerly of the garage, who had just gone home to Trenton.

> Dear Piper,
>
> I just asked about you. I'm so happy to receive a letter + some pictures from you. My sister said I was fatter when I was in there. I told her it's just the clothes. Anyway, I can't believe you got a shot! Amy wrote me her bunkie went to the SHU, but she didn't tell me you got a shot. That place is really going nuts.

Pom-Pom, whose mother had preceded her at Danbury, had been worried about what would happen when she was released. She had relatives who grudgingly agreed to let her live with them, though she also considered going straight to a homeless shelter.

Now she was back on the outside and she had received a chilly reception. The apartment where she was living was in a neighborhood where gunfire was audible every day—much scarier than the Danbury shooting range. The cupboards had been completely bare, and she had taken the little money she had to stock the house with food, shampoo, and toilet paper. She was sleeping on the floor.

> God, I miss you! It's sad to say I miss that place cause it is crazy out here. . . . All this freedom, but I still feel like I'm locked up. I could truly say y'all was my family. I had a birthday and what did I get? Nothing, and I had to beg for a Thanksgiving dinner. Now you know why I was so scared to come home.

We would have made a big deal about her birthday in the Camp. But Pom-Pom still drew on a deep reserve of good humor, which she'd needed to survive her life so far. She sent me a list of people she wanted me to give her good wishes—her bunkie, Jae, the remaining garage girls—and a heartfelt pep talk on how to make it to my own release. She closed, "Love always, Pom-Pom."

It was the strangest feeling ever, but I wished that Pom-Pom was back with us in prison. I was scared for her out there. At least in the BOP ghetto the perimeter guards were the only ones armed with guns, and they never got out of their trucks.

"Piper?" Amy peeked around my cube doorway. I didn't usually allow company up in my cube, preferring to do my visiting out in the common areas.

"What's up, Monster?" I had started calling Amy "the little monster" back when we worked together in electric. It was a deserved nickname, as she was foul-mouthed and foul-tempered and disrespected just about everyone and everything. But I loved Amy in spite of myself, and she made me laugh. She wanted to be so tough, and she was in a street-urchin way, but I thought of her as a spitting, hissing kitten that you could hold at arm's length by the scruff of its neck. Still, kittens have sharp claws and teeth.

Now Amy rushed to the side of my bunk and scrambled up on my footstool. I could see she was upset. She was supposed to go home before me, to upstate New York. I knew there was uncertainty waiting for her at home too, though not as dire as Pom-Pom's situation. For several weeks she had been trying to sort out her living and work arrangements over the phone, and she was stressed out. She was trying to get hold of her father with increasing desperation, and having trouble with the phone system. As she explained her frustration, the words spilled out faster and faster, until she choked on them, hiccupping.

"Come up here, Amy." I made room on my bed, and she scrambled up. "I'm sorry things are uncertain right now. It's going to be okay, you're going to be home soon." I put my arm around her while she cried.

She buried her head in my lap. "I want my daddy!"

I shushed her and patted the blond curls she was so proud of, and inside I grieved angrily over the insanity of locking up children, and then returning them to neighborhoods that were more desperate and dangerous than jails.

I SAW on the callout that I was scheduled to spend my afternoon in a mandatory prerelease class on housing, and my blood pressure started to rise. All federal prisoners are required to go through a series of prerelease classes before they reenter society. This made perfect sense. Many of the women in Danbury had been cloistered away in prison for years, and despite the harshness of being institutionalized, it was also infantilizing. The idea that they were going to hit the ground running and be able to cope with the day-to-day requirements of life "on the outs" was ridiculous.

I had been pretty curious about what the reentry classes would convey to us. The first one I was required to attend was on health. I showed up in the visiting room at the appointed time; chairs had been set out for twenty women, and a CO who worked in food services down in the FCI was there to lead it. I leaned over and asked Sheena, seated next to me, why he was teaching.

"He used to play professional baseball," she replied by way of explanation.

I thought about that for a minute, as if there were any sense to it. "But why is someone from Danbury teaching this class—and why not someone from health services?" Sheena rolled her eyes at me. "Are all the classes taught by the prison staff? They don't work on the outside, with ex-offenders. They spend all their time here. What do they know about reentry?"

"Pipes, you're looking for logic in all the wrong places."

The guy from food services was very nice and very funny. We liked him a lot. He told us that it was important to eat right, exercise, and treat your body as a temple. But he didn't tell us how to get health care services that people with no money could afford. He didn't tell us how we could quickly obtain birth control and other reproductive health services. He didn't recommend any solutions for behavioral or psychiatric care, and for sure some of those broads needed it. He didn't say what options there might be for people who had struggled with substance abuse, sometimes for decades, when they were confronted by old demons on the outside.

Another class had been titled "Positive Attitude" and was taught by the former warden's secretary. We liked her very little, as she was deeply condescending toward us. Her talk detailed her epic struggle to diet her way into a fancy dress for a holiday party. Tragically, she had not been able to lose the weight, but she still had fun at the party, because she had managed to keep her positive attitude. I looked around the room in disbelief. There were women in there who had lost their parental rights and would have to battle to reunite with their children; women who had nowhere to go and so would be heading to homeless shelters; women who had never worked in the mainstream economy and must find real jobs or end up back in prison. I had none of these concerns, because I was so much luckier than the majority of the women I'd been living with in Danbury, but I felt disrespected by how trivial these classes were turning out to be. The next one was led by the dour German nun who ran the chapel and was so vague it's hard to recall but dealt with "personal growth."

Next we heard about housing. Housing, employment, health, family—these are the factors that determine whether a person returning home from prison will succeed or fail as a law-abiding citizen. I knew the guy who was leading this session from CMS—he was a nice enough guy. And he talked about what he knew—which was insulation, and aluminum siding, and the best kind of roof to put on your house. He talked about interiors too. I was so disgusted with the BOP's farcical prerelease program that I just shut my eyes and waited for it to be over.

One woman raised her hand. "Um, Mr. Green, that's cool and all, but I need to find an apartment to rent. Can you talk a little bit about how to get an apartment, and if there are any programs we could qualify for, you know, affordable housing and stuff? Someone told me I should go to a homeless shelter. . . ."

He looked not irritated, but unsure. "Yeah, well, I don't really know too much about that. The best way to find an apartment is in the paper, or there are websites now that you can search."

I wondered how big the BOP's budget for reentry was.

I STARED intently at Larry across the card table. He looked worn out, with deep dark circles under his eyes. I remembered something Yoga Janet had said to me about our boyfriends: "They do the time with us."

Every visit now focused on a single topic: me coming home. It didn't matter if it was Larry, my mother, my brother, or a friend. Among my people there was a collective sense of relief, a feeling that we were almost out of the woods. I didn't want to be a killjoy, so I tried to hold my sense of dread about the possibility of Chicago in check.

It seemed like half the people in the visiting room would be going home soon—Pop, Delicious, Doris, Sheena. Big Boo Clemmons had gone home after Thanksgiving, and her girlfriend Trina had taken to her bed for a week.

Camila was going too, but not home yet. The Camp was about to send another group down the hill to the drug program, and she was among them. Nina was supposed to come back in January, having completed the program, before being released. I hoped that I would see her before I left.

I sat in Camila's cube, watching her sort through her stuff. She had just given me a pair of big black work boots. The drug program was very strict, so she had to dispose of contraband before she went, and give away excess clothing. Camila was in a good mood. The drug program would cut her sentence by a year, from seven to six. I worried about her mouth; more than most of the women in the Camp, Camila would talk back to the guards if they made her mad, and she had a temper. The program was strict, and people got kicked out of it all the time.

"I'm going to miss you. Who will I do yoga with?"

She smiled. "You're going home, tomorrow almost!"

"Camila, you have to promise me you will bite your tongue down there. It's no joke."

She made a perplexed face at me. "Bite my tongue? Why would I do that?"

"Bite your tongue. It's an expression. I mean you can't talk shit to the officers down there. Even if they're like Welch or that asshole Richards."

True to his word, Officer Richards was doing his best to make everyone's life miserable in the Camp. If DeSimon had reminded me of a lost detachable penis, Richards was like a furious one. He was ludicrously angry; he always looked like his shiny bright pink head might explode at any moment. He was petty, refusing to give a prisoner her letters if she had not been present at mail call, and rigidly enforcing the TV hours, much to the displeasure of the insomniacs. I didn't care about most of his new-sheriff activities, although Pop was bitter about having foot massages only when he was not on duty.

But he had one habit so evil that I wished debilitating illness would befall him. He screamed on the mic. All the time. The PA system was wired throughout the entire building, with multiple loudspeakers in all the Dorms. These were hung just feet from some women's beds. And he would get on the PA and just scream invective at us, all evening long, at painful volume. Poor Jae's bunk was right under a speaker. "Pipes, you think you can bring your electric skills over here?" That was something I was not confident I could do, or get away with, without electrocuting myself or going to the SHU. So we all had to listen to his abuse, and the word *torture* took on new meaning.

As CHRISTMAS Day neared, Larry delivered the bad news from my lawyer: I would be called as a witness to Chicago. I felt ill. What if I missed my halfway house date? Actually, there was no question that I was going to miss my halfway house date. Right down to the wire, my past would get in the way of my freedom. And what if I saw Nora? No way were they summoning me and not calling her.

I was nervous, but no one noticed; the Camp was in the midst of holiday mania. It had been building since before Thanksgiving, but now it burst out in force with a team of prisoners busy preparing for the annual Christmas decoration contest. Every unit in the FCI competed—there were a dozen units down in the prison, and the Camp was considered one unit. Leftover decorations from previous years were already hung around the Camp, giant signs that proclaimed NOEL and PEACE in dingy red and white tissue. But the 2004 decorating crew had something new, something big up their khaki sleeves. They toiled in secret, hour after hour in an off-limits television room that had been officially commandeered for them. All we got a glimpse of were the strange papier-mâché creatures they were preparing. "Check out my faggot elf!" one volunteer boasted happily, showing me an odd little humanoid.

The day before Christmas the Camp decorating crew's handiwork was revealed. It was, frankly, incredible: they had transformed a dingy beige television room with gray linoleum floors into a dazzling Christmas village on a winter night. The particleboard ceiling was concealed by an inky blue starry-night sky, a village was spread out as if in a mountain valley, and the workshops, the barroom, even the carousel were populated by little elves of debatable sexual preference. They frolicked in sparkling snow that drifted across the linoleum. Everything twinkled. Awestruck, we all examined the handiwork with glee. I still have no idea how they pulled it off.

We waited nervously all afternoon for the judging to come down. When the verdict was made public, for the first time ever the Camp was victorious! The guards assured us that the competition had been stiff—down on the compound the Puppy Program was housed in Unit Nine, which also included the psych unit, and they had fashioned antlers for all the Labrador retrievers and created a herd of reindeer. *A herd of reindeer!*

A special screening of *Elf,* with free popcorn to boot, was the entire Camp's prize. Faith, my bunkie, surprised me in our cube: "Piper, do you want to watch *Elf* together?"

I was taken aback; assuming things went as they always did, I would be watching the movie with Pop, or maybe with the Italian Twins. But it was clearly important to Faith.

"Sure, bunkie. That would be cool."

The movie was being screened in a different room than was typical, with several showings. Faith and I got our popcorn, grabbed two good seats, and settled in to watch together. We would not be making Christmas cookies, or picking out the perfect tree to decorate, or kissing the people we loved under mistletoe. But Faith could claim her special place in my life, and I had one in hers, especially at Christmastime. And it was cool.

ON DECEMBER 27 people got their Sunday *New York Times* in the Monday mail. I sidled up to Lombardi and asked, "Hey, could I have the Styles section?"

I scurried up to my bunk with the paper; Larry had a piece in it, and not just any piece. It was the "Modern Love" column, the weekly personal essay about love and relationships. He had been working on it for a long time, and I knew it was about our long-delayed decision to get married. Other than that, I had no idea what the *Times* readers and I had in store.

He described, with great humor, our untraditional courtship, and why neither of us really thought it was important to get married, although we'd been to twenty-seven weddings together. But something had changed.

THERE was never a tipping point, no eureka moment when I realized that doing the most traditional thing possible was a good idea. Some guys say they know immediately She's the One. Not me. Whether it's a sweater or software, it takes some time for me to know if I want to keep something, one reason I always save receipts. I can't say there was an instance when I looked into the pale blue eyes of the girl I met over corned

beef hash at a cafe in San Francisco and thought, "This is it."
Now, after eight years, I know.

When did I know? Was it the way she helped me deal
with the death of my grandfather? The relief I felt when she
finally answered her cellphone on Sept. 11? That great hike in
Point Reyes? Because she sobbed with joy when the Sox finally won? The way my nephews greet her like a rock star
when she walks into the room?

Perhaps I should have known right from the start, that
morning in the middle of our cross-country trip, when she
required one last stop at Arthur Bryant's in Kansas City for a
half slab of ribs for breakfast (and 10 minutes into the feast
saying to me, "Hey, baby, why don't you pop open a beer?").

Or did I not truly know until seven years later when we
found ourselves forced apart for more than a year? Who can
say? It's the big moments, maybe, but it's the little moments as
much or even more.

I could of course conjure up every one of those instances in perfect detail, right down to the chewy tang of those ribs and how good
that beer had tasted.

Slow as ever, yet indeed as sure as it gets, it dawned on me:
She wants to get married. And if that's true, then I want to get
married. To her. This is perhaps the least original idea I've had
in a long time, but I needed to get here myself, on my own
terms. And after all these years one thing I actually had going
for me was the element of surprise.

So what the hell, let's do it. I still don't believe marriage
is the only path to happiness or completeness as a person, but
it's the right thing for us. So I asked her. Or, more accurately,
what I said, sitting next to her on that silly island in a scene
straight out of *Bride's* magazine, was something about love
and commitment and not going anywhere and here's these

rings I got you, and if you want actually to make it official, that's cool, and if you don't, that's cool, too. And if you want to have a wedding, I'm into it, and if you don't, who needs it. She's still unclear what it was I was asking, exactly, but when she got done laughing, she said yes. And then she threw off her clothes and jumped in the water.

My friends joke that I've been to 27 weddings and now it's finally time for one funeral—for my singlehood. Which is sad like any funeral, sure, but this death is no tragic accident. I look at it more like euthanasia I'm performing on myself, a mercy killing.

I'm ready, babe. Pull the plug.

Even here, without him, I couldn't imagine any sweeter Christmas present.

I ALWAYS found New Year's Eve a bore on the outside, but on the inside it held greater interest, and I was very conscious and grateful that it would be my only one at Danbury. It made sense that turning the calendar forward would make a prisoner feel more optimistic. Watching those numbers tick suggested progress.

Much more than any New Year, even the Millennium, it felt for me like something was coming to a definitive end. Pop cried as we counted down at midnight—it was her thirteenth New Year's in prison, and her last. As I watched her, I tried to imagine the conflicting rush of emotions when you considered so much survival, regret, resilience, and lost time.

It seemed like half the Camp was focused on getting Pop home in one piece. She was supposed to be finished working in the dining hall—weirdly, prisoners do earn and accumulate vacation days in the BOP—but she didn't even make it one day. I caught her back in the kitchen and had a fit, but she just told me to go fuck myself. She didn't know what to do with herself if she wasn't working. The funny, salty, heavily accented earth mother who had helped me through so much was a bundle of nerves—she was less than two weeks from leaving for the halfway house.

So I felt terrible when I got the call on January 3—"Kerman! Pack out!"

Packing out meant you packed up your shit, because you were going somewhere. The prisoner is provided with army-issue duffel bags to temporarily hold her possessions. I elected to give most of my accumulated treasures away: my hot-pink contraband toenail polish, my prized white men's pajamas that Pop had given to me, my army-green jacket, and even my precious headset radio. All my books went into the prison library. Given my secrecy until this point, my fellow prisoners were surprised by my impending departure. Some assumed I had won early release, but those who heard that I was going on Con Air were full of curiosity, concern, and advice.

"Wear a sanitary pad. They won't always let you use the bathroom. So try not to drink anything!"

"I know you're picky about food, Piper, but eat whatever you can, because it might be the last edible meal you get for a while."

"When they shackle you, try to flex your wrists so there's a little more room, and if you try to catch the marshal's eye when he's chaining you, maybe he won't cuff you so tight your circulation goes. Oh, and double up your socks so the restraints don't make your ankles bleed."

"Pray they don't send you through Georgia. They stick you in a county jail, and it's the worst place I've ever been in my life."

"There are tons of cute guys on the airlift. They will love you!"

I went to talk to the Marlboro Man. "Mr. King, they're shipping me out on a writ, to Chicago." I actually succeeded in making him look surprised.

Then he laughed. "Diesel therapy."

"What?"

"Around here we call the airlift 'diesel therapy.' "

I had no idea what he was talking about.

"Well, you take care of yourself."

"Mr. King, if I come back before my release date, can I have my job back?"

"Sure."

As IT turned out, I didn't get shipped out for two days. I called Larry one last time—other prisoners had warned me not to say anything about the details of prison travel over the phone: "They're listening, and if you give specifics sometimes they think that you're planning to escape." Larry was bizarrely chipper, and I felt like he didn't really understand what was happening, even though I told him I might not be able to talk to him for a long time.

I bade goodbye to Pop.

"My Piper! My Piper! You're not supposed to go before me!"

I hugged her and told her she was going to be fine in the halfway house, and that I loved her.

Then I walked down the hill and began my next misadventure.

CHAPTER 17

Diesel Therapy

||||

Like much airline travel these days, flying Con Air involved a lot of stewing in your own juices. Exactly eleven months since I had first set foot in R&D, I was brought back there, and I waited. One by one guards brought other women in to wait with me. A skinny, dreamy-eyed white girl. A pair of Jamaican sisters. An unpleasant hick from the Camp whom I worked with in CMS, and who was headed back to western Pennsylvania for a court case. A big dykey-looking black woman with a wicked scar that began somewhere behind her ear, wound around her neck, and disappeared down below the collar of her T-shirt. There was little talking.

Finally a prison guard whom I knew from the Camp appeared. Ms. Welch was a food service officer and knew Pop very well. I felt some measure of relief that she would be involved in our departure—much better than the guard who had welcomed me to Danbury. She issued us all new uniforms, the same khaki hospital scrubs and wussy canvas shoes I had been clad in upon arrival. I was sad to give up my steel-toes, even though they already had cracks in the soles. One by one she began to shackle us—chain around the waist, handcuffs that were then chained to your waist, and ankle cuffs with a foot of chain between them. I had never been cuffed in my life outside my boudoir. I thought about the fact that I had absolutely no choice in the matter; I was going to be shackled whether I was cooperative, disgruntled, or prone with a knee in the small of my back or a boot on my chest.

I looked at Ms. Welch as she approached me. "How are you doing, Kerman?" she asked. She sounded genuinely concerned, and I flashed on the fact that we were "theirs," being sent out into the great unknown. She knew what the next few hours held for me, but the rest was probably as much of a mystery to her as it was to me.

"Okay," I answered in an uncharacteristically small voice. I was scared, but not of her.

She started to chain me up, chatting in a distracting way, almost like a dental hygienist who knows she is doing something that causes discomfort. "How is that—too tight?"

"A little too tight on this wrist, yes." I hated the gratitude in my voice, but it was genuine.

We had all been packed out—all of our personal belongings had been gone through by a prison guard (in my case, the same sneering midget I had encountered on my first day) and stored. The only thing you were allowed to bring on the airlift with you was a single sheet of paper that listed your property. On the back I had written all my important information—my lawyer's phone number and the addresses of my family and friends. Also scrawled on the paper in many handwritings was the contact information for my friends in the Camp—and if they were due to go home soon, a street address; if they were down for a long time, their inmate registration number. It hurt to look at the list. I wondered if I would ever see any of those women again. I kept the paper in the breast pocket of my scrubs vest with my ID.

We were lined up and started to shuffle, clinking, out of the building toward a big unmarked bus that was used for prisoner transport. When your legs are chained together, you are forced to adopt a short, tippy-toe cadence. As we were waiting in one of the chain-link-fence chambers between the prison and the bus, the town driver's van came speeding up. Jae hopped out, with duffel bags.

The big black dyke perked up. "Cuz?"

Jae blinked in disbelief. "Slice? What the hell is going on??"

"Fuck if I know."

We were all herded back into the FCI so they could pack Jae out and truss her up—she was joining our motley little crew, and I was really glad to have a friend along for the ride.

Finally, at gunpoint, we were loaded onto the bus and headed into the outside world. It was disorienting to see suburban Connecticut rushing by, eventually giving way to the highway. I had no idea where we were heading, though the odds were on Oklahoma City, the hub of the federal prison transport system. Jae caught up with Slice, her actual cousin, on the bus. Neither of them would cop to knowing why they were being transported, but they were probably codefendants, as the guard had been concerned that they should have extra restraints.

"Naw, naw, we cousins, we love each other!" they protested.

The guard had also indicated that they were headed to Florida, which was most worrisome. "Piper, I don't know shit about Florida, I'm from the Bronx, I been to Milwaukee, and that's it," declared Jae. "No fucking reason I should be going to Florida unless they be taking us to Disney World."

We finally arrived at what seemed like an abandoned industrial vacant lot. The bus stopped, and there we sat, for hours. If you think that it is impossible to sleep in shackles, I am here to prove you wrong. They gave us chicken sandwiches, and I had to help the Pennsylvania hick eat—the guard had not been as kind to her as to me and had chained her tightly and put her in an extra "black box" restraint that immobilized her thumbs—this to protect her codefendant, a woman with whom she was now excitedly gossiping. Finally the bus rumbled to life and pulled onto a huge tarmac. We had company—there were at least a half-dozen other transport vehicles, another bus, unmarked vans and sedans, all idling in the cold winter dusk. And then quite suddenly an enormous 747 landed, taxied briefly, and pulled up among the vehicles. In a moment I recognized that I was in the midst of the most clichéd action thriller, as jackbooted marshals with submachine guns and high-powered rifles swarmed the tarmac—and I was one of the villains.

First they unloaded about a dozen prisoners from the plane, men in a variety of shapes, sizes, colors, and attires. Some of them appeared to be wearing paper jumpsuits, not the best deal in the biting January wind. Disheveled and cold, they seemed pretty interested in our little group huddled next to the Danbury bus. Then the armed figures were shouting at us over the wind to line up, with plenty of room between each of us. We performed the tarmac jig that is done when one is trying to move as quickly as possible against restraints. After a rough pat-down, a female marshal checked my hair and my mouth for weapons, and the hop was on to the stairs up to the plane.

On board were more marshals, enormous beefy men and a handful of weathered-looking women in navy blue uniforms. As we clinked and clanked into the passenger seating area, we were greeted by a wave of testosterone. The plane was packed with prisoners, all of whom appeared to be male. Most of them were very, very happy to see us. Some were making a lot of noise, declaring what they would like to do to us, offering critiques as we shuffled up the aisle as directed by the marshals. "Don't you look at them!" the marshals shouted at us. Clearly, they had calculated that it was much easier to focus control on the behavior of a dozen females than two hundred males.

"What are you scared of, Blondie? They can't do anything to you!" shouted the male prisoners. "Over here, Blondie!" They were proven wrong in my mind later in the trip when a big man rose from his seat, loudly protesting that he needed a bathroom, and the marshals promptly tasered him. He flopped around like a fish.

Con Air is like a layer cake of the federal prison system. Every sort of prisoner is represented; sad-looking middle-aged upper-class white men, their wire-rim glasses sometimes askew or broken; proud cholos looking vaguely Mayan and covered in gang markings; white women with bleached-out hair and very bad orthodontia; skinhead types with swastika tattoos on their faces; young black men with their hair bushed out because they had been forced to undo their cornrows; a skinny white father-and-son pair, obvious because they were the spitting image of each other; a towering black man in extra-heavy restraints who might be the most imposing figure I have ever seen; and of course, me. When I was escorted for a bathroom break (difficult to manage when one's wrists are chained to one's waist), in addition to lascivious invitations and threatening catcalls, I was treated to more than one "Whatcha doin' HERE, Blondie?"

I was feeling more positively about everyone's shackles. I was so glad that Jae was next to me, craning her head to see everything too. Still, it was unnerving that she and her cousin didn't know what legal proceeding they were headed toward. We all agreed that if, God forbid, they had "caught another case" (been charged with another crime), they should have been told. But maybe not. They didn't have high-end representation like me.

Con Air does not fly direct. The jumbo airliners act more like puddle-jumpers, stopping hither and yon to pick up convicts being transported all over the country for all kinds of reasons—court appearances, facility transfers, postsentencing designation. Some prisoners appeared to be fresh off the street, still in civilian clothes. They brought on a Spanish guy with long black hair who would have resembled Jesus were his face not so hard; he was so good-looking, it was like a kick in the gut. At one stop more women got on. One of them paused in the aisle, waiting for a marshal to tell her where to sit. She was a scrawny little white woman, missing teeth, with a cloud of hair that was an indeterminate shade somewhere between gray and peroxide. She looked like a woebegone yard chicken, like she had led a hard life. As she stood there, some wiseass called out, "Crack kills!" and half the plane, which must have contained some crack dealers, busted out laughing. Her homely face fell. It was like the meanest thing you ever saw on the schoolyard.

At about eight P.M. we landed in Oklahoma City. I believe that the Federal Transfer Center sits at the edge of the airport there, but I can't be completely sure, as I never saw the outside world—the planes taxi right up to the prison to unload their heavily tattooed cargo. By default and necessity, it is a maximum-security facility that houses many prisoners during the course of their airlift experiences. Until I reached Chicago, this would be my new quarters.

We arrived at our new unit hours later, approximately twenty exhausted women who were issued sheets, pajamas, and small packets of hygienic necessities and ushered into a triangular cavern lined with two tiers of cells. It was darkened and deserted, because its inhabitants were already in lockdown. The CO was a ferocious six-foot Native American woman who barked out our cell assignments. I had never been in an actual cell before, let alone locked in with a cellie. I crept into my assigned spot, about six by twelve feet with a bunk bed, a toilet, a sink, and a desk bolted to the wall. I could see in the dim fluorescent light that someone was asleep in the top bunk. She rolled over and gave me the eye, then rolled away and went back to sleep. I crawled in and dozed off, grateful to have running water and free range of movement.

Thudding, shouting, and my cellmate vaulting out of her bunk awakened me. "Breakfast!" she said over her shoulder, disappearing. I got up and stepped cautiously out of the cell, wearing the washed-out hospital-green pajamas I had been given the night before. Women were scurrying from the numbered cells to get into line on the other side of the unit. Not one of them was in her pajamas. I hurried to get back into yesterday's nasty clothes and headed toward the line. After receiving a plastic box, I located Jae and Slice, who had claimed a table near my cell. Our boxes contained dry cereal, a packet of instant coffee, a packet of sugar, and a clear plastic bag of milk that struck me as one of the strangest things I had ever seen. But when you mixed the coffee powder with the milk and sugar in a green plastic mug and put it in the unit microwave (an ancient contraption that looked like it belonged on a *Lost in Space* episode), it tasted okay. I pretended that it was cappuccino. "We're going to starve," Slice declared. Jae and I feared she was right. We discussed our predicament, and Slice, who was a hungry woman of action, departed on a recon mission. Jae and I retreated to our respective cells.

I finally got a formal introduction to my new bunkie. "What's your name?" she drawled. I introduced myself. She was LaKeesha, from Atlanta, and on her way to . . . Danbury! The minute she heard I was coming from Danbury, she had a million questions. Then she crawled back into her bed and went to sleep. I soon discovered that LaKeesha slept about twenty-two hours a day, getting up three times to eat and, mercifully, shower. She always looked disheveled, though, emerging from our cell with her twists sticking out in all directions. "Peeper, what's wrong with your bunkie? She looks like Celie in *The Color Purple!*" cracked Slice.

I was totally wired on my first day in Oklahoma City—it was a brand-new scenario to get the hang of, with all new rituals and routines. Unfortunately, there was absolutely nothing to do. There were three TV rooms without chairs, and one little rolling bookshelf filled with a bizarre assortment of volumes—Christian books, ancient copies of John D. MacDonald, Shakespeare's *Antony and Cleopatra,* a handful of romances, and two Dorothy L. Sayers novels. A weird structure in the middle of the unit looked like a reception desk and contained nothing but stubby little pencils and various forms of scrap paper. Next to three pay phones there was an outdoor room where smokers shivered, and you could see a slice of the sky over a partial wall topped with razor wire. The unit felt like a train or bus station, but without a newsstand or a coffee shop. I tried to use the pay phone to call Larry or my parents to tell them I was alive, but the phone would place only collect calls, and no one's phone service would accept them, which intensified the feeling that I had been dropped into a plane of being that didn't exist to the rest of the world.

Women came and went quietly. The place was subdued and spotlessly clean. The unit seemed to be at most half full, maybe sixty women in the breakfast line. At eleven A.M. the CO brought in large rolling carts, signaling that lunch was going to be served. I watched a woman emerge from a cell on the top tier and descend the stairs on the opposite side of the unit. That curly hair, that fireplug shape . . . glasses. Something stirred in my belly; I sat up very straight. What was Nora Jansen doing in here with me?

I had been certain that a "separation order" would be placed on my codefendants and me, but apparently I was wrong. I stared at her as she got in the chow line. "Come on, Peeper!" Slice nudged me to get my lunch. Despite her obvious misgivings about befriending skinny white girls, she was willing to accept me as Jae's buddy, especially given that I didn't eat much. I trailed behind my two companions, drawing a bead on the woman who I thought was Nora.

In the past eleven months I had occasional thoughts of Nora—bad thoughts. I wanted to be certain before I made a move. I had fantasized about confronting the woman I'd followed down the wrong path, the woman who had likely ratted me out. In my head I usually set the moment in a lesbian bar in San Francisco and imagined much smashing of bottles with pool cues and breaking of pug noses and general bloodletting. Now the real moment had arrived. What was I going to do?

The short, curly-headed, and decidedly middle-aged woman received her lunch box and turned to head to a table. It was the same woman I had followed to Indonesia, to Zurich, to the Congress Hotel. If I had never met her, I wouldn't be sitting here now holding a bag of lukewarm milk and wearing government clothing. It was the same French bulldog face ten years later—ten apparently long, hard years. She looked like hell. She glanced at me as she passed, and I saw the shock of recognition cross those flattened features. I held my breath, my pulse pounding.

At the table with my companions, I hissed, "Jae! I think I see one of my codefendants!"

Jae looked at me, very serious. Almost all drug prisoners have codefendants, and that can have a host of meanings, but Jae knew immediately from my tone that this was not a good thing.

"What's up?" asked Slice, catching that there was a problem.

"Piper thinks she got one of her codefendants here, and she's surprised."

"Where?"

I indicated without pointing.

They relaxed a little. "That old lady?" "Shee-it, Peeper, what kind of gangster is you anyway?"

I glared at them. "Jae, I think that bitch ratted me out."

All levity ceased. Slice studied Nora. Jae thought for several moments, then spoke deliberately.

"Piper, you do what you need to do, knowhatmsayin', but know this—you will be in the SHU the rest of the time here. If it sucks like this here, imagine what the SHU is like. And fuck knows what else is gonna happen to you. You about to go home, to your man who you know loves you, he got his ass up in the visiting room every damn week. Is that bitch worth it to catch another case? I'ma back you up *to a point*. I'm telling you f'real though, I am not going to the SHU, but I respect that you gotta do what you need to."

Slice piped in, "I'm not going to the SHU either, not for some white girl I don't even know. No offense, Peeper. But do your thing."

I did nothing. Jae kept a worried eye on me. Slice procured a full deck of playing cards from another prisoner and began to shuffle them. I couldn't stand it, though. I took a break and lay on my bunk and stared at the cinder-block wall. The woman who had landed me here was finally within my grasp, and I was paralyzed. Would I really do nothing?

I left my cell and stalked around the unit, which took about three minutes. Nora was nowhere to be found. Jae gestured me over. "C'mon, Piper, play with us."

Jae and her cousin riffed back and forth as we played cards. Slice was full of very funny accounts about the life of a bulldagger on the make in the FCI back in Danbury, including the story of being caught in the act in the middle of the night by a guard we all knew. "I froze, man, he's got his flashlight on us, and it wasn't the kinda situation where you can deny, know what I mean? And he just said, 'Let me watch.' Soooooooo . . ." and she indicated getting back to business. It was the same guy who had bird-dogged me for giving Pop an innocent foot massage. Filthy pig.

By the time the dinner cart showed up after the four o'clock count, we were laughing our asses off. When we took the lid off the plastic trays, the stench made us slam them back on immediately. Jae spoke up, after a beat: "We're gonna have to kill one of these bitches and eat her, or starve."

I was crossing the unit to return my tray when I saw Nora headed toward me. I squared my shoulders and adopted my most arctic ice-queen stare. As we passed, she looked at me uncertainly.

"Hi," she said, almost under her breath.

I stalked by her.

"What happened?" asked Jae, concerned.

"Tried to say hello to me." I shook my head, and we started playing cards again. "You know, the thing I can't figure out is why she's here and her sister isn't."

"Her sister?"

"Yeah, her sister's my codefendant too. She's doing time in Kentucky."

The next morning at breakfast, there was Hester. That was the way it was in Oklahoma—new people materialized in the middle of the night while you were locked down in the cells. They popped up at breakfast, a day-making novelty. I witnessed the sisters' reunion from my turf—they hugged ecstatically and headed to a corner to confer.

My companions took note. "You need to kill sis, too?" asked Slice.

"Nah, I never had any beef with Hester—she's all right."

Time had been kinder to Hester. She looked more or less the same, perhaps due to her old chicken bone charms: long reddish curly hair, a faraway but quizzical expression, and a witchy, mystical demeanor.

For the weeks that we spent in Oklahoma City, I refused to acknowledge the sisters' presence. Max lockdown was torturous in its monotony and lack of stimulation; the hours and the days crawled by. Flights arrived and departed almost every day, but you never knew when you might be put on one. It was the perfect realization of limbo—departure from one realm of being, waiting to arrive at another. Oklahoma City made me homesick for the Danbury Camp, a surreal and disturbing feeling. I was accustomed to hours of strenuous activity every day, between working construction, running, and the gym. Here the only options were push-ups and yoga in my cell and "walking the tiers," actually circling the tiers hundreds of times in my canvas slippers until my blisters bled. Back in Danbury Sister Platte had used the hall as a makeshift treadmill during inclement weather.

I would sometimes fall into step next to her. She moved pretty fast for a sixty-nine-year-old, and her constant good spirits amazed me. "How are you holding up, dear?" the little nun would ask me.

I was lucky to have Jae by my side to share the stress and uncertainty and to blow off steam, and her cousin was funny as hell and a reassuring (if also menacing) presence. I asked Jae one day about her cousin's scar.

"Guy jumped her, tried to rape her, and he cut her with a box cutter. Hundred stitches." Pause. "He's in jail now." And the nickname? "It's her favorite drink!"

It was easy to lose track of what day it was—there were no newspapers, no magazines, no mail, and since I avoided the TV rooms, no significant way to tell one day from the next. You can only play so many games of gin. I tried to count off which day was January 12, when Pop would be released from Danbury. I couldn't talk to Larry on the pay phone, and there were no clear windows, so I couldn't even watch the progression of the sun. I wasn't remotely interested in messing with prison pussy, one of the only available distractions. I learned dominoes. And I learned to understand the true punishment of repetition without reward. How could anyone do significant amounts of time in a setting like this without losing their mind?

No one was all that inclined to be social with strangers, but some limited intrigue took place around cigarettes. In Danbury, the opportunities for hustle were many. But in Oklahoma City, the only things on the market were sex, other people's psych meds, and, most important, nicotine. Prisoners who volunteered as orderlies got to "shop," but all there was to buy were cigarettes. Once a week, when the cigarettes got doled out, there would be frenzy right below the surface, threatening to bust out. The orderlies were either companionable and split their cigs up into smaller "rollies," to be shared out of the milk of human kindness, or were paid in psych meds, which would help you sleep away the days like LaKeesha. I found the whole deal completely stressful and was glad I didn't smoke. My hair was turning into a rat's nest absent conditioner—all we had were little packets of shampoo. Finally, I turned to scavenging packets of mayonnaise, which made my locks greasy, but at least I could get a prison-issue little black plastic comb through it.

Suddenly Jae and Slice got shipped out. At four A.M. Jae and I said goodbye through the thick glass rectangle in my door. "Stick next to Slice!" I said. "I'll track you down after I get home!"

Jae fixed me with her huge liquid brown eyes, sweet and sad and scared. "Be careful, Piper!" she said. "And remember the Vaseline trick I told you!"

"I will!" I waved goodbye through the inches of glass. When they let us out for breakfast two hours later, I felt truly alone, left to navigate the seas myself. I missed my girls, and I glared across the unit in Nora's direction. I knew that whatever my immediate future held, it included her.

A few days later my bunkie LaKeesha left for Danbury. I was jealous. As she was scrambling into her clothes, I instructed her, "When you get to the Camp, tell Toni, that's the town driver, that you saw Piper in Oklahoma City and she's okay, she says hello."

"Okay, okay . . . wait, who is Piper?"

Why wasn't I surprised? I sighed. "Just tell them you met a white girl who does yoga from Danbury and she's all right!"

"That I can remember!"

I had a couple of days of total privacy in the cell. I cycled through my yoga poses repeatedly, gazing at the opaque window that let some daylight in; it was the full height of the room and about six inches wide. I would save my bag of milk at breakfast and put it at the bottom of the window, where it stayed cold for hours. The milk was the one guaranteed edible thing every day. I had also learned to sleep against the wall with my arm shielding my eyes from the fluorescent light that was on in the cell twenty-four hours a day. For the first time I had a bottom bunk, a strange novelty.

Then a new bunkie showed up, a young Spanish girl. She was from Texas, on her way to a prison in Florida. She had never been down before, was wide-eyed and full of questions. I played the role of seasoned prisoner and told her what I thought she could expect. She reminded me of Maria Carbon from Room 6 and the construction shop, which made me sad.

Finally, a week later there was a thud on my door at four A.M. "Kerman, pack out!" I had no possessions to pack other than my now-crinkled paper from Danbury with its scribbled reminders of the people I knew there. I practically danced into my khaki uniform, at this point ready for anything that would get me out of there, Nora or no Nora. Per Jae's instructions, I fished my precious contraband store of Vaseline out of its hiding place in a sock and tucked gobs of it into the curves of my ears. During the long hours of travel on the flight largely without water, I could dab it on my lips to keep them from cracking.

As I shuffled onto the airplane, shackled again, one of the feds who had also been on my previous flight stared at me. "What's wrong, Blondie?"

I was stone-faced.

"You better improve your attitude, Blondie," he advised sharply.

The marshals made me sit next to Nora on the plane. At this point I wasn't even surprised at my bad fortune, though I was rigid with fury. Shackled, with Vaseline in my ears, and sitting next to the cow who got me into the whole mess, I refused to look at her. We maintained a wall of uncomfortable silence between us as the flight stopped in Terre Haute, Detroit, and other snow-covered midwestern wastelands. At least I had the window seat.

Descending into a sunny, wintry Chicago, I felt, despite my extreme agitation and acute physical discomfort, a quiet thrill. I retained a tiny shred of humor with which to appreciate the irony of the whole situation. Here was the city that was the hub of this whole mess, and it seemed somehow fitting that I should be here, with her next to me.

THE TARMAC in Chicago was lively and bitterly cold. I was freezing in my thin khakis. Convicts were hopping every which way in shackles under the direction of the marshals, and Nora and Hester grew excited at the sight of one floppy-haired white boy. "It's George!" they exclaimed.

I looked closely, as he turned our way and cheerfully indicated greeting with his chin before being hustled onto a bus. If that was Hester's old friend George Freud, he had lost some weight in ten years. It seemed that the whole gang was being recalled to Chi-town for the big event of Jonathan Bibby's trial. We were loaded into a passenger van with a bunch of guys and whisked downtown through rush-hour traffic in a phalanx of unmarked and heavily secured white vehicles.

Hester was seated next to me, and she gazed into my eyes intently for a moment. "Are you doing all right?" she asked, very genuinely, in her flat midwestern tone. I muttered that I was okay, and looked out the window, unnerved by her kindness.

As we headed into the Loop, I tried to anticipate how best to handle myself at the Chicago Metropolitan Correctional Center, aka federal jail, where people are typically held before their cases are resolved—unless, like Lil' Kim, they do all their time there. Jae had been locked up in the Brooklyn MCC for two years before coming to Danbury and had described that situation as far better than what we experienced in Oklahoma City. "Two units in Brooklyn, about two hundred females, and you could have a job and everything, there was stuff to do. In Chicago MCC you'll be able to fade back, hook up with someone normal, and just lay low, probably even get in a different unit or dorm than your codefendants."

We were driven into the base of a tall, triangular fortress on a city block in the crowded Chicago Loop. Unloaded from the van, shuffled into an elevator, we were deposited in a filthy, decrepit, and disorganized R&D. The building was disorienting; the floor felt tiny and even more constricting because it was cluttered. It was lined with holding cells, populated by men in orange, most of them brown-skinned. We were quickly locked into an empty holding cell, also filthy.

During the next five hours I paced the cell and tried to ignore the sisters. They were polite and did not say much, seeming to give deference to my coiled, stymied rage. After several hours I was lying prone on a hard narrow bench, practicing nothingness, and Nora cleared her throat.

"Piper?"

"What?"

"Do you even know Jonathan Bibby?"

"NO."

Several moments passed in silence. "You must be *pissed*."

"YEAH."

A female guard issued us ill-fitting orange men's jumpsuits. Mine snapped up the front and had short sleeves and weirdly cropped legs, like convict clamdiggers. I had almost made it through the year without lapsing into total cliché but had now missed the mark. Finally, it seemed that they would escort us to our resting place for the night. I was so goddamned tired, I assumed anything would be an improvement over this filthy, uncomfortable cell, especially if it was far away from Nora.

The three of us rode in silence up in the elevator to the twelfth floor. We exited through clanging security gates, until the last gate slid open to reveal the women's unit.

Psych ward. That was my overwhelming first impression. Dueling televisions blared at opposite sides of the small room. A cacophony of voices vibrated in the close, crowded space. Women, disheveled and stooped, blinked at us like moles. Although there was nothing playful about the place, it had an infantilized, nursery-school vibe. As we entered, everything seemed to stand still, and every eye turned to us. A guard in an ill-fitting uniform, who telegraphed "ineffectual," approached us. He seemed utterly surprised by our arrival. I turned and looked at Nora and Hester, and then I started to laugh, a disbelieving and desperate laugh. In an instant, the iceberg between me and my codefendants melted. "Oh, *hell*, no!" And they laughed too, with relief and recognition, and I saw the same look of disbelief mixed with disgust and exhaustion in their eyes. They were in the same boat as me. And right here and now, all of a sudden I knew that they were all I had.

Most changes in perception are gradual: we grow to hate or love an idea, a person, or a place over a period of time. I had certainly nursed a hatred of Nora Jansen over many years, placing much of the blame for my situation on her. This was not one of those instances. Sometimes, rarely, the way we see something is subject to alchemy. My emotions changed so rapidly, and I felt so strongly all the things I had in common with these two women, there was no way not to take immediate notice and stock of what was happening. Our troubled history was suddenly matched by our more immediate shared experience as prisoners on an exhausting journey.

We huddled together for a moment while chaos reigned around us, and it occurred to me that they probably knew nothing at all about the last ten years of my life, including the very fact that I was incarcerated. They had both gone to prison before me.

And that's how we broke the ice. "Is Kentucky like this?" I asked Hester.

"Nope."

"Dublin?"

"Hell no. Where are you?"

"Danbury. And it's nothing like this freak show."

The officer reappeared, with housing assignments. We were shown to our respective cells and locked down. My new roommate Virginia weighed 350 pounds and snored like nothing I had ever heard before. It was like there was a wild, rabid animal in the bunk below me. As I tossed and turned on the plastic mattress, trying to cover my head with the pillow, I realized that this was what Pop meant when she said "real prison," as in "You girls don't have any idea what *real prison* is like." I remembered a college professor who had told me that lack of sleep, or sleep only in short intervals, will eventually bring on hallucinations.

Virginia was an amateur astrologer who rarely showered. She informed me that she was planning on defending herself in court. When I refused to tell her my birth date so she could "do my chart," she was deeply insulted. I thought of Miss Pat and Miss Philly, two of the more unstable women back in Danbury, and remembered to tread very lightly with crazy people. The next day my initial impression of the unit was confirmed when I realized that a significant percentage of its occupants were under court-ordered psychiatric observation. This was darkly humorous, as the prisoners in Chicago had little to no contact with prison staff or counselors of any stripe—the inmates really seemed to run this asylum.

I also gleaned that just about all of the women in Chicago were on pretrial status—their cases had not yet been resolved, but they did not or could not make bail. So they were captive here while the wheels of justice ground. A couple of them had been here for months without being charged with a crime. This made their lives uncertain on every level, and those who were not already crazy were acting pretty wacko, driven nuts by rage and instability. I had been dropped into a snake pit. Virginia warned me, "See Connie over there?" She indicated a catatonic-looking woman. "She's gonna ask you for your razor. Promise me you won't give it to her! She's only dangerous to herself, don't worry." I promised.

None of the accepted rules of prison behavior that I had learned seemed to apply here. There was no welcome wagon with shower shoes and a toothbrush; there was no understanding of inappropriate or *verboten* questions; there was no sense of solidarity or recognition of the sanity-saving value of personal routine or order or self-respect. Goddammit, you couldn't even rely on the tribe system—the white women weren't worth a damn. Most of them were drooling on meds to keep them from killing themselves (or their neighbors).

My de facto tribe was Nora and Hester (who was going by her given name of Anne these days). At least they understood the official and unofficial rules of incarceration. Warily I sat down with them and slowly began to feel out the situation, including what each of us knew about the upcoming trial and exactly why this place was so freaking miserable. They too were staggered by how awful the Chicago MCC was; we agreed that it was hard to believe it was a federal facility. There was enormous ground for the three of us to cover just on the prison front, but that wasn't really what I was interested in. I wanted Nora to cop to ratting me out and to tell me why she did it.

. . .

FINALLY WE met what passed for the Welcome Wagon—Crystal. Crystal was a tall, skinny black woman in her fifties and the de facto mayor of the women's unit. She appeared to be perfectly sane and was in charge of issuing uniforms and basics to new arrivals. She led us to a jumbled closet, where she began burrowing in boxes for more orange uniforms and some towels. They were short on underpants, and she handed me two pairs. I looked at them. "Crystal, these are . . . not clean."

"I'm sorry, sweetie, that's all we got. You put 'em in the laundry that goes out tomorrow. They'll probably come back."

There were no pajamas for us, no shampoo, not even eating utensils. I was relieved to hear that we could shop commissary once a week, but of course my ability to do that was going to depend on someone in this building doing their job and completing my paperwork, which seemed like a fantasy.

I was thrilled to discover that there were two private showers, though I was disgusted when I saw them. Before surrendering I had been warned never, ever to go into the shower without shower shoes. My feet had not touched tile in almost a year, but I had no shoes. I was dying to bathe. I turned on the water and gingerly stepped out of my canvas slippers and into the gross shower stall, holding a little bar of motel soap. My skin crawled, and icy water stung my back as I tried to get clean.

NORA WAS cautious around me but was almost pathetically grateful that I wasn't outright hostile. I certainly felt entitled to be nasty; when I was, she took it without resistance. Hester/Anne was bemused but didn't interfere. I guess she figured her big sister could fend for herself, or that she had it coming. I learned that Nora had taught in a vocational program they had in Dublin; Hester/Anne was in the Puppy Program in Lexington. Before she'd been locked up, Hester/Anne had gotten sober, got married, and quietly embraced Jesus as her personal savior. Nora was just as I remembered her—funny, scheming, curious, and sometimes an insufferably egotistical pain in the ass in need of a takedown.

Finally, I cut to the chase. "So why don't you fill me in on everything that happened after we broke up in 1993?"

According to Nora, many months after my departure from her life, she did some soul-searching and tried to get out of the business with Alaji, who told her in no uncertain terms, no dice, and warned her of the consequences if she did walk. "I'll always know where your sister is," he threatened her. A while later, when a pair of drug couriers got arrested—separately in San Francisco and Chicago—things began to get messy and ugly, and of course the whole operation collapsed.

With her drug money Nora had built her dream home in Vermont—or at least it was her dream until a SWAT team of heavily armed federal agents arrived in jackboots to take her into custody. When the feds sat her down, she claimed, they already had detailed information about the whole enterprise. Someone—I thought probably her slimy business partner Jack—had been singing.

"Did they have my name?" I asked.

"Yes, they knew exactly who you were. But at first I told them you were just my girlfriend and you didn't know anything."

At this point it was hard to know what to believe. I had invested a lot of time and energy into hating Nora and elaborating fantasies of revenge. Her story was plausible, but it could easily be a lie. I believed that she felt terrible about the mistakes she had made, and when she looked across the table at her little sister, or talked about her elderly parents (who had not one but two children in prison), I felt bad for her in spite of myself. My brain and my guts were twisted, a snarled cat's cradle that I would have to pick apart.

I was starting to understand what the Marlboro Man meant by "diesel therapy."

CHAPTER 18

It Can Always Get Worse

||||

Every day in the Chicago MCC began the exact same way: at six A.M. male inmates (who were allowed to have jobs) brought food carts up to the women's unit and through the massive metal security doors. Then the lone CO on duty would go around the unit unlocking the female prisoners' doors. When the bolts clicked, everyone would vault out of bed and rush out into the unit to stand in line for breakfast. The line was not a happy place; no one spoke, and faces were hard and set or just stuporific. The food was usually cold cereal and a half-pint of milk and sometimes some bags of bruised apples, handed out by an inmate named Princess. Every now and then there were hard-boiled eggs. It was clear why everyone always got up: as in Oklahoma City, breakfast was the only meal of the day that was guaranteed to be edible.

As quickly as everyone had appeared, the room would empty. Almost everyone went back to bed. Sometimes they ate their breakfast or sometimes they just stashed it, sticking the milk on ice in a scavenged receptacle. The unit would remain quiet for several hours, and then the women would start to stir, the televisions would go on, and another miserable day in the high-rise fortress would begin.

EVERYBODY WHO loved me wanted me to be innocent—tricked, duped, all unawares. But of course, that was not the case. All those years ago I wanted to have an adventure, an outrageous experience, and the fact of it being illegal made it all the more exciting. Nora may have used me all those years ago, but I had been more than ready to take what she was offering.

The women I met in Danbury helped me to confront the things I had done wrong, as well as the wrong things I had done. It wasn't just my choice of doing something bad and illegal that I had to own; it was also my lone-wolf style that had helped me make those mistakes and often made the aftermath of my actions worse for those I loved. I no longer thought of myself in the terms that D. H. Lawrence used to observe on our national character: "The essential American soul is hard, isolate, stoic, and a killer. It has never yet melted."

Women like Allie, Pom-Pom, Pennsatucky, Jae, and Amy melted me. I recognized what I was capable of doing and how my choices affected the people I was now missing; not only Larry and my family but all my fellow penitents whom I had crossed paths with in this year, this season in hell. I had long ago accepted that I had to pay consequences. I am capable of making terrible mistakes, and I am also prepared to take responsibility for my actions.

Yet you still had to resolve not to believe what the prison system—the staff, the rules, even some of the other prisoners—wanted you to think about yourself, which was the worst. When you chose to do otherwise, when you acted like you were a person worthy of respect, and treated yourself with respect, sometimes they did too. When doubt and shame or worse crept in, the letters and books and visits from my friends and lover and family were powerful proof that I was okay, more effective than charms or talismans or pills to fight those terrible feelings.

The Chicago MCC was a different story. I'd been taken away from all the people who'd helped me to do my time, people on the outside and the inside, and I was completely off-balance. The misery of the women surrounding me rattled me, as did the pointlessness of every day that passed here, and the complete disrespect and indifference with which we were treated. The COs who worked the unit were in fact often pleasant, if unprofessional, but they couldn't do anything. Interacting with "the institution" in Chicago MCC was like staring at a concrete wall. Questions went unanswered. Underpants were not provided. My bedrock sense of myself was in some danger. Food, sometimes edible, was brought on a regular schedule, and in this new universe that was really all you could count on as a stable principle. My phone calls to Larry and my parents took on a desperate edge. For the first time in the year I had been in prison, I said the words, "You've got to get me out of here."

I THREATENED to drown Nora in a toilet.

We had settled into a companionable antagonism, wherein I threatened to kill her several times a day, as we three codefendants would sit and play cards, reminisce, compare notes on our respective prisons, or just complain. It was very, very strange. I still had overwhelming flashes of hostility toward her, which I did not swallow. I didn't really trust her, but I realized that it didn't matter. Regardless of whether she was honest with me, I wanted to forgive her.

It made me feel better about myself, better about the crazy shithole we were currently residing in, and honestly, better about the fact that I was going home soon. She was going to be in prison for many more years. If I could forgive, it meant I was a strong, good person who could take responsibility for the path I had chosen for myself, and all the consequences that accompanied that choice. And it gave me the simple but powerful satisfaction of extending a kindness to another person in a tough spot.

It's not easy to sacrifice your anger, your sense of being wronged. I still cautioned Nora regularly that today might be the day she drowned, and she laughed nervously at my mock-threats. Sometimes her sister offered to help with the drowning, if Nora was being annoying. But we were able to settle into a feisty rapport, like all ex-lovers who have a lot of water under the bridge but have elected to be friends. The things that I had liked about her over a decade earlier—her humor, her curiosity, her hustle, her interest in the weird and transgressive—all those things were still true; in fact, they had been sharpened by her years in a high-security prison in California.

We served each other as a barrier against the freaks, of which this small unit had an astonishing array. In addition to poor suicidal Connie, there were several bipolar arsonists, an angry and volatile bank robber, a woman who had written a letter threatening to assassinate John Ashcroft, and a tiny pregnant girl who would seat herself next to me and start running her hands through my hair, crooning. I saw more temper tantrums and freakouts in a few weeks than I had in many months in Danbury, all of which the CO basically ignored. There was no SHU for women in Chicago (we were one floor above the men's SHU), so the only disciplinary action that could be taken against us was sending a female off to the Cook County Jail, the largest in the nation at ten thousand inmates. "You do not want to go there!" warned Crystal, the mayor, who seemed to know what she was talking about.

Now that we had been in the MCC for a couple of weeks, the sisters and I saw that there were in fact some sane women present. At first no one really came near us; it took a while to realize that some of the residents of the twelfth floor were scared of us—after all, we three were hardened cons from *real prison*. But after a bit they must have recognized that we were "normal" like them, and then they made eager overtures: a couple of sweet and friendly Spanish mamis, a very short sports fanatic, and a hilarious Chinese lesbian who introduced herself to me hopefully with the line "I like your body!"

We were instantly elevated as authorities on anything and everything involving the federal prison system. When we explained that in fact "real prison" was much more bearable than our present surroundings, they were perplexed. They also wanted legal advice, lots of it, and I found myself repeating, "I am not a lawyer. You have to ask your attorney . . ." But all of them had court-appointed lawyers who were rarely accessible. There was a bizarre black Batphone on the wall, which was supposed to tap directly into the public defender's office. "Fat fucking lot of good that does us," complained one of the arsonists.

I did not have the representation problems of my fellow prisoners. One day I was called out of the unit, told I was going "to court," and sent down to R&D to sit in a holding cell for hours. Finally I was handed off to my escorts, two big, young Customs agents, federal cops. I'm not sure what they were expecting, but it wasn't me. When I turned my back to them to be cuffed, the guy doing the honors got rattled.

"She's too small. They don't even fit her!" He sounded anguished.

His counterpart stuck a thick finger between the cuffs and my wrist and said he thought we were good.

In the worldview of these burly, clean-cut young guys, I was clearly not supposed to be resident in this fortress. I probably looked too much like their sister, their neighbor, or their wife.

After being locked away for so many weeks, I enjoyed the ride through the streets of Chicago. At the federal building on South Dearborn, I was taken upstairs to a nondescript conference room and deposited, with the less-rattled officer to guard me. We sat across the table from each other, in silence, for fifteen minutes. I wasn't looking at him, but I could tell he was watching me, which I guess was his job. He seemed to be getting agitated. He shifted in his chair, looked at the clock, looked at me, shifted again. I thought he was just bored. With prison Zen, I waited for whatever was going to happen next. Finally he couldn't stand it anymore.

"You know, we all make mistakes," he said.

I turned my eyes to him. "I know that," I replied.

"What were you, an addict?"

"No, I just made a mistake."

He was silent for a moment. "You're just so young."

This amused me. It must be the yoga. He was definitely younger than me.

"My offense is more than eleven years old. I'm thirty-five." His eyebrows shot toward his hairline. He had no idea what to do with this information.

Mercifully the door opened, ending the conversation. It was my lawyer, Pat Cotter, with the Assistant U.S. Attorney and a roast beef sandwich. "Larry said roast beef was your favorite!"

I wolfed it down in as ladylike a fashion as I could muster. I had almost forgotten about my orange attire, but now I felt a little self-conscious. He also brought me a root beer. This is what a top-shelf, white-shoe criminal defense gets you. I was very happy to see him.

Pat explained that because I would appear as a government witness, the AUSA, the woman who had put me in jail (well actually, that was me; she just prosecuted) got to prepare me. He again reminded me that my plea agreement obligated me to cooperate. He would stay with us, but I had no legal protection per se. Nor was I in any legal risk, as long as I didn't perjure myself. I assured him I had no plans for that, then pressed him about getting me out of the MCC and back to Danbury. He said he would see what he could do; Jonathan Bibby's trial date had already been pushed back twice. I knew that meant "Fat chance."

I was very tired when I got back to our fortress prison. "You'll get your turn," I told Nora and Hester/Anne. We had managed to get moved into a six-person cell with three other women, so now in addition to everything else, we were roommates. I went to sleep.

THE BIGGEST problem with the MCC was that there was nothing to do. There was a pathetic pile of crap books, decks of cards, and the infernal televisions, always on, always at full volume. There had been nothing to do in Oklahoma City either, but there the surroundings were spotless and serene, with about ten times as much space. Mercifully in Chicago we received mail, and letters and books began arriving for me. I shared my books with my bunkies.

When you are deep in misery, you reach out to those who can help, people who can understand. I picked up a pen and wrote to the only person on the outside who could begin to grasp my situation, my pen pal Joe, the ex–bank robber. He wrote me back immediately.

Dear Piper,

Got your letter. Thanks for reminding me of how much I hated the Los Angeles Metropolitan Detention Center (MDC). I laughed like a mental patient when you told me you are withholding your birth date from your chatty, amateur astrologist bunkmate. That's hilarious. Must be driving her nuts.

So I officially met your boy Larry when I was in NYC last month. A cool guy. We chilled at a nice coffee shop near where you live. It's good that you have a loving place to land when you are officially released altogether from the halfway house.

Talk about places to land, I was trapped in Oklahoma City (during my transfer from California to Pennsylvania) for 2 months. And I was a high-security risk so I spent that entire time locked in the hole. In the middle of summer. I suffered. I'm so fucking happy that I'm done with doing time. I got good at it, but I never want to be good at it again. That's one talent I don't mind squandering.

You mentioned seeing your old crimeys, that it was chilly at first. It's amazing how misery can instantly bond folks. Once upon a time I was doing time in a California prison but had to go to a county jail to receive another sentence. I was at the county jail for a month and couldn't wait to go back to the state prison. I wanted my old routine, my old friends, my own clothes, better food. So I understand your desire to go back to Danbury. I once felt the same thing.

Anyway, stay strong, Piper. You're almost done and then you can put this thing behind you in a large way. Not completely, but mostly.

Until next time,

Peace.

Joe Loya

. . .

THE MCC tested my endurance and tolerance. At least we had feminine hygiene items, all emblazoned with Bob Barker's name. I finally was allowed to buy shampoo, conditioner, stamps, and food from the commissary, plus tweezers. My brows were in a shocking state, and as there were no mirrors in the MCC, the Jansen sisters and I had to play beauty parlor. I did push-ups and crunches, but there was no place to do yoga without someone eyeballing me, certainly not in our six-woman cell. It contained the three of us, an Eminemlette, a cheerful six-foot-four giantess called Tiny, and a new Spanish mami named Inez who was also in Chicago on a writ.

When Inez had first been arrested, another woman in the county jail had thrown cleaning solution in her eyes and blinded her. After nine operations she had recovered partial sight, but she was extremely light-sensitive and so was allowed to wear gigantic wraparound sunglasses. Inez had just celebrated her fiftieth birthday; we tried to make it cheerful.

Now I didn't just miss Danbury, I also missed Oklahoma City. The Jansen sisters agreed. We talked longingly about doing "the shackle dance" on the tarmac again. Our shared mantra became "It can always get worse." We literally repeated it aloud every day, as a charm to ward off the possibility that our situation might grow even more unpleasant.

The women's unit was granted "privileges" only once a week, such as recreation time in what resembled a 1970s elementary school gym with dead basketballs and no weights, just one medicine ball, and access to a law library that contained cheesy paperbacks in addition to ancient legal texts. We were escorted by a CO to and from these activities like a kindergarten class. During these journeys we always encountered male prisoners at work; they had far more freedom of movement than we did, which infuriated me. To get to the gym we had to pass the kitchens, where some hopeful-looking guys were always waiting to catch a glimpse of us.

"You ladies need anything up there?" one of them asked one day as we were being herded onto the elevator.

"More fruit!" I shouted.

"I'm gonna send you some bananas, Blondie!"

I COULD barely contain myself when I got the news that Larry was going to visit me. It took all my self-restraint not to climb up onto one of the unit tables and pound my chest and scream. But the most dangerous thing in prison—jealousy—was not something I wanted to tangle with right now. So I kept it on the down-low. Plus, I was growing skeptical that anything would ever go right for me again.

On the Saturday he was supposed to come from New York, I took a hot shower. Another prisoner had tipped me off that there was one window of time in the morning when for some reason we could get hot water. My wet hair hung down my back—no hair dryers in the MCC. I went into the bathroom and stared at myself in the metal plate that was bolted over the sinks in lieu of a mirror. It was probably for the best that I couldn't really see what I looked like. I noted the pencil scrapings on the wall, where other prisoners had made makeshift eyeliner by mixing the lead powder and Vaseline. I didn't have that kind of skill.

Visiting hours were very short in Chicago. I sat nervously watching the clock. The Jansen sisters sat nervously watching me. "He'll be here," they assured me. It was sort of touching how invested in his visit they were, how they had started to talk about Larry as if they knew him. I felt bad that Hester/Anne's husband was not able to come visit her in Chicago—he lived not far from the prison where she was serving her seven-year sentence.

After over an hour of the visiting time had elapsed, I was beside myself. I knew what was happening. The morons who ran the MCC had turned him away. I was sure of it—these people were completely incompetent in every way I had observed so far; why on earth would visitation be any different? I was beaten and furious, a horrible combination.

And then the security door opened, and a CO walked in and conferred with the CO on duty in the unit. "Kerman!"

I bolted across the room.

When I finally got into the big, dirty visiting room, I felt calmer. There were a lot of prisoners with their families in there, and at first I didn't see Larry, but when I did, I felt faint. I hugged him, and he looked a little faint too.

"You wouldn't believe what they put me through. These people are just unreal!" he almost shouted. We sat where we were told, facing each other on molded plastic chairs. I felt truly calm for the first time since I left Danbury.

The remaining hour flew by. We talked about how on earth I was going to get home, what was going to happen. "We'll figure it out, babe," he soothed me, squeezing my hand.

When the guards called "time," I wanted to cry. After I kissed Larry goodbye, I practically backed out of the room so I could see him as long as possible. And then I was being herded into a room with a handful of female prisoners. Everyone had the postvisit glow of happiness, and they all looked a lot better for it.

"Piper, you had a visit?" someone asked.

"Yeah, my fiancé came to see me." I grinned like a fool.

"He came all the way from New York to see you? Wow!" It was as if he had come from the moon.

I just nodded. I didn't want to be boastful of my great fortune to have a man like Larry.

I HAD been hearing about the roof since I got to the MCC. Apparently there was a recreation area up on the top of the building, and when the weather was agreeable, an officer might bring us up there. I had been indoors for weeks now; I was dreaming about the track and the lake at Danbury every night. Finally one day it was announced that we could sign up for roof time. As many women crammed into the elevator as could fit. At the top there were nylon coats we could throw on, and then we were out, high in the sky, al-

beit caged under razor and chicken wire. There were a couple of basketball hoops up there, and the temperature was in the forties. I immediately got hiccups from the oxygen differential and just breathed
as deeply as I could. The roof reflected the building's triangular foot-
print, and you could see far in every direction. In one direction were
railway yard tracks. A nearby building had a fabulous art deco statue
at its pinnacle. And to the southeast I could see the lake.

I walked to the south side of the rec deck, which was fenced
with black iron. The bars were wide enough apart that I could wedge
my face between them. I stared out at the lake, scanning the city
below me.

"Hey! Nora. Come here!"

"What?" She came over.

I pointed through the bars. "Isn't that the Congress Hotel?"

She stared through the bars for a moment, trying to find the spot
where she had packed a suitcase full of money for me to carry, more
than ten years before. "I think you're right. You are right. Jesus."

Neither of us said anything for a moment.

"What a dump."

THE TRIAL finally began. Jonathan Bibby, the guy who had taught
Nora how to smuggle drugs way back when, claimed that he had
been an innocent art dealer who happened to hang out with a lot of
convicted drug smugglers. But the feds had detailed evidence against
him, including records of him traveling to Africa on the same flights
as Nora, Hester/Anne, and others. Hester/Anne was taken away to
appear in court first. She had known the defendant for years. She
came back teary-eyed; the defense attorney had ripped her apart.

Nora went out next. I remembered that George Freud was somewhere in the building; I figured there was no way they weren't calling other codefendants as well. On February 14 I was called to R&D.
"Happy Valentine's Day," cracked Nora. She had no idea how close to
drowning she was.

My escorts to court this time were older, burlier, and more confident. They were also solicitous. "Is there anything we can get you, Piper?"

I was stumped by that one. I didn't smoke. I was pretty sure they weren't going to give me scotch. "I would love a good cup of coffee?"

"We'll see what we can do."

I had never seen Jonathan Bibby until I was marched into the courtroom in my best orange jumpsuit and stepped into the witness box. Yet I spent what seemed like hours on the stand recounting my own experience, while the jury listened. I wondered what they made of what they were hearing. All of the defense attorney's questions to me centered on Nora, so it was obvious that she was the star witness. I truly hated testifying for the government, but I was also pretty peeved that this jackass didn't have the good grace to plead guilty as his codefendants had and spare us all this hassle and discomfort.

On my ride home my escorts pulled over under the El. One of them hopped out and returned with a piping-hot cup of Dunkin' Donuts coffee. He uncuffed me. "There's sugar and cream in there, I wasn't sure how you take it."

They sat in the front seat and smoked while I enjoyed every sip of that coffee. I listened to the roar of the train above and watched people going about their lives on the street. I wondered if this was as weird as it was going to get.

When it was all over—the jury found Bibby guilty—no one felt good. All I wanted to do was go back to real prison, meaning Danbury. And then go home.

WITHIN THE stifling women's unit, Crystal "the mayor" made an effort to maintain a faint semblance of prison protocol. Of course, this involved the Lord. Crystal was a big fan and liked to listen to a local minister's daily morning TV broadcast turned way up loud. She was a much more persistent proselytizer than any prisoner I had known in Danbury. Every week she would swing by when they called for the church group to go out of the unit, Bible in hand. "Coming to church, ladies?"

The Jansen girls would scowl. Although Hester/Anne had been born again, she shared my distaste for prison religious ceremonies. "No thanks, Crystal."

She wasn't giving up easily. I figured you had to fight fire with fire. The next time they called us for gym time, I went looking for Crystal.

"You coming to the gym, Crystal?"

Looking at me as if I had lost my rabbit-ass mind, she squawked with outrage, "What? Gym? You won't find me in no gym, Piper. Tire myself out!"

That Sunday she was back, optimistic as ever. "You comin' to church, Piper? It's a good one this week!"

"I tell you what, Crystal. You go on to church, and I'm gonna ask you to pray for me. And this week when I go down to the gym, I'm gonna work out for you. Is that a deal?"

She thought that was the funniest thing she had heard in months. She cackled all the way out the door. From then on, whenever they called our respective faiths to action, we would sing out to each other:

"Work it out for me, Piper!"

"Pray for me, Crystal!"

I CORNERED the unit manager in his office during his once-a-week appearance on the women's floor. I tried to remain calm as I explained that March 4, my release date, was drawing close, and I needed to know what was going to happen next. Would they ship me back to Danbury? Would they release me from Chicago?

He had no idea. He didn't know anything about it. He was not concerned.

I wanted to break everything in his office.

Nora and Hester/Anne cast worried eyes on me as I emerged

after my conversation. I had kept the fact that my release date was just a week away a secret from everyone in Chicago, especially them. They both had years left to do. Plus I didn't trust any of the other prisoners not to mess with me in some way, a very typical prison paranoia. So as far as the sisters were concerned, I was losing it over Con Air, which was very un-Zen of me.

"Let's make dinner," said Hester/Anne. I went to retrieve the hard-boiled eggs that had been on ice since breakfast that morning. Anne carefully sliced each oval in half, and Nora mixed the yolks with packets of mayo and mustard, plus generous dashes of hot sauce from the commissary.

I tasted it. "Needs something."

"I know." Nora produced a packet of hot dog relish.

I wrinkled my brow. "Are you sure?"

"Trust me." I tasted again. It was perfect. Now I carefully filled each half of the egg whites.

Nora sprinkled a bit more hot sauce on the top.

"Not too much!" said Hester/Anne.

Deviled eggs. We had a feast. The other women admired our dinner, wishing they had saved their eggs too. The three of us had carved out a place among the few sane women in Chicago. But my God it was hard.

I SAID goodbye to the sisters when the next Con Air flight left days later—with them on it. They were mystified as to why I had not been called with them to do the shackle dance on the tarmac. They said goodbye to me with sadness and pity in their eyes. I was so upset that I could barely look at them. Part of it was that I wanted so badly to be on that airplane escaping from Chicago. Part of it was that I knew I would probably never see them on the outs. It felt like there was a lot more to say.

When they were gone, I got under a blanket on my bunk and cried for hours. I didn't think I could keep going. Although I was days away from my release date, I wasn't sure of what was going to happen.

It was totally irrational, but I was beginning to feel like the BOP would never let me go.

As a child, a teen, a young adult, I developed a firm belief in my solitude, the not-novel concept that we are each alone in the world. Some parts self-reliance, some parts self-protection, this belief offers a binary perspective—powerhouse or victim, complete responsibility or total divorcement, all in or out the door. Carried to its extreme, the idea gives license to the belief that one's own actions do not matter much; we traverse the world in our own bubbles, occasionally breaking through to one another but largely and ultimately alone.

I would seem to have been ready-made for prison time then, as a familiar jailhouse trope says "you come in alone and you walk out alone," and common counsel is to keep to oneself and mind your own business. But that's not what I learned in prison. That's not how I survived prison. What I discovered was that I am emphatically not alone. The people on the outside who wrote and visited every week and traveled long distances to come and tell me that I wasn't forgotten, that I wasn't alone, had a tremendous impact on my life.

However, most of all, I realized that I was not alone in the world because of the women I lived with for over a year, who gave me a dawning recognition of what I shared with them. We shared overcrowded Dorms and lack of privacy. We shared eight numbers instead of names, prison khakis, cheap food and hygiene items. Most important, we shared a deep reserve of humor, creativity in adverse circumstances, and the will to protect and maintain our own humanity despite the prison system's imperative to crush it. I don't think any of us could have managed those survival techniques alone; I know I couldn't—we needed each other.

Small kindnesses and simple pleasures shared were so important, whether given or received, regardless of what quarter they came from, that they brought home to me powerfully that I was not alone in this world, in this life. I shared the most basic operating system with people who ostensibly had little in common with me. I could connect—perhaps with anyone.

Now here, in my third prison, I perceived an odd truth that held for each: no one ran them. Of course, somewhere in those buildings, some person with a nameplate on their desk or door was called the warden and nominally ran the place, and below them in the food chain there were captains and lieutenants. But for all practical purposes, for the prisoners, the people who lived in those prisons day in and day out, the captain's chair was vacant, and the wheel was spinning while the sails flapped. The institutions putzed along with the absolute minimum of staff presence, and the staff that were there invariably seemed less than interested in their jobs. No one was present, interacting in any affirmative way with the people who filled those prisons. The leadership vacuum was total. No one who worked in "corrections" appeared to give any thought to the purpose of our being there, any more than a warehouse clerk would consider the meaning of a can of tomatoes, or try to help those tomatoes understand what the hell they were doing on the shelf.

Great institutions have leaders who are proud of what they do, and who engage with everyone who makes up those institutions, so each person understands their role. But our jailers are generally granted near-total anonymity, like the cartoon executioner who wears a hood to conceal his identity. What is the point, what is the reason, to lock people away for years, when it seems to mean so very little, even to the jailers who hold the key? How can a prisoner understand their punishment to have been worthwhile to anyone, when it's dealt in a way so offhand and indifferent?

I SLUMPED onto a hard plastic chair, watching BET. The video for Jay-Z's single "99 Problems" was playing. The grim, gritty black-and-white images of Brooklyn and its hood-life citizens made me feel homesick for a place where I had never even lived.

My last week in prison was the hardest. If I had been shipped back to Danbury, I would have received a boisterous welcome back into the fold and a hasty, tearful send-off into the outside world. In Chicago I felt terribly alone; separated from all the people and the jubilant going-home rituals I had known in Danbury and had assumed I would one day partake in. I wanted to celebrate my own strength and resilience—my survival of a year in prison—around people who understood me. Instead what I felt was the treacherous anger that takes over when you don't have one bit of control over your life. The MCC still would not confirm that I would be released on March 4.

Yet even the BOP can't stop the clock, and when the day arrived, I was up, showered, and ready. I knew that Larry was in Chicago, that he was coming to get me, but no staff in Chicago had acknowledged that I was going to be released; no paperwork had been shown to me. I was deeply hopeful, but also deeply skeptical, about what would happen that day.

My fellow prisoners watched the early morning news broadcast of Martha Stewart's midnight release from Alderson Prison Camp, and soon it was business as usual, with BET music videos battling Lifetime at top volume on the two TVs. I sat on one of the hard benches, watching the guard's every move. Finally at eleven A.M. the phone rang. The guard picked it up, listened, hung up, and barked, "Kerman! Pack out!"

I leaped up, rushed to my locker, retrieving only a small manila envelope of personal letters, leaving behind toiletries and books. I was intensely aware that the women I shared the cell with were all at the beginning of their prison journey, and I was at the end of mine. There was no way to give them all the things I now carried in my head and my heart.

"You can have anything in my locker, ladies. I'm going home."

THE FEMALE guard in R&D explained that they had no women's street clothes, so she gave me the smallest pair of men's jeans they had, a green polo shirt, a windbreaker, and a cheap pair of fake-suede lace-up shoes with thin plastic soles. They also provided me with what she called "a gratuity": $28.30. I was ready for the outside world.

A guard led me and another prisoner, a young Spanish guy, to an elevator. We looked at each other as we rode down.

He nodded to me. "How much time you do?"

"Thirteen months. You?"

"Twenty."

When we got to the bottom, we were in the service entrance. The guard opened the door to the street, and we stepped out. We were on an empty side street, a canyon between the fortress and some office buildings, with a slice of gray sky above us. Homie's people were waiting directly across the street in an SUV, and he broke for the car like a jackrabbit and was gone.

I looked around.

"Isn't anyone coming to get you?" asked the guard.

"Yeah!" I said, impatient. "Where *are* we?"

"I'll take you around to the front," he said, reluctant.

I turned and started walking briskly ahead of him. Ten yards farther, and I saw Larry, standing in front of the MCC, talking on his phone, until he turned and saw me. And then I was running, as fast as I could. No one could stop me.

Afterword to the Paperback Edition

||||

So I came home, unshackled on the airplane, and landed late at night. Larry brought me to an unfamiliar apartment in Brooklyn and I ate a slice of pizza at one in the morning.

The federal probation office in downtown Brooklyn was where I had to go the next day, beginning two years of supervised release. Probation involved urine tests, copious amounts of paperwork, occasional surprise visits from my probation officer at home or at work, and travel permission if I needed to leave the city. I was in the home stretch of nearly nine years of supervision or imprisonment by the federal government.

Work began a week later, at a marketing job created just for me at a tech company that was run by a friend. His executive board, who had approved my employment, regarded me with some curiosity; my co-workers, mostly young guys, were welcoming and enthusiastic. For most people, checking the felony conviction box on a job application ends their shot at employment. Every day, when I rode the subway to work, or went to the deli to pick out whatever I wanted for lunch, or walked the nighttime streets of New York, I felt overwhelmed by my good fortune. As I ran in Prospect Park in the cold March sunshine, tears would suddenly well up and stream down my face.

I was only one of the more than 700,000 people who return home from American prisons and jails every year, but I was hyper-conscious of my opportunities "on the outs," in stark contrast to most of those other men and women. I had a safe and stable place to live; a network of family and friends with many resources to help me come home; and a precious job, with health insurance. I thought often of the plans other women from Danbury had been making: homeless shelters, family court, uncertain prospects for work. I had watched hundreds of women leave prison with optimism and a resolve to change their lives going forward, and I knew that most of them would have to find a way to make those changes with very little help.

Lack of empathy lies at the heart of every crime—certainly my own—yet empathy is the key to bringing a former prisoner back into the fold of society. What happens in our prisons is completely within the community's control. The public expects sentences to be punitive but also rehabilitative; however, what we expect and what we get from our prisons are very different things. The lesson that our prison system teaches its residents is how to survive as a prisoner, not as a citizen—not a very constructive body of knowledge for us or the communities to which we return.

When you're on federal probation, you are not to have contact with other people who have a criminal record. I've been done with probation for many years, and now I hear from or about many of the remarkable women I met in prison. Some are married, with new children or grandchildren and quiet lives; some are working and going to school, hopeful about their futures; some are ill, and struggling. Some are activists who are determined to change the criminal justice system, and some have gone back into the system, back to prison. I can hear their voices and see their faces in my head, and sometimes on the subway I search the crowd, half-expecting to see Natalie, or Yoga Janet, or any of the hundreds of women whose paths crossed mine.

Before I went to Danbury a friend of a friend of a friend who had served a year in federal women's prison spoke to me about what to expect, and she said something that stayed with me: "Not a day goes by that I don't think about prison in some way." Now I serve on the board of the Women's Prison Association, a nonprofit that has been helping women who've had criminal justice involvement change their lives since 1845. And not a day goes by that I don't think about prison in some way, too. In the course of my work I have spoken with groups of prisoners and prison staff, probation and parole officers, public defenders, prison volunteers, and justice reform advocates; whether they consider themselves reformers or law enforcement, everyone agrees that we must do a better job of changing lives and improving the system.

The United States has the biggest prison population in the world—we incarcerate 25 percent of the world's prisoners, though we are only 5 percent of the world's population. This reliance on prisons is recent: in 1980 we had about 500,000 Americans in prison; now we have more than 2.3 million people locked up. A huge part of that growth is represented by people like the women I did time with—low-level offenders who have made serious mistakes but pose little threat of violence. Most of the women I know from prison have lived lives that were missing opportunities many of us take for granted. It sometimes seems that we have built revolving doors between our poorest communities and correctional facilities, and created perverse financial incentives to keep those prisons full, at taxpayers' expense. America has invested heavily in prisons, while the public institutions that actually prevent crime and strengthen communities—schools, hospitals, libraries, museums, community centers—go without.

Incredible things can happen behind prison walls because people are so remarkably resilient; we can survive almost anything, one of the reasons that harsh punishment alone doesn't bear fruit. In order for prisons to truly serve the public, the people who run them would do well to aspire to the words of Thomas Mott Osborne, the storied warden of New York's Sing Sing Prison in the early part of the twentieth century, who vowed, "We will turn this prison from a scrap heap into a repair shop."

Acknowledgments

||||

Most of all, I would like to thank my husband, Larry Smith, whose ferociously stubborn love sustains me and without whom I would not have written this book. I'd also like to thank the women of the Danbury FCI, and the other prisons I traveled through, because they changed my life.

I am deeply grateful for the love and support of my mother, father, and brother and all of my family, and to Carol and Lou and the entire Smith family.

Thanks to my agent, Stuart Krichevsky, for his belief in this project, his patience, and his hard work, and to Shana Cohen, Jennifer Puglisi, Danielle Rollins, and Howard Sanders. Thank you to my incredible editor, Julie Grau, who always understood the book I wanted to write and challenged me to make it so much better; and to Cindy Spiegel, Laura Van der Veer, Hana Landes, Steve Messina, Donna Sinisgalli, Christopher Sergio, Rachel Bernstein, London King, Anne Tate, Avideh Bashirrad, and the great team at Spiegel & Grau and Random House.

Special thanks to my best friend, Kristen Grimm, who knows every step of the journey recounted in this book and has never stopped helping me through it. To my readers Trish Boczkowski, David Boyer, Robyn Crawford, and Ellen DeLaRosa, I say thank you each for your unique help and counsel.

I'm grateful to each and every person who wrote me letters, sent me books, and helped me in so many other ways while I was in prison; the enormous kindness of friends and strangers is humbling. I especially would like to thank Earl Adams, Zoe Allen, Kate Barrett, Michael Callahan, Jeff Cranmer, Cheryl Della Pietra, Gabriella DiFilippo, Dave Eggers, Arin Fishkin, Victor Friedman, John Garrison, Noah Hatton, Liz Heckles, Steve Huggard, Joe Loya, Kirk and Susan Meyer, Leonid Oliker, Julie Oppenheimer, Ed Powers, Brie Reeder, Ted Rheingold, Kris Rosi and the Rosi family, Jon Schulberg, Shannon Snead, Tara Stiles, Ty Wenger, Penelope Whitney, Kelly Wyllie, and Sam Zalutsky.

Huge thanks to my defense attorney, Patrick J. Cotter, and to my other legal eagles, Dave Corbett, Wallace Doolittle, and Eric Hecker.

Tim Barkow, the creator of www.thepipebomb.com, is a kind friend and generous tech genius, as is Teresa Tauchi, the creator of www.piperkerman.com. Thank you to my friend and enthusiastic photographer, John Carnett. Thank you also to Lisa Timothy, for her insight on discussion questions.

Returning to the workforce after prison is a daunting proposition. Thank you for the generosity and the warm welcome of Dan Hoffman and the entire M5 team. Thanks also to my enthusiastic and bighearted colleagues at Spitfire Strategies.

Without the generous hospitality of Jean Brennan and Zach Rogers, Paul and Erica Tullis, and Liz Gewirtzman, this book would probably not have been written. And thank you to the entire Above and Beyoncé crew for tireless cheerleading and well-timed diversions.

To all of these people, I am so very grateful.

Justice Reform Resources

| | | |

In 1980, there were approximately 500,000 people in prison in the United States. Today there are 2.3 million, and, according to the 2008 U.S. Bureau of Justice Statistics, a total of over 7 million people are on parole or probation or locked up. A great number of these people have committed nonviolent offenses, and this dramatic change is due to laws and sentencing guidelines related to the "war on drugs," which has not reduced rates of drug addiction or abuse in this country. Overincarceration in America destabilizes families and communities, making life outside the mainstream more likely by limiting opportunities for change. We have a racially biased justice system that overpunishes, fails to rehabilitate, and doesn't make us safer.

Fortunately, there are many people around the country who are working to change our criminal justice system so that we'll have fewer Americans in prison without compromising public safety. Here are just a few organizations that are helping to make our justice system work properly for all of us. I am always adding to the list at www.piperkerman.com/justice-reform and at www.facebook .com/orangeisthenewblack.

WOMEN

Alabama Women's Resource Network

401 Beacon Parkway West
Birmingham, AL 35209-3105
(205) 916-0135, ext. 501
www.awrn.org
Alabama Women's Resource Network works to reduce the number
of women in prison in Alabama by promoting investment in neighborhood resources and community-based alternatives to prison.

California Coalition for Women Prisoners

1540 Market Street, Suite 490
San Francisco, CA 94102
(415) 255-7036, ext. 4
www.womenprisoners.org
California Coalition for Women Prisoners is a grassroots social justice
organization, with members inside and outside prison, that prioritizes
the leadership of the people, families, and communities most affected
by the prison system in building a movement.

The Center for Young Women's Development

832 Folsom Street, Suite 700
San Francisco, CA 94107
(415) 703-8800
www.cywd.org
The Center for Young Women's Development is one of the first nonprofits in the United States run and led entirely by young women.
The center organizes young women who are the most marginalized
in San Francisco—those in the street economies and the juvenile
justice system—to design and deliver peer-to-peer education and
support.

A New Way of Life Reentry Project

P.O. Box 875288
Los Angeles, CA 90087
(323) 563-3575
www.anewwayoflife.org

Led by Susan Burton, a CNN Hero of 2010, A New Way of Life Reentry Project provides housing, support services, and leadership development to formerly incarcerated women in South Central Los Angeles, facilitating a successful transition back to community life.

Power Inside

P.O. Box 4796
Baltimore, MD 21211
(410) 889-8333
www.powerinside.org

Power Inside is committed to building self-sufficiency and preventing incarceration among women and families in Baltimore through direct client services, advocacy, leadership development, and public education.

Women and Prison: A Site for Resistance

Beyondmedia Education
4001 North Ravenswood, #204B
Chicago, IL 60613
(773) 857-7300
www.womenandprison.org

Women and Prison: A Site for Resistance is a website that makes visible women's experiences in the criminal justice system. Documenting these stories in women's own voices is essential to a true understanding of the reality of women's experiences in prisons and jails. The stories are supported by a collection of resources, such as lists of organizations, reports, essays, and links to a wide range of information on women and prison.

Women in Prison Project
c/o The Correctional Association of New York
2090 Adam Clayton Powell Boulevard, Suite 200
New York, NY 10027
(212) 254-5700
www.correctionalassociation.org/WIPP/index.htm
The Women in Prison Project is dedicated to addressing the effects of
New York's criminal justice policies on women and their families.
The Project advocates for a shift in government priorities away from
prison and toward alternative programs where a woman can stay connected to her family, address underlying issues, and become a productive member of society.

Women on the Rise Telling HerStory
c/o The Osborne Association
809 Westchester Avenue
Bronx, NY 10455
(917) 626-8168
www.womenontherise-worth.org
WORTH (Women on the Rise Telling HerStory) is an advocacy and
consultant group comprising incarcerated and formerly incarcerated
women who have the expertise and understanding to engage, navigate, and challenge policies and perceptions concerning incarcerated
women.

Women's Prison Association
110 Second Avenue
New York, NY 10003
(646) 292-7740
www.wpaonline.org
The Women's Prison Association, founded in 1865, is the nation's
oldest service and advocacy organization committed to helping
women with criminal justice histories see new possibilities for themselves and their families. WPA offers a host of useful information and

resources on issues facing these women and our families, in addition to housing, health, employment, and family services and leadership and advocacy training.

THE NATIONAL Institute of Corrections and the Women's Prison Association have partnered to create a searchable online **National Directory of Programs for Women with Criminal Justice Involvement**. This database provides a place where practitioners, policy makers, and community members can find information on programs and services for women in the criminal justice system. The database includes state-by-state programs and services for women at all stages of criminal justice involvement, both in correctional facilities and in the community: www.nicic.gov/wodp.

CHILDREN

Angel Tree
Prison Fellowship Ministries
44180 Riverside Parkway, #100
Leesburg, VA 20176-1709
(703) 478-0100; (800) 55-ANGEL
www.angeltree.org
The faith community has worked long and hard to provide services to current and former prisoners and address injustice. Prison Fellowship believes that the way our government handles crime and punishment affects all of us, and advocates for reform. Its related programs include Angel Tree, which serves the children of prisoners at Christmastime and throughout the year.

308 | Justice Reform Resources

Children of Inmates
(888) 757-5439
www.childrenofinmates.org
Children of Inmates is a collaborative effort among nine Miami-Dade County organizations. They identify, encourage, and refer families to the services that will meet the needs of the children of inmates, based on their development and circumstances.

Corporation for National and Community Service
Mentoring Children of Prisoners, Online Resource Center
www.nationalserviceresources.org/service-activities/mentoring-children-of-prisoners
The Corporation for National and Community Service is a federal agency that engages more than 5 million Americans in service through Senior Corps, AmeriCorps, Learn and Serve America, and United We Serve.

Family and Corrections Network
National Resource Center on Children
and Families of the Incarcerated
93 Old York Road, Suite 1, #510
Jenkintown, PA 19046
(215) 576-1110
www.fcnetwork.org
Family and Corrections Network's National Resource Center on Children and Families of the Incarcerated works to connect program providers, policy makers, researchers, educators, correctional personnel, and the public with the families of the incarcerated for advocacy, action, and planning. It provides information on children of the incarcerated, programs for parenting from prison, prison visiting, help for incarcerated fathers, hospitality programs, and a variety of other topics.

Legal Services for Prisoners with Children
1540 Market Street, Suite 490
San Francisco, CA 94102
(415) 255-7036
www.prisonerswithchildren.org
Legal Services for Prisoners with Children advocates for the human
rights and empowerment of incarcerated parents, their children, their
family members, and people at risk for incarceration. LSPC responds
to requests for information, trainings, technical assistance, litigation,
community activism, and the development of more advocates. Its
focus is on women prisoners and their families, and it emphasizes that
issues of race are central to any discussion of incarceration.

Reclaiming Futures National Program Office
Portland State University
527 SW Hall, Suite 400
Portland, OR 97201
(503) 725-8911
www.reclaimingfutures.org
Reclaiming Futures helps young people in trouble with drugs, alcohol, and crime by reinventing the way police, courts, detention facilities, treatment providers, and the community work together (now in
twenty-six communities around the country). Juvenile justice reform
is a critical lever for changing the U.S. prison crisis for the better.

WRITING and BOOKS

Book 'Em
The Thomas Merton Center
5129 Penn Avenue
Pittsburgh, PA 15224
(412) 361-3022
www.bookempittsburgh.org

Book 'Em sends educational books and quality reading material to prisoners and prison libraries all over the United States.

Books Through Bars
4722 Baltimore Avenue
Philadelphia, PA 19143
(215) 727-8170
www.booksthroughbars.org
Books Through Bars provides book distribution to prisoners and education programs throughout the mid-Atlantic region. It also created a great online resource with contact information for other prison book programs throughout the United States: www.books throughbars.org/pbp.

PEN American Center Prison Writing Program
588 Broadway, Suite 303
New York, NY 10012
(212) 334-1660
www.pen.org/prisonwriting
The PEN American Center Prison Writing Program believes in the restorative and rehabilitative power of writing, and serves hundreds of prisoners across the country. The program sponsors an annual writing contest, publishes a free handbook for prisoners, provides one-on-one mentoring to inmates whose writing shows merit or promise, conducts workshops for former inmates, and seeks to get inmates' work to the public through literary publications and readings.

Women's Prison Book Project
c/o Arise Bookstore
2441 Lyndale Avenue South
Minneapolis, MN 55405
www.wpbp.org
The Women's Prison Book Project provides women and transgender-identified persons in prison with free reading materials covering a

wide range of topics from law and education (dictionaries, GED, etc.) to fiction, politics, history, and women's health.

NATIONAL RESOURCES

Council of State Governments Justice Center
100 Wall Street, 20th Floor
New York, NY 10005
(212) 482-2320
www.justicecenter.csg.org
The Council of State Governments Justice Center is a national non-profit organization that serves policy makers at the local, state, and federal levels from all branches of government. Staff provides practical, nonpartisan advice and consensus-driven strategies—informed by available evidence—to increase public safety and strengthen communities. As part of their work they focus on mental health, justice reinvestment, and national reentry resources (www.national reentryresourcecenter.org/library).

Families Against Mandatory Minimums
1612 K Street NW, Suite 700
Washington, DC 20006
(202) 822-6700
www.famm.org
Families Against Mandatory Minimums is the national voice for fair and proportionate sentencing laws. It shows the human face of sentencing, advocates for state and federal sentencing reform, and mobilizes thousands of individuals and families whose lives are adversely affected by unjust sentences. FAMM works to change mandatory sentencing laws through the legislative process on the federal and state levels, through participation in precedent-setting legal cases, and by educating the public.

The Innocence Project

100 Fifth Avenue, 3rd Floor
New York, NY 10011
(212) 364-5340
www.innocenceproject.org

The Innocence Project works to exonerate wrongfully convicted people in the United States and to reform the justice system so that innocent people do not go to jail. Since 1992, more than 250 innocent people have been exonerated through DNA testing (which is available in only a small fraction of criminal cases), including 17 who were at one time sentenced to death.

Just Detention International

3325 Wilshire Boulevard, Suite 340
Los Angeles, CA 90010
(213) 384-1400
www.justdetention.org

Just Detention International is a human rights organization that seeks to end sexual abuse in all forms of detention. Just Detention works to ensure government accountability for prisoner rape; to transform ill-informed public attitudes about sexual violence in detention; and to promote access to resources for those who have survived this form of abuse.

National H.I.R.E. Network

225 Varick Street
New York, NY 10014
(212) 243-1313
www.hirenetwork.org

The National H.I.R.E. (Helping Individuals with criminal records Reenter through Employment) Network is both a national clearinghouse for employment information and an advocate for policy change.

The Pew Center on the States
Public Safety Performance Project
901 E Street NW, 10th Floor
Washington, DC 20004-1409
(202) 552-2000
www.pewcenteronthestates.org/publicsafety
The Pew Center on the States Public Safety Performance Project
helps states advance fiscally sound, data-driven policies and practices
in sentencing and corrections that protect public safety, hold offenders accountable, and control corrections costs.

PrisonMovement's Weblog
http://prisonmovement.wordpress.com
From a tireless reformer. Her blogroll is extensive.

Reentry Central
Box 411
New Haven, CT 06513
(203) 468-6589
www.reentrycentral.org
Reentry Central provides a centralized national news and information site for professionals in the fields of ex-offender reentry and related criminal justice areas.

Restorative Justice Online
Centre for Justice and Reconciliation
Prison Fellowship International
P.O. Box 17434
Washington, DC 20041
(703) 481-0000
www.restorativejustice.org
Restorative Justice emphasizes repairing the harm caused by crime.
When victims, offenders, and community members meet to decide
how to do that, the results can be transformational. This is very differ-
ent from retribution, and is grounded in cultures around the world.

Thousand Kites

91 Madison Avenue
Whitesburg, KY 41858
(276) 679-3116
www.thousandkites.org
Thousand Kites is an innovative community-based performance, Web, video, and radio project centered on the United States prison system. It integrates radio broadcasts, phone calls from and to prisoners, and individuals' stories to serve families affected by incarceration and create human context for what happens in our prisons.

Vera Institute of Justice

233 Broadway, 12th Floor
New York, NY 10279
(212) 334-1300
www.vera.org
The Vera Institute of Justice is an independent, nonpartisan, nonprofit center for justice policy and practice. Its projects and reform initiatives, typically conducted in partnership with local, state, or national officials, are located across the United States and around the world. It helps leaders in government and civil society improve the systems people rely on for justice and safety.

Washington State Institute for Public Policy

110 Fifth Avenue SE, Suite 214
P.O. Box 40999
Olympia, WA 98504
(360) 586-2677
www.wsipp.wa.gov/pub.asp?docid=06-10-1201
The Institute's 2006 report "Evidence-Based Public Policy Options to Reduce Future Prison Construction, Criminal Justice Costs, and Crime Rates" is eye-opening in terms of what really delivers.

ORANGE
Is the New
BLACK

| | | |

PIPER KERMAN

A READER'S GUIDE

INTERVIEW:

PIPER KERMAN,

author of *Orange Is the New Black*

SMITH Magazine
April 6, 2010

By Whitney Joiner

"Memoirs are often about difficult things in a person's life. In my situation, my story starts with about the stupidest, most immoral thing I've ever done, one with terrible consequences."

In 1993, Piper Kerman, a recent graduate of Smith College, made a reckless decision that would alter the course of her life: she accompanied her then-girlfriend, "an impossibly cool" older woman named Nora, who earned her unending stack of cash through drug smuggling, on a handful of lengthy trips. While Nora met up with her "connections" in Europe and Asia, Kerman roamed the streets and hit the beaches. But, after carrying a suitcase of cash across the Atlantic, Kerman realized she was in over her head and she escaped to San Francisco to piece her life back together.

Five years later, she was happily living in New York City with her then-boyfriend (and now husband, SMITH founder Larry Smith). Her period of criminal activity was short, nonviolent—and behind her. Or so Kerman thought. Then in May 1998, two Customs agents arrived at her door. Years of legal delays later, she was sentenced to fifteen months in a federal prison, thirteen months with good behavior. After serving time in three facilities—including a trip on Con Air—she was released in March 2005.

Orange Is the New Black: My Year in a Women's Prison is Kerman's poignant and powerful memoir of those months. It's fascinating to follow Kerman as she navigates the endless lists of rules, petty prison guards, repetitive jobs for pennies an hour (used to buy soap or a radio at the commissary), and that all-important mail call that make up life in the correctional facility in Danbury, Connecticut. But it's her rendering of her fellow prisoners—their surprise birthday parties with homemade cards and microwave cheesecake, the ways they bring hope and humor to the inside, and the makeshift families they create—that allows *Orange* to transcend the prison genre and become a story about the remarkable capacity for strength and resilience of Kerman and the women she met in prison.

I spoke with Kerman over the phone from her home in Brooklyn about her decision to focus on her time behind bars, what emotional blank spot is at the bottom of almost every crime, and why more than 7 million Americans can directly relate to her book.

WHITNEY JOINER: When did you first start writing about your experience in prison?

PIPER KERMAN: I've never been a daily diary person, but when I was in prison, I would occasionally write in a journal. And I wrote hundreds of letters. Then, shortly after I came home, I sat down and started writing some of the stand-alone narratives that are within the book—like what was that first day like, or about my neighbor Vanessa, who'd been a man and was now a woman. All of those things ultimately went into the book.

WJ: How did you move from writing those pieces to deciding to try a cohesive narrative—a whole book?

PK: Even before I sat down to write, as soon as I got home, people wanted to hear—in great detail—about the experience. There was a clear appetite for insight into this hidden world, which was really encouraging. I think people are fascinated by prison. And the very dramatic fact of transgression and punishment is engrossing, regardless of whether it's men or women.

My own experience was, in many ways, dramatically different from the popular conception and prevailing narrative about prison: who's there, why they're there, and what life there is like. When I came home, people would ask me, "Did you get beaten up every day?" There's an expectation of violence. There's definitely violence in prison, but it wasn't a central part of my own experience. I just felt like there's a much more complete and complex picture to be presented about who's in the prison, why they're there, and what happens.

WJ: Do you mean that your experience was dramatically different than popular conceptions of prison because you were in a minimum-security facility, or because you're a middle-class white woman with a much more privileged background than most of the women you were incarcerated with?

PK: Neither. Those things are true, but I think the popular image of prison, *Oz* and *Cops,* is very narrow—and intended to justify the strengths of the prison system and its out-of-control growth. If everyone in prison is an uncontrollable and irredeemably violent person, then it's totally justified to have a massive and massively expensive prison system because, you know, public safety at any cost.

But if in fact everyone in prison is not irredeemably violent, if their lives have meaning and value, then suddenly you really call into question whether our government is doing the right thing. It's important for people who have been prisoners to have a voice, and to say in a more authentic way what life is really like. Otherwise, someone else is telling our story.

WJ: You didn't keep a daily journal at Danbury. How else did you reconstruct your time there?

PK: I wrote and received many, many letters. A lot of my friends saved my letters, and sent me copies. In my office here I have these giant binders. One of primary documents: letters I wrote, paperwork from the prison, things I received from other prisoners, like notes and birthday cards. In another binder, I put together the letters I received, which helped me understand my relationship to the outside world.

The first draft I wrote was literally a month-by-month—every chapter was a month. That was really helpful and instructive in terms of really cataloging the experience. I think it was a little painful to read. My editor, in one of her notes in that first draft, was like, "Here I think you're trying to capture the incredible tedium . . ." That rubric was shelved after that first draft.

WJ: You've worked in the communications and media arena, but you hadn't written for publication before. Were you worried about that at all?

PK: When I finished the first draft, I thought, *Well, I wrote a book! I don't necessarily know if it's a good book, but it's a book!* Then there were many subsequent drafts to make it a better book. But there were times, especially in the thick of it, where I thought, *How am I going to do this?* But I had a great support system and a wonderful editor.

You just have to put your head down and do your best. You can't get involved in a downward spiral of self-doubt. For me, Julie Grau, the editor who I was ultimately lucky enough to work with, was very challenging, right from the beginning, and said, "Your ability to capture detail and paint a vivid picture is very strong; you need to work on connecting what you're describing to your own emotional life and to see yourself as a participant and not an observer." That was the most challenging thing, and the thing I had to work on the most.

WJ: What were your perceived pros and cons before you launched into the project?

PK: I think the biggest con seemed like the loss of privacy, and I'm actually a private person. I talked to my family quite seriously to make sure that I would have their blessing. It's a huge level of self-exposure. Memoirs are often about difficult things in a person's life. In my situation, my story starts with about the stupidest, most immoral thing I've ever done, one with terrible consequences. It's a high level of self-exposure, but that's true for anyone who chooses to write about their own experience in a nonfiction format.

WJ: You spend only a bit of time on what happened before your conviction, the decisions you made that landed you there. What was your process of working with that material—explaining your period of criminal activity to readers?

PK: Every human being makes mistakes and does things they're not proud of. They can be everyday, or they can be catastrophic. And the unfortunate truth of being human is that we all have moments of indifference to other people's suffering. To me, that's the central thing that allows crime to happen: indifference to other people's suffering. If you're stealing from someone, if you're hurting them physically, if you're selling them a product that you know will hurt them—the thing that allows a person to do that is that they somehow convince themselves that that's not relevant to them. We all do things that we're not proud of, even though they might not have as terrible consequences. That's something that anyone can understand. So I thought it was really important, especially in those early chapters, to both help the reader maybe understand how one makes really bad decisions, but also to take responsibility. And I hope that it's really clear that I do take responsibility for my actions.

WJ: It's clear how awful it is to spend any time in a federal prison, especially when you discuss the power dynamics between the guards and the prisoners. But I was surprised by the ways in which it seemed livable: friendships with fellow prisoners, and the daily and weekly rituals that mark how you slog through.

PK: Prison's pretty horrible. First of all, I have to reemphasize—I had a very short sentence in relation to that of many of the women that I was serving time with. And I went into it—especially after almost six years of waiting—thinking, *One year is one year, and you can survive anything for one year.* First and foremost I walked in the prison gates with that mentality.

But the way that I did my time was by focusing on what positive things I could find, either in myself or other people, and that is reflected in the book. I didn't focus on the people I really didn't like. I didn't focus on feeling bad for myself. And when you start talking to people who are doing so much more time than you, and it seems like the only reason is the color of their skin and that they're from a poor neighborhood or family, it's pretty damn hard to feel bad for yourself.

It does unsettle me when folks say, "Oh, it doesn't sound so bad." It's *awful*. Prison is a horrible thing. If you have to go to prison for one year, you're just unbelievably grateful for the fact that you're out. And I had an easy road home in comparison to most people who return home from prison. But the focus on the positive that the book offers is really about finding that value in humanity and warmth in a setting where we're constantly told there's none to be found— people are irredeemable, terrible people. And that's not the case.

WJ: The reader certainly comes away with a sense of the waste within the system—the fact that the U.S. spends a ton of money to incarcerate nonviolent offenders, often for low-level drug charges. And we get a sense of the waste within prison itself, the lack of rehabilitative services. But you don't rail against the drug war or the prison system; you weave it in throughout the narrative.

PK: The reader is definitely able to draw her own conclusions from that. Right now, with the economy in chaos and state governments in chaos, it's 60 billion a year in taxpayer dollars that we can't afford economically. But it's also not something we can afford socially; it's devastating to communities that are already vulnerable. And it's not one we can afford morally, because of that warehousing aspect. I think there's this expectation that confinement alone will create the incentive and the means for an individual to make a change in their life. But it doesn't.

WJ: The women who are serving time with you are such a huge part of the book. Did you have any contact with them while writing this?

PK: I've heard from some people who I knew, and they've expressed excitement. I don't know if everyone who reads it who lived in Danbury will be excited or not, but I hope so.

It's really rare for prisoners to have an opportunity to tell their own story. Almost all the personal narratives out there are by men, especially full-length books. There are a lot of anthologies of women's writing from prison, but there's not that much out there. I really hope that more people get the opportunity to tell their story, because my story is so specific and narrow. It's a sprawling prison system— almost 2.5 million Americans in federal prisons, state prisons, county and city jails. Seven million Americans are either in prison, on probation, or on parole, and then all of their families.

That's one of the reasons I wanted to tell the story. I think my own story is relevant to that of millions of Americans, even though there's no question that middle-class white women are far from the majority of the prison system. Still, I think we only benefit from gaining a complete understanding: prison is a huge government entity that affects millions of Americans, and if the people who are most affected don't have a voice, that's really questionable.

WJ: The book's been getting a lot of buzz, including a blurb by Dave Eggers, who wrote, "Don't let the irreverent title mislead: This is a serious and bighearted book." Why did you choose that title?

PK: The title is obviously a play on the classic orange jumpsuit that prisoners wear (which also takes on a personal meaning based on a letter a friend sent me, something I recount in the book). But it also refers to the fact that women are the fastest-growing segment of the prison population in this country. Most of those rising prisoner numbers are women who are nonviolent drug offenders.

WJ: Your previous Six-Word Memoir was "In and out of hot water." What is it now?

PK: I kind of feel that it'll always be that! That memoir probably would've been true on a smaller scale before all of this. That's the nature of life: you get yourself into hot water, and then you manage to get yourself out.

Questions for Discussion

||||

1. Piper, a graduate of Smith College and, arguably, an unlikely candidate for incarceration, gets involved in a drug ring shortly after graduation. This dangerous activity stands in sharp contrast to her previously safe, law-abiding life. What do you think precipitated Piper's foray into crime? What might have made the drug world so enticing?

2. In Chapter 2, Piper seeks refuge from the underworld in San Francisco. What support does Piper have that allows her to change the direction of her postcollegiate life successfully? How do her circumstances contrast with those of the women she meets in Danbury?

3. Piper is indicted for a crime she committed several years earlier and is sentenced to more than a year in prison. At the time of her incarceration, she is a self-aware woman with a steady job and solid, fulfilling relationships. Once Piper meets other prisoners, she expresses consternation over many of their sentences, which often seem disproportionate to the crimes committed. For example, prisoners receive fifty-four months for Internet fraud and two years for a marijuana charge, but a guard convicted of sexually abusing prisoners receives one month. Women from poor communities often seem to be serving much longer

sentences than middle-class prisoners. How do these sentences, including Piper's, fit in with your idea of prison's role in society, and the purpose of punishment? What are the biggest crimes in this story, who commits them, and what is their punishment?

4. Many crimes related to the sale of illegal drugs are nonviolent crimes; how do they compare with the sale of legal products that are unhealthy or dangerous, like cigarettes or guns? Nonviolent drug offenses are the reason the majority of the women in the book are in prison; should low-level nonviolent drug offenders be put in prison?

5. Piper's first taste of prison comes when she surrenders herself to the guards at Danbury. Throughout the memoir, the prisoners endure a number of humiliating tasks at the hands of the guards—arguably, the most vivid being the naked squat/cough ritual after every visitation. Interestingly, though, the incidents that most affect Piper seem to be when one guard refuses to call her by her last name at mail call, sexual harassment from her boss on the electrical job, and a gruff, uncomfortable gynecological exam. Why do you think that is? How do these humiliating encounters shape her view of prison life and of the psychic effects of incarceration on prisoners?

6. The women in the prison have a very definite social system of their own. What purposes do those social systems serve for the prisoners? How do things like food and humor play a role in prisoners' survival? What special strengths and vulnerabilities do women have when they are in tight-knit single-sex communities such as Danbury? How do you think the needs (emotional and otherwise) of incarcerated men and women differ, and how do their needs differ once they return home?

7. Piper has to learn the ins and outs of prison quickly. Her fellow inmates are nothing if not savvy prisoners. While the coping

skills they teach Piper come in very handy behind bars, they don't translate well into the free world. What kind of education were these women missing in prison? What skills could they have been given that would have helped them establish themselves as productive members of society? How can people convicted of felonies be successfully reintegrated into society?

8. At the end of Chapter 8, Piper discusses the relationship between guards and prisoners. How do you think prison guards can maintain their humanity when the very requirement of their job is to restrict the rights of individuals? Are there any guards or persons of authority in Piper's story who favorably distinguish themselves by their behavior?

9. Clearly the author's race, education, and socioeconomic status have an impact on her experience. Should that matter when we consider her story? Do those factors make her story more or less credible? What's the difference between Danbury FCI, where the author spends most of her time, and the correctional facilities she is transferred to toward the end of the story? Does Piper change in these harsher environments?

10. Should prisons be run by private, for-profit corporations as they are in many states? It is currently legal to make a profit imprisoning the mentally ill, poor, and addicted—but is it ethical?

11. After reading *Orange Is the New Black,* do you think our prison system is successful? Do you think its dramatic growth over the last thirty years—nearly 400 percent more Americans in prison—is a good thing for the country? Why or why not? What do you think the author is trying to accomplish by telling her story?

PHOTO: SAM ZALUTSKY

PIPER KERMAN is a vice president at a Washington, D.C.–based communications firm that works with foundations and nonprofits. A graduate of Smith College, she lives in Brooklyn with her husband.

ABOUT THE TYPE

This book was set in Baskerville, a typeface which was designed by John Baskerville, an amateur printer and typefounder, and cut for him by John Handy in 1750. The type became popular again when the Lanston Monotype Corporation of London revived the classic Roman face in 1923. The Mergenthaler Linotype Company in England and the United States cut a version of Baskerville in 1931, making it one of the most widely used typefaces today.